SOUTHWEST
THE BEAUTIFUL COOKBOOK

RECIPES FROM AMERICA'S SOUTHWEST

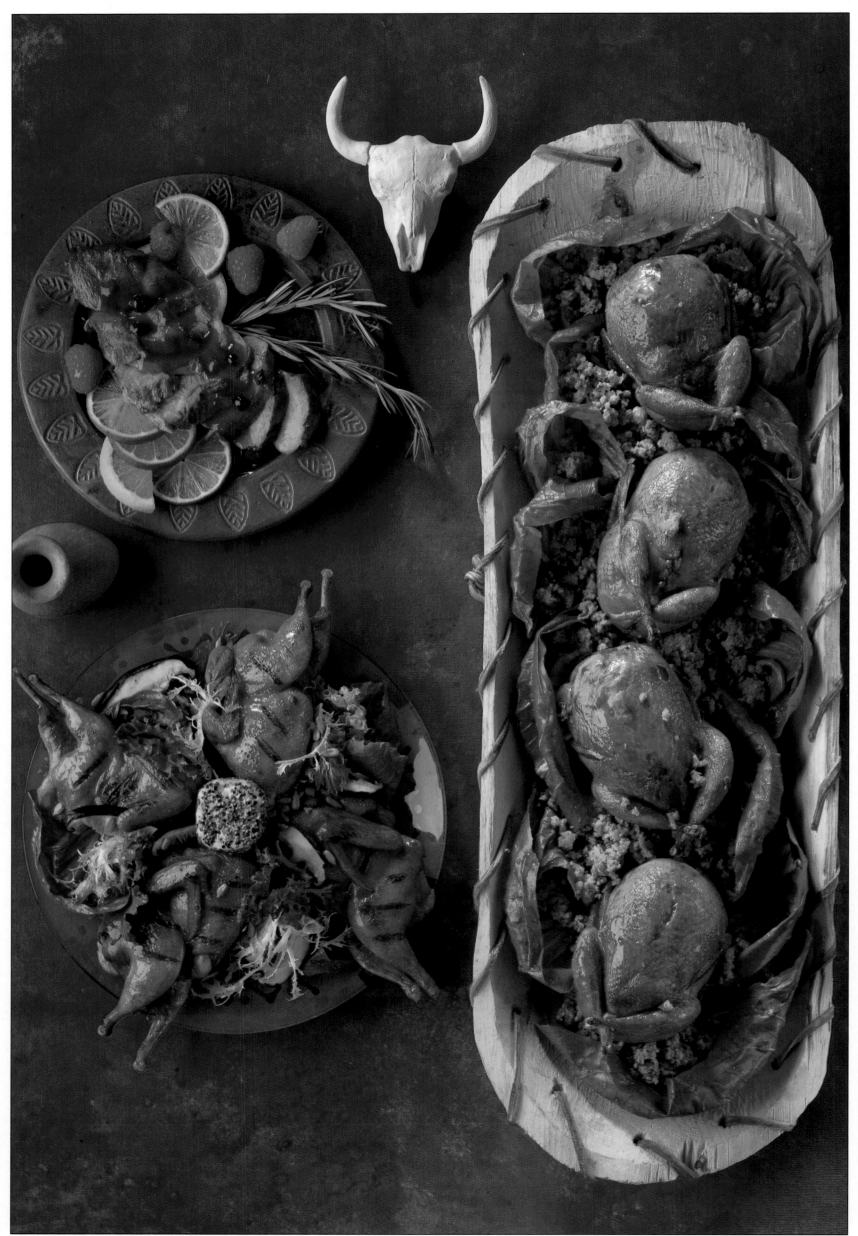

Clockwise from bottom left: Quail Salad with Toasted Pumpkin Seeds (recipe page 117), Duck Breasts with Juniper Berries in Red Wine Sauce (recipe page 120), Stuffed Roasted Quail (recipe page 102)

RECIPES FROM AMERICA'S SOUTHWEST

SOUTHWEST
THE BEAUTIFUL COOKBOOK

RECIPES BY
BARBARA POOL FENZL

TEXT BY
NORMAN KOLPAS

FOOD PHOTOGRAPHY BY
E. JANE ARMSTRONG

CollinsPublishersSanFrancisco
A Division of HarperCollinsPublishers

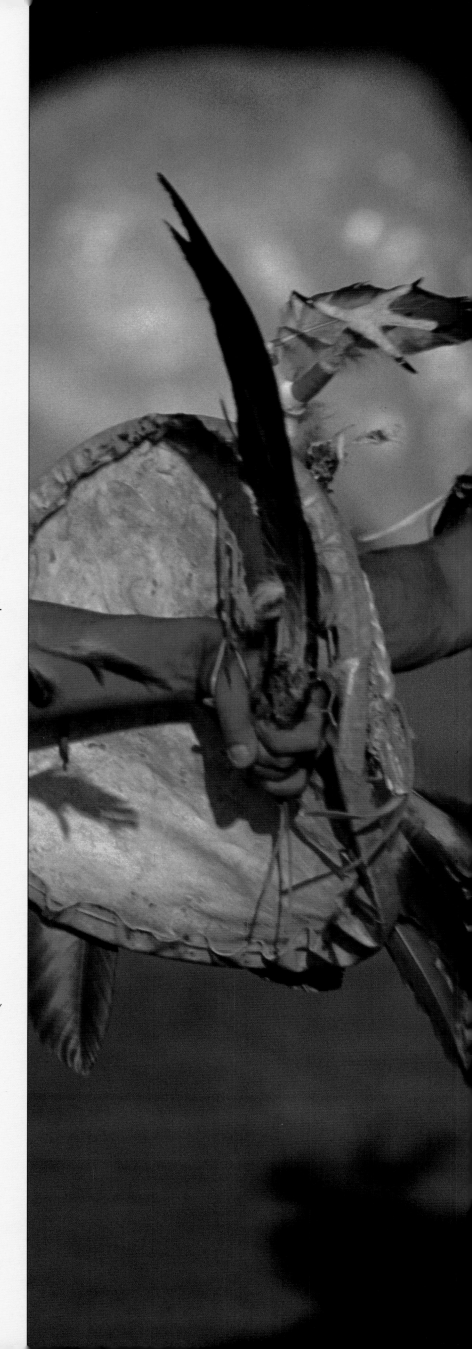

First published in USA 1994
by Collins Publishers San Francisco

Produced by Weldon Owen Inc.
814 Montgomery Street
San Francisco, CA 94133 USA
Phone (415) 291-0100   Fax (415) 291-8841

Weldon Owen Inc.:
President: John Owen
Publisher: Jane Fraser
Managing Editor: Anne Dickerson
Editorial Assistant: Jan Hughes
Copy Editor: Carolyn Miller
Proofreader: Jonathan Schwartz
Production: Stephanie Sherman, Mick Bagnato,
    James Obata
Design: Tom Morgan, Blue Design
Design Assistant: Jennifer Petersen
Design Concept: John Bull, The Book Design Company
Map: Kenn Backhaus
Illustrations: Diana Reiss-Koncar
Index: Ken Dellapenta
Photography Assistant, Studio Manager: Greg DeBoer
Stylists: Diana Isaiou, Patty Wittmann, Phyllis Bogard

Library of Congress Cataloging-in-Publication Data:

Southwest the beautiful cookbook : authentic recipes
    from the Southwest / recipes by Barbara Fenzl ; text
    by Norman Kolpas ; food photography by
    E. Jane Armstrong.
            p.   cm.
        Includes index.
        ISBN 0-00-255348-1
        1. Cookery, American—Southwestern style.
    I. Fenzl, Barbara. II. Kolpas, Norman.
    TX715.2.S68S69   1993
    641.5979—dc20   93-35996
                                             CIP

Produced by Phoenix Offset
Printed in China

A Weldon Owen ◆ Production

*Endpapers: More than 300 petroglyphs decorate the face of Newspaper
Rock State Historical Monument in southeastern Utah. Scholars suspect
they were produced over a period of 3,000 years by the prehistoric Archaic,
Basket Maker, Anasazi and Fremont peoples; by the Ute and Navajo;
and even by white settlers.*

*Page 2–3: Wind and rain etch soft mudstone surrounding more resilient
rock to form the towering buttes and dramatic spires of Arizona's
Monument Valley.*

*Right: The ancient White Buffalo Dance is vibrantly rendered by the
Acoma Inter-Cultural Dancers at the Traditional American Indian Feast
Day festival in New Mexico's Gran Quivera ruins.*

*Pages 8–9: Clockwise from left: Black Beans and Black Bean Cakes
(recipes page 162), Habanero Pilaf (recipe page 169), Corn on the Cob
(recipe page 177).*

*Pages 12–13: In striking contrast to the surrounding desert, Havasu Falls
forms an enchanting oasis in the western region of the Grand Canyon.*

Light bathes the undulating walls of Antelope Canyon near Page, Arizona, revealing intricate sandstone patterns.

CONTENTS

Cholla cactus grows in Arizona's Organ Pipe National Monument.

INTRODUCTION

The modern world with its pressures, hectic pace and burgeoning cities makes many of us long for a simpler life in touch with the earth's natural wonders. Maybe that explains our ever-growing fascination with the American Southwest.

Nowhere does the earth present a more consistently dramatic repertoire of sights and experiences. In northwestern Arizona, the Colorado River slices through the awesomely wide chasm of the Grand Canyon, a vision still capable of rendering the most sophisticated travelers dumbstruck. To the north and east, the Colorado Plateau encompasses not only the Grand Canyon but the megalithic sculptures of Bryce Canyon, Arches National Park and Monument Valley, and the sheer cliff sides of Mesa Verde and Canyon de Chelly.

Two hundred miles to the south stretches the austerely beautiful Sonoran Desert, its arid vastness punctuated by jagged peaks and saguaro cactuses, whose forms possess a noble, near-human presence. North to south through New Mexico, the southern trailings of the Rockies cleave the state in half, as the Rio Grande descends from high mountain valleys to low basins of rich, fertile soil. At the Southwest's easternmost extremes, the Great Plains sweep down across New Mexico and the Texas Panhandle, breaking up into the precipitous bluffs of the Llano Estacado. And where Texas meets Mexico, the Rio Grande marks the boundary between two countries.

The spell cast by the Southwest today is also partly due to its distinctive foods. Southwestern cuisine captures, in microcosm, the appeal of the vast region: corn tortillas and boiled pinto beans, as rugged and earthy as the desert; fresh and dried chilies, as searing as the sun overhead; piñon nuts harvested from wild piñon trees whose smoke scents the air of New Mexico; meat and game seared over glowing coals of wood from mesquite trees, whose gnarled forms decorate almost every vista. And the colors of this food—tawny yellow or slate-blue corn, purple-brown and black beans, bright-green fresh chilies or the deep brick-red of dried chilies—come from the same palette used by nature to paint the features of the region.

Southwestern cuisine today is the sum of the myriad cultures who have lived in this region, from prehistoric tribes to today's native Americans, from the first Spanish explorers to later Mexican settlers, from Anglo pioneers to the many people who have made or found modern-day Edens in the deserts and mountains. As such, it is far more complex than the stereotypical dishes of tacos, enchiladas, burritos, guacamole, rice and beans.

Thousands of years ago, the first humans came to the Southwest, probably crossing the land bridge of the

Arizona's Grand Canyon, one of the world's great natural wonders, offers a rare glimpse into the vast geological history of the earth, with some layers dating back as far as 2 billion years.

15

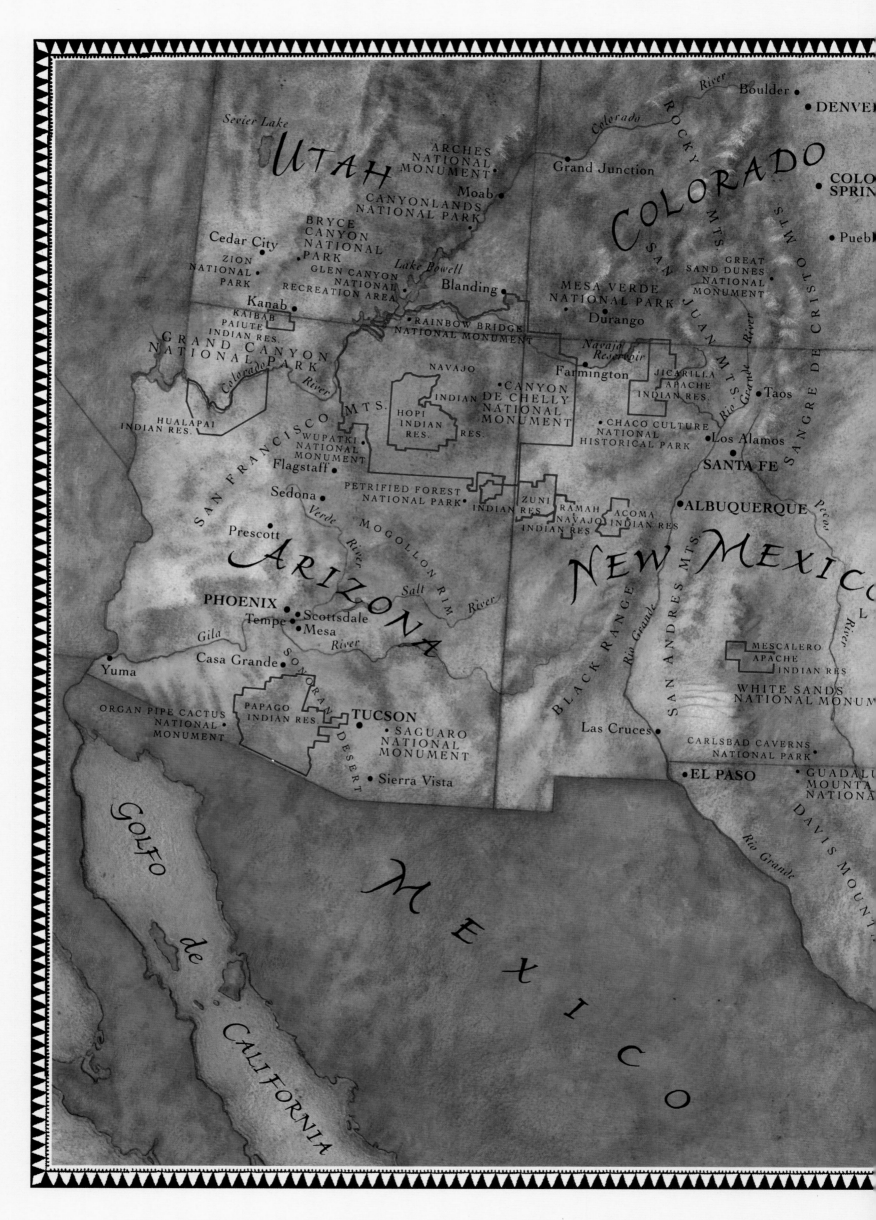

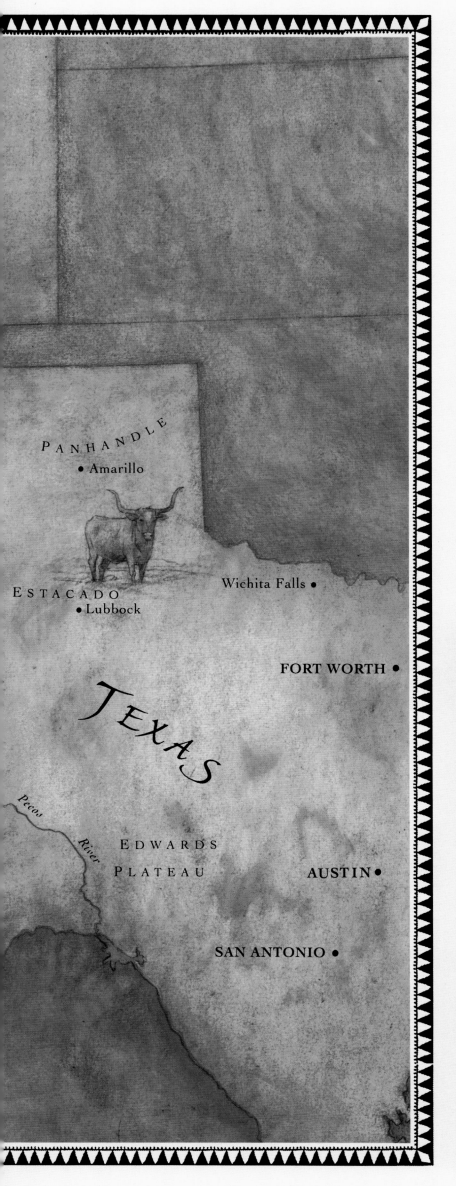

Bering Sea from Asia. Subsisting by hunting animals and gathering plants from the wild, those who settled here found ample food to sustain themselves in the varied geography of desert and mountains, basin and range. Deer and elk wandered the highlands. Trout glided silently through mountain streams. Across the plains roamed herds of American bison, more familiarly known today as buffalo. Everywhere, jackrabbits and cottontails, wild turkeys and piglike peccaries provided other steady sources of protein. The earth, too, provided abundant blessings. Southwestern tribes learned to extract nourishment from the pulp and fruit, beans, seeds and nuts of such wild plants as agave and prickly pear cactus, saguaro and yucca, mesquite and piñon, acorn and sunflower.

They also soon learned to gain more reliable, consistent sustenance from plants they could grow, irrigate and harvest themselves: the culinary holy trinity of corn, squashes and beans. With the more settled life that such early agricultural efforts engendered, three great, sometimes interlinked cultures developed in the Southwest. In the Sonoran Desert and near the Mogollon Rim of southern and central Arizona, the Hohokam built villages that featured intricate networks of irrigation canals. Covering the southwestern third of New Mexico and reaching well into central Arizona and northern Mexico, the Mogollon people developed multiroomed villages and dug ditches to water their crops.

The center of a Navajo wedding basket, used in nuptial ceremonies, signifies the beginning of life moving outward.

*San Geronimo Mission at the entrance of Taos Pueblo is a testament
to the influence of early missionaries who came to the Southwest in
search of converts.*

18

Most sophisticated of all, perhaps, were the Anasazi, who occupied the Colorado Plateau and what is today called the Four Corners area, where Arizona, New Mexico, Colorado and Utah meet. Such archaeological sites as Mesa Verde, Canyon de Chelly, Chaco Canyon and Bandelier reveal their architecturally dazzling cliff-side dwellings and a wealth of cave paintings, stone carvings and other artifacts that offer tantalizing glimpses of their daily lives.

By the fifteenth century A.D., these peoples had begun to evolve into more than two dozen separate, sometimes related tribes that today give the Southwest such a diversity of native cultures, including familiar groups like the Hopi and the Zuni, the Pima and the Papago. At that time, they were joined in the region by yet another culture from the north, the nomadic Athabascans, who later became the Navajo and Apache nations.

These were the diverse peoples Spanish conquistador Francisco Vasquez de Coronado encountered when, between 1540 and 1542, he and his men searched for the fabled golden Seven Cities of Cíbola—becoming, in the process, the first Europeans to set foot in the Southwest. No treasure found, they left to the Franciscan friars the territory of Nuevo México and its wealth of native souls ready for converting. The missionaries, in turn, were followed in 1598 by Don Juan de Oñate, who founded the territory's first permanent Spanish settlement near the present-day site of Española, New Mexico.

Old World Mexican traditions live on in the Southwest; here, mariachis serenade in traditional costume.

Gathering storm clouds reflect the light of the setting sun over Saguaro National Monument in Arizona.

19

Thus began a dynamic interchange of culinary cultures. Spanish and Mexican missionaries and settlers brought herds of cattle and sheep to the region, as well as horses to assist in the arduous work of ranching; beef, lamb, milk and cheese became parts of the regional cuisine. They introduced wheat, preferring breads made from its flour to the coarser native corn breads. They planted fruit orchards—most notably peaches and apricots. And they established the first vineyards, precursors of the excellent but little-known wines produced today in many parts of the Southwest.

Most significantly, they brought with them the chili. Not that it was entirely new to the Southwest: growing wild in the Sonoran Desert, the plains of western Texas and no doubt elsewhere were the tiny, berrylike pods of the chiltepín, whose seeds were scattered and spread by birds. Many native tribes of the region used this fiery spice to season their foods. But the active cultivation and hybridization of the chili in all its different forms was introduced from farther south in Mexico, along with such other now-familiar Southwestern agricultural ingredients as tomatoes and avocados.

Mexican independence from Spain opened the Southwest to trade with the United States starting in the 1820s. With the passing years, and especially after the region became U.S. territory following the Mexican-American War in 1848, more and more non-Spanish-speaking settlers arrived—many coming along the famous Santa Fe Trail, leading from Kansas to the New Mexican capital. As varied as the American people had already become, so too was that variety infused into the culture of the Southwest. The cowboy chuck wagon cook grilling a beefsteak at day's end on the Llano Estacado; the German sausage-maker tending his shop in the Texas Hill Country; the Mexican-American *abuelita* stirring her chili-laced stew in San Antonio—each in his or her own way, along with countless others, made a tangible contribution to the cuisine of the Southwest.

Anthropologists believe the Navajo migrated from the Great Plains to the Southwest in the sixteenth century.

Organ Pipe National Monument protects Arizona's unusual plant and animal life in its 500-square-mile nature preserve.

Yet, the Southwest remained a sparsely populated region deemed inhospitably stark, hot and dry. Ironically, those very same qualities attracted a stampede of settlers in the twentieth century. Artists and writers, most notably D.H. Lawrence and Georgia O'Keeffe, found ravishing beauty there to inspire them. Architect Frank Lloyd Wright constructed Taliesin West, his winter headquarters, on a hillside in Scottsdale, Arizona, creating "a desert building . . . nobly simple in outline as the region itself is sculpted." Collectors like Standard Oil heiress Millicent Rogers and Arizona-transplanted Chicago businessman Dwight Heard became so excited about the native arts of the region that they went on to establish outstanding museums that today bear their names in, respectively, Taos and Phoenix.

America's efforts to develop nuclear weapons during World War II found the perfect top-secret site in Los Alamos and a rich source of uranium in mines in the Four Corners area. Retirees seeking a place in the sun; convalescents requiring a dry, allergy-free climate; wandering souls in search of higher spiritual truths—all have found permanent havens in the great Southwest.

And all, in turn, have subtly changed the way people eat there. Visiting the Southwest today, you'll encounter a wide variety of dining experiences. There are the purveyors of tamales and enchiladas, posole and chimichangas, to be sure. Particularly in Texas, you can bet your life on great barbecue and chili con carne. But count, as well, on finding food to please most any craving: Chinese, Japanese or Thai; rustic Italian or nouvelle French; all-American greasy spoon or New Age vegan.

The delicate flowers of the claret-cup cactus belie its fierce struggle to adapt to the harsh conditions of the desert.

A mining settlement since 1871, Silverton, Colorado, enjoyed a reputation as truly "wild" in the Old West with its gambling houses, saloons and brothels.

The San Juan Mountains, in Colorado, lured miners throughout the twentieth century who laid claim to the scattered mineral deposits.

23

More than two million people visit the Grand Canyon annually; here, tourists prepare to saddle up and enjoy a day trip into the canyon on mule-back.

It was inevitable that this cosmopolitan environment would engender a new regional cooking, referred to by such labels as "new Southwestern cooking" and "modern Southwest cuisine"—the latter term most likely coined by Santa Fe–born chef John Sedlar, who pioneered a sophisticated blend of Southwestern and French nouvelle styles in the mid-1980s at his now-departed Saint Estèphe restaurant in Manhattan Beach, California. Soon a galaxy of nationally acclaimed super-star chefs shone in the Southwest, including Vincent Guerithault in Phoenix; Janos Wilder in Tucson; Mark Miller in Santa Fe; Robert Del Grande in Houston; and Dean Fearing in Dallas. The food they prepare to such great acclaim bears the hallmarks of contemporary cooking everywhere: impeccably fresh ingredients from a gallimaufry of world cuisines, quickly and simply cooked to highlight their natural qualities, then arranged on the plate in presentations that approach high art.

Add to that the traditional ingredients and vernacular of the Southwest and you have such intriguing creations as blue cornmeal soufflés, pinto bean purées, lobster tacos and chocolate chiles rellenos. No wonder food-lovers in droves have taken notice. Fittingly, such modern encounters with Southwestern cooking have often led them to seek out the authentic roots of the cuisine.

This book aims to assist in that pursuit. While by no means exhaustive—it would take several volumes this size to even approach such a goal—it offers a comprehensive overview of the enchanted region, the people who live there and the foods they eat. Organized by course and by ingredients, this collection of more than 200 recipes spans the years and embraces the Southwest's many peoples to include ancient preparations and contemporary creations alike; and the brief essays that introduce each chapter attempt to place the recipes in their historic, regional and cultural contexts.

Above all else, the intention of this book is to bring to the reader a sense of the vivid beauty of the landscape and the cuisine of the Southwest.

25

The subtle beauty of the desert emerges when an almond tree blooms against the stark backdrop of Arizona's Painted Desert.

BASIN AND RANGE DESERTS

lished in 1870, named after the mythological bird to symbolize the city's
rise from the ruins of the prehistoric Hohokam civilization.

United Bank of Arizona

29

The natural gardens of the Southwest vibrantly remind a patient
observer that the seemingly barren desert teems with life.

30

provided protein. Saguaro cactuses, still found today in vast numbers in the 120,000-acre Saguaro National Monument west of Tucson, yielded their egg-sized fruit, whose sweet pulp is said to resemble a combination of watermelon and fresh figs. The hard seeds of the mesquite tree were boiled to make a broth or dried and ground into a coarse, flavorful flour.

Several centuries before Christ, the Hohokam began to build networks of irrigation canals at such settlements as Snaketown, on the north bank of the Gila, supporting rudimentary agriculture that provided two crops a year of corn, squashes and beans. By analyzing skeletons at Hohokam sites, archaeologists have found intriguing evidence of corn's importance in their diets. Their teeth were worn down by the rocky grit that mixed with cornmeal during milling, and the bones of the women's hands were strong and well-developed—a result of hefting heavy grinding stones day after day.

Though the Hohokam dispersed by about A.D. 1450, the Pima and Papago tribes that replaced them in the region continued to grow corn, beans and squashes. In years when rainfall was plentiful, or on riverside lands where the water table was high, they practiced their agriculture without benefit of irrigation; at other times or places, they dug ditches off the river or threw logs across it to divert water to their fields.

The Papagos and Pimas seasoned their food with chiltepíns: small wild chilies that still grow in microclimates where the basin meets the range. Indeed, these chilies were so important to some tribes that the Papagos went on pilgrimages each year to gather the best and most abundant in Mexico's Sierra Madre range.

Diets grew more varied with the arrival of Spanish missionaries. Jesuit priest Eusebio Kino, who lived in the region from 1683 until his death in 1711, and founded many churches and missions, (including the magnificent San Xavier del Bac in Tucson) detailed in his journal that he had distributed to the natives "wheat, chick peas, bastard chick peas, lentils, cow peas, cabbages, lettuce, onions, leeks, garlic, anise, pepper, mustard, mint, melons, watermelons and cane, also grapevines, roses and lilies, plum, pomegranate and fig." The wheat at the top of that list came over time to exceed corn in popularity, and today more wheat flour tortillas than corn tortillas are eaten in this part of Arizona.

At the same time, the natives' options for dietary protein increased with the introduction by the Spanish of chicken, sheep, pigs, goats and cattle. Dairy animals in turn introduced cheese into the local diet, which remains a popular ingredient here.

In return, the natives introduced the missionaries to some of their indigenous ingredients—sometimes with unexpected results. "I could not say a word and believed I had hell-fire in my mouth," wrote Fr. Ignatz Pfeffercorn in 1794, after his first taste of a chiltepín.

Those chilies, or milder ones, may be used in the preparation of a signature dish of Tucson that developed from the interaction of Spanish and native cuisines. The dry air and prevailing sunshine of the Sonoran Desert had always provided an ideal means

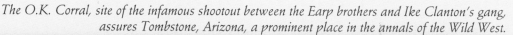

The O.K. Corral, site of the infamous shootout between the Earp brothers and Ike Clanton's gang, assures Tombstone, Arizona, a prominent place in the annals of the Wild West.

The glistening white stucco walls of the Spanish Baroque-style San Xavier Mission in Tucson, Arizona, were constructed in the late eighteenth century.

for preserving wild game: Just cut it into thin strips, season it, set it outside and let it shrivel. Applied to beef, the technique yielded carne seca—literally, dried meat—which today, in myriad restaurants within hailing distance of San Xavier del Bac, is sautéed with onions, garlic, chilies and tomatoes to make a savory filling for burritos, tacos, enchiladas or the deep-fried tortilla packets known as chimichangas. Outside of Tucson, a similar effect is achieved simply by stewing a fresh, tough cut of beef with those same ingredients to make a dish known as machaca.

In the nineteenth century, Anglo settlers of many national origins brought their own foods to the Sonoran Desert region, from Dutch-oven-baked cobblers to the sourdough of pioneer and cowboy chuck wagons, to live fresh oysters shipped from the East Coast, packed in barrels of ice and fed with sprinklings of cornmeal. But the greatest impact they made here came in 1868, when frontiersman Frank Swilling and his Swilling Irrigation Canal Company began making new use of the centuries-old abandoned Hohokam irrigation ditches in the Salt River Valley. Like the namesake mythical bird that rose from the ashes of its own pyre, the town of Phoenix was born, and by 1870 there were thirty-five thousand acres ready for planting. In the years that followed, great orchards of citrus fruit, pecans and dates sprang from the desert. So did real estate developers, inspired by the area's beautiful mountain-fringed geography and clear skies to rename it the Valley of the Sun. Residential tracts, resorts and retirement communities

thronged Phoenix and the adjoining arts enclave of Scottsdale, which together rank as the greatest metropolitan area of the Southwest.

With that ranking comes a cosmopolitan approach to food and dining. In Phoenix you can enjoy cowboy steaks and Sonoran-style Mexican food as well as Provençal and Hunanese fare; fresh-squeezed Arizona orange juice as well as fresh fish flown in from the Pacific, the Gulf and the Atlantic. Pioneering local chefs find new and creative ways to combine traditional ingredients and dishes with the cutting edge of culinary invention.

That level of sophistication may be found in many establishments in Tucson as well. Yet locals in both cities also continue to pursue the dishes of the past with missionary zeal. The annual Tucson Meet Yourself festival, held each October, is so dominated by food that locals have come to call it "Tucson Eat Yourself." A weekly newspaper there set up a "green corn tamale hotline" to gather reader reports on the best-available examples of that specialty. A homecoming to either city invariably centers on a visit to a favorite purveyor of tacos or enchiladas. And among the food cognoscenti of Phoenix and Scottsdale, the name and phone number of someone who privately makes and sells the best-ever tamales will pass from friend to friend as furtively yet speedily as a hot piece of gossip.

All these behaviors are the actions of confirmed addicts. And a newcomer's first taste of the local cuisine of the Southwest's basin and range deserts is likely to swell those hordes of food-addicts by one more person still.

The majestic saguaro cactus, found only in the Sonoran Desert, grows 2 feet every 25 years and can live as long as 200 years.

Appetizers and Salads

The fine art of preparing piki, a paper-thin ceremonial corn bread, was a skill to be mastered before a young Hopi woman was considered eligible for marriage.

APPETIZERS AND SALADS

Among the many customs carried by Spanish settlers to the New World was the one of serving appetizers as a sign of hospitality and as a gracious start to a meal. Throughout the Southwest today, snacks and nibbles are inescapable, whether you stroll into a bar in El Paso, a chic restaurant in Santa Fe or a Hopi pueblo home in northeastern Arizona.

Many of these appetizers will be versions of Mexico's traditional *antojitos,* the varied forms of street food. The subtle differences and elaborations on this theme found north of the border are the product of good old-fashioned American ingenuity as well as of geography and history.

Take the generous group of appetizers based on the tortilla, for example. In Mexico, the term *quesadilla* usually describes a small, handmade tortilla of fresh cornmeal masa folded around a filling of cheese and other ingredients, then fried in hot lard or oil. The quesadilla of the Southwest, on the other hand, calls for a large tortilla made of white wheat flour (itself an adaptation for Europeans used to eating raised bread), filled with cheese and cooked on a griddle or grill until lightly charred. And few traditional Mexican cooks would countenance such contemporary American fillings as goat cheese, chutney, smoked salmon, grilled chicken and tropical fruit.

The best-known Southwestern elaboration of a Mexican snack is undoubtedly nachos. Throughout Mexico, corn tortillas are cut into wedges and deep-fried to make crisp *totopos,* better known in the United States as tostaditas, or tortilla chips; these are used as crunchy scoopers for salsas, guacamole or the melted-cheese-and-chilies dip known as *chiles con queso.* Some sources credit the idea of pouring melted cheese *over* the chips and topping them with pickled jalapeño chilies to the World War II–era Victory Club in Piedras Negras, Mexico, just across the Texas border from Eagle Pass; others claim it originated with an establishment in Ciudad Acuna, across the river from Del Rio. Whoever deserves the kudos, Southwesterners popularized that topsy-turvy creation, making it standard fare in ballparks, cocktail bars and restaurants nationwide. Perhaps only American cooks, unbound by centuries of tradition, could have added so many optional extras for toppings that a pile of nachos can now constitute a meal in itself.

To be sure, such cross-cultural culinary influences work in both directions. You can see Mexico's influence on the appetizers hosts offer their guests at gatherings in Scottsdale and Sedona, Albuquerque and San Antonio. At the hands of a Midwestern cook, for example, a deviled egg may derive its devilry from a dash of mustard; but here, roasted chilies and zesty taco sauce add a hotter fire. Popular party dips find fresh inspiration in the creamy consistency of refried beans, especially when the bean dip is decoratively

Previous pages, left to right: Artichoke Sunflower (recipe page 43),
Eggs Diablo (recipe page 46), Fiesta Shrimp (recipe page 40)

36

layered with guacamole, chilies, cheeses and other ingredients to form the popular Arizona appetizer known as an Aztec Calendar. Crab cakes, a specialty of the Mid-Atlantic states, take a Southwestern turn when a robust salsa of avocado and fresh corn replaces the traditional tartar sauce. Even that Mediterranean transplant, the artichoke, may be arranged to resemble a sunflower, a plant cultivated by native tribes since ancient times.

Southwestern salads of today display the same innovative level of give and take between the region's varied cultures. Half a millennium ago, before colonization, there were really no salads to speak of here—at least, not in the form that we now think of them. Doubtless, prehistoric hunter-gatherers of the deserts and mesas picked wild greens to serve with their roasted game. Some of these plants even possess a certain cachet among modern gourmets: the Hopi's *peehala,* known throughout New Mexico today as *verdolagas,* is the mild, sweet and succulent purslane much beloved of the French; the delicately flavored plant the French call *mâche* grows throughout the region and is known as *quelites.*

Still, it took an influx of European settlers to add their traditional salad ingredients and to transform local

Red chilies dry in the autumn sun before they are strung together to make the garlands called ristras.

Sacred to native Americans of the Southwest, corn is traditionally planted and harvested with elaborate ceremonies.

raw materials into an imaginatively dressed and artfully presented dish. The first tentative stages in that interplay of cooking habits may be seen in the mid-nineteenth-century comments of Father Latour, the future Archbishop of Santa Fe, as imagined by Willa Cather in her novel *Death Comes for the Archbishop:*

> I brought him a bottle of olive-oil on my horse all the way from Durango (I say 'olive-oil,' because here 'oil' means something to grease the wheels of wagons!), and he is making some sort of cooked salad. We have no green vegetables in winter, and no one seems ever to have heard of that blessed plant, the lettuce.

Modern agriculture has long since bestowed the blessing of lettuce on the Southwest. And the region has returned the blessing, elaborating salads with its own abundant indigenous ingredients. Tiny baby greens of tumbleweed and dandelion, even tender yucca blossoms, now find their way into the Southwestern salad bowl. The immature pads of the prickly pear cactus, known as nopales, are carefully scraped of their spines and trimmed to yield a vegetable reminiscent of zucchini, ideal for tossing with lettuces. A specialty of tropical Mexico, jícama contributes its own refreshing crispness.

Even simple Southwestern touches yield dramatic effects. Toasted pumpkin seeds, a favorite nibble in Mexico and throughout the Southwest, add color, texture and flavor to a marinated mixture of black beans and corn. Hot chilies spike the dressings for such all-American standards as Caesar salad, potato salad and coleslaw, producing eye-opening (and sometimes sinus-clearing) new dimensions of flavor. In these and many other ways, enterprising cooks of the region continue to demonstrate the synergy that can occur when two or more cuisines happily intermingle.

Left to right: Gazpacho Salad, Smoked Salmon Quesadilla

GAZPACHO SALAD

Like the classic Spanish soup, this salad features cucumber, tomatoes and peppers. Full of color and taste, it is a zesty starter to any meal or a satisfying summer main course.

SALAD

1 ripe avocado, peeled, pitted and diced
1 tablespoon fresh lemon juice
1 large cucumber, peeled, seeded, quartered and sliced
1 green bell pepper (capsicum), cored, seeded and julienned
1 red bell pepper (capsicum), cored, seeded and julienned
1 yellow bell pepper (capsicum), cored, seeded and julienned
3 ripe tomatoes, seeded and diced
1½ cups (6 oz/185 g) grated Monterey jack cheese
¼ cup (1 oz/30 g) sliced black olives

DRESSING

2 tablespoons fresh lime juice
1 garlic clove, minced
1 tablespoon minced onion
2 teaspoons minced fresh cilantro (coriander)
¼ teaspoon cayenne pepper
¼ teaspoon ground cumin
1 jalapeño chili, seeded and minced
½ cup (4 fl oz/125 ml) olive oil
salt and freshly ground pepper to taste
tortilla chips for garnish

❋ In a large bowl, toss the diced avocado with the lemon juice. Add the remaining salad ingredients and toss together.
❋ In another bowl, whisk together the lime juice, garlic, onion, cilantro, cayenne pepper, cumin and jalapeño. Slowly whisk in the olive oil and season with salt and pepper.
❋ Toss the dressing into the salad ingredients just before serving. Garnish with tortilla chips.

SERVES 6–8

SMOKED SALMON QUESADILLA

The combination of flavors in this robust appetizer is quintessential modern Southwest cuisine. Goat cheese and cream cheese pair with roasted chilies and salmon to create a delectable and filling first course. Chilies, the culinary gold of the New World, were believed by the Aztecs to be a powerful sexual stimulant, so be careful where and to whom you serve this.

¼ cup (2 oz/60 g) mild fresh goat cheese
¼ cup (2 oz/60 g) cream cheese at room temperature
3 flour tortillas (8 in/20 cm in diameter)
1 poblano chili, roasted, peeled, cored, seeded, and cut into strips (see glossary)
1 red bell pepper (capsicum), roasted, peeled, cored, seeded, and cut into strips (see glossary)
1 avocado, peeled, pitted, and cut into thin slices
¼ cup (2 oz/60 g) minced shallots
2 oz (60 g) smoked salmon, cut into strips

❋ In a small bowl, mix together the goat cheese and cream cheese until smooth and creamy. Spread one third of the mixture over half of each flour tortilla.
❋ Divide the poblano and red bell pepper strips evenly over the 3 halves of the flour tortillas. Layer the avocado slices over the pepper strips and top with the chopped shallots. Divide the salmon evenly among the tortilla halves. Fold the tortillas over, pressing to seal.
❋ Heat a nonstick skillet over medium high heat and toast the folded tortillas until the cheese melts and they are brown on one side. Turn over and brown on the other side.
❋ Cut each quesadilla into 4 wedges and serve immediately.

SERVES 6 (2 WEDGES EACH)

SEVICHE

A classic dish in Mexico, this marinated raw seafood appetizer is perfect for the summer months when it's too hot to cook. The citrus juices "cook" the fish by firming the flesh and turning it opaque. Serve in glass dishes to show off the colors.

8 oz (250 g) scallops, finely diced
8 oz (250 g) firm-fleshed white fish (snapper, turbot, pompano), diced
½ cup (4 fl oz/125 ml) fresh lime juice
¼ cup (2 fl oz/60 ml) fresh lemon juice
2 ripe plum (egg) tomatoes, diced
1 serrano chili, seeded and minced
1 Anaheim chili, seeded and minced
1 tablespoon minced fresh cilantro (coriander)
½ cup (2½ oz/75 g) finely chopped red (Spanish) onion
2 green (spring) onions, finely chopped
2 tablespoons olive oil
½ teaspoon dried oregano
½ teaspoon salt
tortilla chips or crusty French bread

❋ Dip the fish in boiling water for 30 seconds and remove any bones. Put the fish and scallops in a nonaluminum bowl; cover with the lime and lemon juices and allow to stand, refrigerated, for 1 hour. Drain the fish and scallops and rinse in cold water. Stir together all the remaining ingredients except the chips or bread in a nonaluminum bowl; add the fish and scallops and refrigerate, covered, for 1 hour. Serve chilled in cocktail glasses, accompanied with tortilla chips or bread.

SERVES 6

TANGERINE, JÍCAMA AND GREEN SALAD

Sometimes referred to as the Mexican potato, jícama is a large, light brown root vegetable with the appearance of a potato but the texture of a water chestnut. Peeled and julienned, it's delicious raw in salads or with dips as an appetizer, but it is also good cooked because it keeps its crunchy texture.

DRESSING

¼ cup (2 fl oz/60 ml) red wine vinegar
3 tablespoons honey
1¼ teaspoons chili powder
½ teaspoon aniseed, crushed
¼ teaspoon cayenne pepper
7 tablespoons (3½ fl oz/105 ml) corn oil
salt and freshly ground pepper to taste

SALAD

1 small head romaine (cos) lettuce
1 head curly endive (escarole), outer leaves discarded
1 small head red leaf lettuce
4 tangerines or small oranges, peeled and divided into segments
1 avocado, peeled and cut into ½-in (12-mm) cubes
1 cup (6 oz/185 g) coarsely grated jícama (yam bean)
2 green (spring) onions, finely chopped

❀ To make the dressing, mix the vinegar, honey, chili powder, aniseed and cayenne pepper together in a medium bowl. Slowly whisk in the oil until well incorporated; add salt and pepper.
❀ Wash lettuces and spin dry; tear into bite-size pieces and place in a large bowl. Toss in the tangerines or oranges, avocado, jícama and onions. Add enough dressing to coat the lettuce leaves and toss again.

SERVES 6

Left to right: Tangerine, Jícama and Green Salad; Seviche

FIESTA SHRIMP

Many Southwesterners flock to Puerto Peñasco (Rocky Point), Mexico, to vacation on the beach. One of the highlights of a visit here is buying shrimp to bring home; it's delicious in this colorful dish, although any good-quality shrimp will do. For a cocktail buffet, serve this in a glass bowl (to show off the lovely colors), with toothpicks nearby so your guests can spear the shrimp, onions and olives. The marinade may be made well ahead of time, but the shrimp should be added no more than 3 hours before serving.

MARINADE

3 tablespoons vegetable oil
2 garlic cloves, minced
1 teaspoon dry mustard
1 teaspoon salt
¼ cup (2 fl oz/60 ml) fresh lemon juice
1 tablespoon balsamic vinegar
1 serrano chili, seeded and minced
⅛ teaspoon cayenne pepper
2 tablespoons minced fresh cilantro (coriander)
1 lime, thinly sliced

1½ lb (750 g) shrimp (prawns), shelled and deveined
½ cup (2 oz/60 g) thinly sliced red (Spanish) onion
1 lime, halved and thinly sliced
½ cup (2 oz/60 g) black olives, pitted
1 red bell pepper (capsicum), roasted, peeled, cored, seeded and diced (see glossary)

❁ Whisk together all the marinade ingredients in a medium bowl.
❁ Cook the shrimp in boiling salted water just until they turn pink, about 2–3 minutes; drain and rinse in cold water.
❁ In a large bowl, toss together the onion, lime, olives, bell pepper, and marinade. Add the shrimp; cover and refrigerate for up to 3 hours.

SERVES 8–10   *Photograph pages 34–35*

ROMAINE AND PIÑON SALAD

Piñon trees are scattered over the northern parts of Southwest, and their nut-bearing cones are prized among the people who live there. Here piñon (pine) nuts add a unique flavor and texture to a crisp green salad.

DRESSING

2 garlic cloves, boiled in water for 10 minutes and drained
¼ teaspoon salt
1 teaspoon Dijon mustard
2 tablespoons red wine vinegar
⅓ cup (3 fl oz/80 ml) extra virgin olive oil
freshly ground pepper to taste

1 head romaine (cos) lettuce, washed and dried
¼ cup (1 oz/30 g) grated cotija or Parmesan cheese
¼ cup (1½ oz/45 g) piñon (pine) nuts, toasted (see glossary)

❁ In a small nonaluminum bowl, mash the garlic and salt together with the back of a fork. Whisk in the mustard and vinegar; slowly whisk in the oil until the dressing is thick. Add the pepper.
❁ Put the lettuce in a large salad bowl and toss with the dressing. Sprinkle the cheese and nuts over the greens and toss again. Serve immediately.

SERVES 6

GRILLED CHICKEN QUESADILLAS WITH PAPAYA

Quesadillas are flour tortillas covered with cheese then grilled or broiled. Charles Wiley, the executive chef at the beautiful Boulders resort in Carefree, Arizona, embellishes this version of the traditional dish with aged Monterey jack cheese, papaya, chicken and peppers. If aged jack cheese is unavailable, use any good-quality Monterey jack.

½ teaspoon chili powder
½ teaspoon cumin seed, toasted and ground (see glossary)

Left to right: Romaine and Piñon Salad, Grilled Chicken Quesadillas with Papaya

1 whole chicken breast, boned and skinned
kosher salt and freshly ground pepper to taste
2 flour tortillas (10 in/25 cm in diameter)
⅓ cup (1 oz/30 g) grated aged Monterey jack cheese
⅓ cup (1 oz/30 g) grated jalapeño jack cheese
1 Anaheim chili, roasted, peeled, seeded and diced
   (see glossary)
1 red bell pepper (capsicum), roasted, peeled seeded and
   diced (see glossary)
¼ cup (1½ oz/45 g) diced ripe papaya

¼ cup (2 oz/60 g) each guacamole, sour cream and chunky
   salsa for garnish

❃ Prepare a charcoal grill or preheat a broiler (griller). In a

small bowl, combine the chili powder and cumin; mix well. Season the chicken well with the mixture, then add salt and pepper. Grill or broil the chicken until just opaque throughout; dice into ½-in (12-mm) cubes.

❃ Place each tortilla on a medium-hot grill or in 2 skillets over medium-high heat. Divide the cheese between the tortillas, sprinkling it evenly over each one. Sprinkle the chili and red pepper over the cheese, then sprinkle with the papaya and warm chicken. When the cheese is melted and the tortillas are lightly browned, fold them in half and transfer to a cutting board; cut each into 4 slices. Garnish with guacamole, sour cream and salsa; serve at once.

MAKES 8 WEDGES

41

CHAYOTE, CHORIZO AND GREENS SALAD

This warm salad is a terrific dish to start a meal or to serve as a light main course. Chef-owner Donna Nordin has brought national attention to Southwest cooking with her two Cafe Terra Cotta restaurants (in Phoenix and Tucson) as well as her television shows and her cooking classes.

DRESSING

2 tablespoons fresh lime juice
6 tablespoons (3 fl oz/90 ml) olive oil
2 tablespoons chorizo (Spanish sausage) fat
1 jalapeño chili, seeded and minced
1 garlic clove, minced
salt and freshly ground pepper to taste

4 oz (125 g) mild fresh goat cheese
1 tablespoon minced fresh cilantro (coriander)
1 garlic clove, minced
salt and freshly ground pepper to taste
1 teaspoon ground ancho chili powder or regular chili powder, or to taste
12 slices of baguette, ⅛–¼ in (3–6 mm) thick, brushed with butter and toasted in oven
6 cups (6 oz/185 g) mixed lettuces (radicchio, spinach, endive, red leaf, lamb's lettuce and so on)
2 chayote squash (vegetable pears), peeled, sliced and blanched

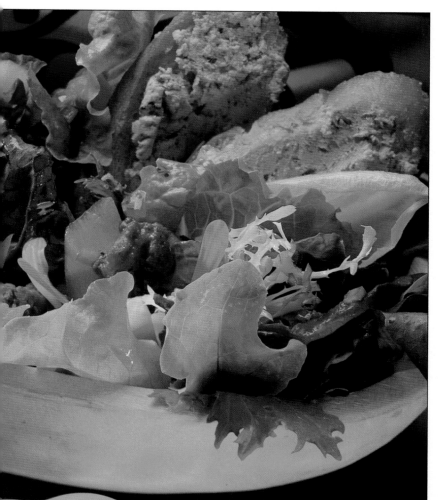

Left to right: Black Bean and Corn Salad with Toasted Pumpkin Seeds; Chayote, Chorizo and Greens Salad

4 oz (125 g) chorizo (Spanish sausage), cooked, crumbled and cooking fat reserved

❀ Mix all the dressing ingredients together in a small saucepan and heat until just warm.
❀ In a small bowl, combine the goat cheese, cilantro, garlic, salt, pepper and chili powder. Spread on the bread slices and place under the broiler (griller) until the cheese is melted and slightly browned, about 2–3 minutes.
❀ Divide the lettuce among 6 salad plates. Top the lettuce with sliced chayote and crumbled chorizo; pour the warm dressing over the salad and place 2 croutons on the side of each salad.

SERVES 6

VALLEY OF THE SUN, ARIZONA

ARTICHOKE SUNFLOWER

Beautiful on a buffet table, this appetizer is always a hit with artichoke fans. When assembled, the leaves of the artichoke resemble a sunflower. Be sure to provide an extra dish for discarded leaves.

1 large artichoke
2 tablespoons vinegar
1 teaspoon vegetable oil
1 bay leaf, crumbled
1 teaspoon salt
1 package (3 oz/90 g) cream cheese at room temperature
¼ teaspoon red hot pepper sauce
1 garlic clove mashed with ¼ teaspoon salt
1 tablespoon milk or heavy (double) cream
8 oz (250 g) very small cooked baby shrimp (prawns)
paprika

❀ Put the artichoke in a saucepan and cover with water. Add the vinegar, vegetable oil, bay leaf and salt. Bring to a boil, cover and simmer until a leaf pulls away easily and the base is tender, 30–45 minutes. Drain and let cool. Remove all the leaves of the artichoke, keeping those that have a good edible portion on the ends.
❀ Mix together the cream cheese, hot pepper sauce, garlic-salt mixture and milk or cream to form a smooth paste. Spread a small amount (about ½ teaspoon) on the base of each leaf and place a small shrimp on top of the paste; sprinkle the shrimp with paprika.
❀ Arrange the finished leaves on a round serving tray in concentric circles, placing the largest leaves along the edge and the smallest in the center. The center leaves should be almost standing up so that they resemble the center of a flower.

SERVES 12–18   *Photograph pages 34–35*

SANTA FE, NEW MEXICO

BLACK BEAN AND CORN SALAD WITH TOASTED PUMPKIN SEEDS

Toasted pumpkin seeds (pepitas), available in Latino markets, add a delicious crunch to this colorful salad. For a special occasion, serve the salad in a hollowed-out tomato or in a yellow, green, or red bell pepper half.

3 cups (21 oz/660 g) cooked black beans
1½ cups (9 oz/280 g) corn kernels
1 green bell pepper (capsicum), cored, seeded and diced
1 red bell pepper (capsicum), cored, seeded and diced
2 jalapeño chilies, seeded and diced
¼ cup (1 oz/30 g) diced red (Spanish) onion
3 cloves garlic, minced
3 green (spring) onions, chopped
½ cup (2½ oz/75 g) unsalted green pumpkin seeds (pepitas), toasted (see glossary)
2 tablespoons extra-virgin olive oil
3 tablespoons fresh lime juice
salt and freshly ground pepper to taste

❀ In a large bowl, stir together the beans, corn, peppers, chilies, onions, garlic and pumpkin seeds. Mix together the olive oil and lime juice and pour over the bean mixture. Add salt and pepper. This salad will keep in the refrigerator for 1 or 2 days.

SERVES 6

Left to right: Southwestern Caesar Salad, Fiesta Rice Salad

SANTA FE, NEW MEXICO

SOUTHWESTERN CAESAR SALAD

A spicy take-off on the classic version, this salad offers a nice balance of flavors and textures. For a main course lunch, add bite-sized pieces of grilled chicken. The fettuccine cutter of a hand-crank pasta machine works well for cutting the tortilla strips.

DRESSING

2 eggs
3 garlic cloves
1 chipotle chili in adobo sauce (see glossary)
¼ teaspoon cumin seed, finely crushed
1 tablespoon Dijon mustard
2 teaspoons anchovy paste
1 tablespoon balsamic vinegar
1 tablespoon fresh lime juice
1 shallot
¼ teaspoon cayenne pepper
⅔ cup (5 fl oz/160 ml) extra-virgin olive oil
⅓ cup (3 fl oz/80 ml) corn oil
salt and freshly ground pepper to taste

vegetable oil for frying
4 corn tortillas (6 in/15 cm in diameter), cut into ¼-by-3-in (6-mm-by-7.5-cm) strips
1 teaspoon chili powder
2 heads romaine (cos) lettuce, washed, separated and torn into pieces
½ cup (2 oz/60 g) crumbled cotija, Parmesan or Asiago cheese

❂ Place the eggs in boiling water for 1 minute. Remove from water and separate; reserve the whites for another use. Place the yolks and all the remaining dressing ingredients except the oils and salt and pepper in a medium bowl and whisk until well blended. Slowly add the olive oil, then the corn oil. Add salt and pepper.
❂ Pour vegetable oil into a small skillet to a depth of ¼ in (6 mm). Heat the oil over medium-high heat. Sprinkle the tortilla strips with chili powder and fry in the hot oil until they are crisp and lightly browned. Drain on paper towels.
❂ Toss the lettuce with the dressing; gently mix in the cheese and tortilla strips.

SERVES 8

VALLEY OF THE SUN, ARIZONA

FIESTA RICE SALAD

For a lovely addition to a buffet table, pack this colorful rice salad into an oiled ring mold, cover and refrigerate. Unmold on a platter and garnish with sprigs of cilantro.

SALAD

1 cup (7 oz/220 g) long-grain white rice
2 cups (16 fl oz/500 ml) water
1 cup (6 oz/185 g) corn kernels
½ cup (2½ oz/75 g) finely chopped red (Spanish) onion
¼ cup (1 oz/30 g) sliced black olives
1 cup (5 oz/ 155 g) diced red bell pepper (capsicum)
1 cup (5 oz/ 155 g) diced green bell pepper (capsicum)
½ cup (¾ oz/20 g) minced fresh cilantro (coriander)

DRESSING

1 garlic clove, minced
¼ cup (2 fl oz/60 ml) olive oil
3 tablespoons red wine vinegar
1½ teaspoons ground cumin
salt and freshly ground pepper to taste

❂ Place the rice and water in a medium, heavy saucepan and bring to a boil. Cover the saucepan, reduce heat to a simmer and cook for 20 minutes, or until the water is absorbed and the rice is tender. Transfer the rice to a large bowl. Add the remaining salad ingredients and toss.
❂ In a small bowl, whisk together the dressing ingredients. Pour over the rice mixture and toss well; season to taste.

SERVES 6–8

SOUTHWEST

PINTO BEAN DIP

Popular throughout the Southwest, pinto bean dip is served warm with tortilla chips. It may also be used in layered appetizers such as the Aztec Calendar (recipe on page 46). Adjust the spiciness by adding or subtracting minced jalapeños or by using jack cheese with peppers instead of Manchego. (Manchego is a rich, mellow-flavored cheese available in Latino markets.)

2 tablespoons vegetable oil
2 garlic cloves, minced
1 cup (5 oz/155 g) onions, finely chopped
2 cups (16 fl oz/500 ml) refried beans (recipe on page 163)
1½ cups (12 oz/375 g) grated Manchego or Monterey jack cheese, plus more for sprinkling if desired
2 jalapeño chilies, seeded and diced
½ teaspoon ground cumin
salt and freshly ground pepper to taste

❂ In a medium saucepan, heat the oil and sauté the garlic and onions until soft, about 5 minutes. Add the beans, cheese, jalapeños and cumin and cook, stirring occasionally, over low heat until the cheese is melted and the beans are warmed through. Add salt and pepper. Transfer to a chafing dish and sprinkle with additional grated cheese, if desired. Serve with tortilla chips.

MAKES ABOUT 4 CUPS (32 FL OZ/1 L)

S C O T T S D A L E ,   A R I Z O N A

ROASTED RED BELL PEPPER DIP

This sunset red dip, with its unique taste of roasted garlic and red bell peppers brings out the best in any raw vegetable, but particularly chayote squash, jícama, broccoli and cauliflower. It is also delicious on baked potatoes or tossed with pasta.

1 teaspoon olive oil
5 unpeeled garlic cloves
3 red bell peppers (capsicums), roasted, peeled, cored and seeded (see glossary)

½ teaspoon ground cumin
4 oz (125 g) cream cheese at room temperature
2 tablespoons crème fraîche or sour cream
salt and freshly ground pepper to taste

❀ Preheat an oven to 350°F (180°C). Sprinkle the olive oil over the garlic cloves and wrap tightly in aluminum foil. Place in the oven for 45–60 minutes, or until the cloves are soft. Let cool.
❀ Squeeze the soft garlic cloves from their peels into a food processor or blender. Add the red peppers and cumin; purée. Add the cream cheese and blend until smooth. Transfer the mixture to a bowl and fold in the crème fraîche or sour cream; add salt and pepper.

MAKES ABOUT 1½ CUPS (12 FL OZ/375 ML)

Top to bottom: Pinto Bean Dip, Roasted Red Bell Pepper Dip

EGGS DIABLO

Flavorful and colorful, these eggs are a great addition to a picnic or backyard barbecue. To make them spicier, use jalapeño jack cheese instead of Monterey jack.

6 hard-cooked eggs
1 Anaheim chili, roasted, peeled, cored, seeded and diced
   (see glossary)
2 tablespoons finely chopped green (spring) onion
2 tablespoons finely shredded Monterey jack cheese
2 tablespoons Taco Sauce (recipe on page 197)
2 tablespoons mayonnaise
salt and freshly ground pepper to taste
24 strips roasted red pepper or pimiento (canned sweet
   pepper) for garnish

❁ Cut the eggs in half lengthwise. Place the yolks in a bowl and the whites on a decorative platter. Mash the yolks with a fork and blend in all the remaining ingredients except the garnish. Divide the yolk mixture among the egg white halves, mounding it evenly. Decorate each egg with 2 strips of red pepper or pimiento. Serve immediately or refrigerate until ready to use.

MAKES 12   *Photograph pages 34–35*

SALAD DE MEXICO

Colorful and lively, this tangy salad delivers the flavors, textures and tastes of the Southwest. Nopales are available year-round in the produce department of Latino grocery stores. The smaller, deep-green pads are the most tender. If you cannot find fresh ones, they are also available in jars or cans.

1 cup (6 oz/185 g) julienned nopales (cactus pads) (if using
   canned, rinse well and drain)
1 cup (6 oz/185 g) julienned jícama (yam bean)
1 small red bell pepper (capsicum), roasted, peeled, cored,
   seeded and julienned (see glossary)
2 navel oranges, peeled and sectioned
1 teaspoon minced jalapeño chili
1 tablespoon minced fresh cilantro (coriander)
1 tablespoon fresh orange juice
1 tablespoon avocado oil, or corn oil
salt and freshly ground pepper to taste

❁ Toss the nopales, jícama, bell pepper, oranges, jalapeño and cilantro together in a nonaluminum bowl. Whisk the orange juice and avocado oil together in a small bowl; stir into the salad. Add salt and pepper. Serve at room temperature.

SERVES 6

AZTEC CALENDAR

A popular appetizer in Arizona, this layered dip is perfect for a large group or a buffet table. When arranged on a large round platter, it resembles the design of an Aztec calendar. Serve it with a variety of corn chips: blue, white, yellow and red.

4 cups (32 fl oz/1 l) Pinto Bean Dip (recipe on page 44)
1½ cups (12 fl oz/375 ml) Guacamole (recipe on page 191)
3 Anaheim chilies, roasted, peeled, seeded and diced
   (see glossary)

4 green (spring) onions, finely chopped
2 cups (8 oz/250 g) grated Cheddar cheese
2 cups (8 oz/250 g) grated Monterey jack cheese
12 pitted ripe olives, sliced
1 large tomato, seeded and diced
shredded lettuce

Left to right: Aztec Calendar, Salad de Mexico

1 teaspoon chili powder
sprigs of fresh parsley for garnish

❀ Evenly cover a large round platter or pizza pan with the pinto bean dip. Spread the guacamole over the layer of beans. Sprinkle the Anaheim chilies and green onions over the guacamole. Combine the cheeses and completely cover the chili-onion layer. Decorate the top by alternating wedges of sliced olives, tomato and shredded lettuce over the cheese so that the wedges of cheese show. Sprinkle chili powder over all and place parsley sprigs around outside of platter. Serve with corn chips.

SERVES 12

47

MARINATED CORN AND LIMA BEAN SALAD

Corn is sacred to many native Americans and is the traditional food of Pueblo peoples. The six colors of corn (yellow, white, red, blue, black and speckled) each represent a different direction in some Pueblo cultures: north, south, east, west, up and down. Native Americans often combine corn and beans, as in this recipe, which is nutritionally sound: combining plant proteins provides the necessary balance of amino acids. If possible, make this salad with more than one color of corn.

3 cups (18 oz/560 g) cooked corn kernels
1 red bell pepper (capsicum), roasted, peeled, cored, seeded and diced (see glossary)
1 green bell pepper (capsicum), cored, seeded and diced
1 cup (5 oz/155 g) finely chopped red (Spanish) onions
1 cup (7 oz/220 g) cooked lima beans

DRESSING

1 teaspoon salt
1 teaspoon chili powder
¼ cup (4 fl oz/125 ml) cider vinegar
⅓ cup (3 fl oz/80 ml) corn oil

❀ In a large bowl, combine corn, peppers, onions and lima beans. To make the dressing, in another bowl, stir together the salt, chili powder and vinegar; slowly whisk in the corn oil. Pour the dressing over the vegetables and mix well. Refrigerate, covered, for at least 2 hours before serving.

SERVES 6

SPINACH SALAD WITH CITRUS

This salad makes good use of grapefruit and oranges from the river valleys of Arizona. The combination of tart fruit and spinach makes this a nice palate cleanser.

DRESSING

2 tablespoons olive oil
1 tablespoon white wine vinegar
1 tablespoon fresh grapefruit juice
½ teaspoon sugar
¼ teaspoon grated orange zest
⅛ teaspoon salt
⅛ teaspoon ground cinnamon

Left to right: Spinach Salad with Citrus, Marinated Corn and Lima Bean Salad

SALAD

4 cups (4 oz/125 g) stemmed fresh spinach, washed
  and dried
1 grapefruit, peeled and sectioned
1 orange, peeled and sectioned
2 tablespoons minced green (spring) onions
¼ cup (1½ oz/45 g) slivered almonds, toasted (see glossary)

❁ Mix together all the dressing ingredients in a small bowl;
cover and chill until ready to serve.
❁ Place the spinach, fruit and green onions in a large bowl.
Toss with just enough dressing to coat the leaves of the
spinach. Sprinkle the almonds over the salad and toss again.

SERVES 6

SAN ANTONIO, TEXAS

SHRIMP STUFFED WITH COTIJA AND CILANTRO

*The combination of Mexican cheese and shrimp from Puerto
Penasco (a fishing village and resort town on the Gulf of California
in Mexico) is a winning one, and these look beautiful on a colorful
platter for a buffet. If you don't have a pastry bag, cut a corner off
a sealable plastic bag, place the cheese mixture in the bag and
squeeze the mixture through the cut.*

4 oz (125 g) cream cheese at room temperature
4 oz (125 g) cotija, feta or mild fresh goat cheese
2 tablespoons fresh lemon juice
2 tablespoons chopped fresh cilantro (coriander)
¼ teaspoon cayenne pepper
salt and freshly ground pepper to taste
1½ lb (750 g) medium to large shrimp, peeled

❁ In a food processor or blender, mix the cheeses until
smooth. Add the lemon juice, cilantro, cayenne, and salt and
pepper to taste. Blend thoroughly.
❁ Bring a large pot of salted water to a boil. Cut a deep slit
down the length of the outside curve of each shrimp and
devein. Put the shrimp in the boiling water and cook until
they turn pink, about 2 minutes. Drain, plunge into a bowl
of ice water, drain again and pat dry.
❁ Scoop the cheese mixture into a pastry bag fitted with a
star tip; pipe the mixture into the slit of each shrimp.
Arrange on a platter and chill until the filling is firm, about
1 hour.

MAKES 25–30 SHRIMP

TUCSON, ARIZONA

PASTEL OF SHRIMP, AVOCADO AND TOMATO WITH CAVIAR

*Pastel in Spanish translates to "cake." This elegant appetizer, the
creation of Janos Wilder, chef-owner of Janos restaurant in Tucson,
gets its name from the cakelike layering of ingredients.*

1 cup (1 oz/30 g) loosely packed fresh cilantro
  (coriander) leaves
2 ripe Haas avocados, peeled, pitted and finely diced
¼ cup (2 fl oz/60 ml) fresh lime juice
1 cup (6 oz/185 g) fresh corn kernels, lightly blanched
  and drained
16 shrimp (prawns), peeled, deveined and steamed or grilled
10 yellow pear (egg) tomatoes, halved
2 oz (60 g) Beluga caviar (optional)

*Top to bottom: Shrimp Stuffed with Cotija and Cilantro; Pastel of Shrimp,
Avocado and Tomato with Caviar*

VINAIGRETTE

1½ oz (45 g) wild mushrooms
1 garlic clove, minced
7 tablespoons (3½ fl oz/105 ml) extra-virgin olive oil
2 tablespoons balsamic vinegar
salt and freshly ground pepper to taste

2 tablespoons finely diced red bell pepper (capsicum)
2 tablespoons finely diced yellow bell pepper (capsicum)
2 tablespoons finely diced purple bell pepper (capsicum)

❁ Center a ring mold (3 in/7.5 cm in diameter, 1½ in/4 cm
high) on each of 4 plates. In a medium nonaluminum bowl,
toss the cilantro, avocados and lime juice together. Pack the
bottom ⅓ in (9 mm) of each ring mold with a layer of the
avocado mixture. Pack the next ⅓ in (9 mm) of each mold
with a layer of the corn. Arrange 4 shrimp in concentric circles on top of the corn in each mold. Arrange the tomatoes
decoratively on top of the shrimp. Garnish with caviar, if
desired.
❁ To make the vinaigrette, toss the mushrooms with the
garlic and 1 tablespoon of the olive oil and quickly grill over
hot coals, or sauté in a hot, dry skillet over high heat. Put
the grilled mushrooms and remaining olive oil in a blender
and purée until smooth. Turn into a small bowl and whisk
in the balsamic vinegar; add salt and pepper.
❁ Sprinkle the diced peppers on the plates surrounding each
mold; drizzle the peppers with vinaigrette and carefully
remove the molds.

SERVES 4

Mexican Pizza

Hearty enough for a light meal, this pizza may be varied in a number of ways. Instead of using the crust described here, use a large flour tortilla broiled on one side, turned over and covered with the toppings and placed under the broiler until the cheese is melted. You may also use cooked chicken or shrimp in place of sausage and try different types of cheeses.

CRUST

½ cup (4 fl oz/125 ml) warm (110°F/45°C) water
1 package active dried yeast
1 teaspoon sugar
1½ cups (7½ oz/235 g) unbleached all-purpose (plain) flour
¼ teaspoon salt
1 tablespoon yellow cornmeal
1 tablespoon olive oil

TOPPING

1 cup (8 fl oz/250 ml) Ranchero Sauce (recipe on page 190)
8 oz (250 g) hot sausage, cooked, crumbled and drained on
   paper towels

1½ cups (12 oz/375 g) grated Monterey jack cheese
½ cup (2 oz/60 g) thinly sliced red (Spanish) onion
1 red, yellow or green bell pepper (capsicum), cored, seeded
   and thinly sliced
1 pickled jalapeño chili, seeded and diced

❀ Preheat an oven to 500°F (260°C). Lightly oil a 12-in (50-cm) pizza pan.
❀ To make the crust, in a small bowl, mix the warm water, yeast and sugar together; let sit until the yeast activates, about 3 minutes. In a large bowl, stir together the flour, salt and cornmeal; add the yeast mixture and olive oil and knead to a smooth dough. On a board sprinkled with cornmeal, roll the dough out into a 13-in (32.5-cm) circle and line the prepared pizza pan with the dough.
❀ Spread the ranchero sauce evenly over the pizza dough. Cover the sauce with the cooked sausage and sprinkle the cheese over all. Evenly distribute the red onion, bell pepper and pickled jalapeño over the cheese.
❀ Bake the pizza in the lower third of the oven until the crust is browned and the cheese is melted, about 15–20 minutes.

SERVES 6 AS AN APPETIZER, 3 AS A MAIN COURSE

Mexican Pizza

Blue Crab Cakes with Avocado-Corn Salsa

BLUE CRAB CAKES WITH AVOCADO-CORN SALSA

One of the first modern Southwestern chefs, Vincent Guerithault has put Phoenix on the culinary map with his creative cuisine. This is one of the most popular dishes at the restaurant bearing his name, and the salsa is delicious on its own with tortilla chips.

CRAB CAKES

1 lb (500 kg) fresh blue crab meat or thawed and well-drained frozen crab meat
1 tablespoon minced shallots
1 tablespoon diced red bell pepper (capsicum)
1 tablespoon diced yellow bell pepper (capsicum)
1 tablespoon diced green bell pepper (capsicum)
2 extra-large eggs
1 teaspoon plain low-fat yogurt
salt and freshly ground pepper to taste

1 tablespoon brioche bread crumbs
olive oil for sautéing

AVOCADO-CORN SALSA

1 cup (6 oz/185 g) fresh corn kernels, steamed
1 cup (6 oz/185 g) diced avocado
1 teaspoon chopped fresh cilantro (coriander)
1 teaspoon diced tomatoes
1 teaspoon chopped shallots
1 teaspoon chopped red bell pepper (capsicum)
1 teaspoon chopped yellow bell pepper (capsicum)
1 teaspoon chopped green bell pepper (capsicum)
1 teaspoon fresh lemon juice
salt and freshly ground pepper to taste

❁ Mix all the crab cake ingredients together except the bread crumbs and form 8 cakes of equal size. Dust each with brioche bread crumbs and sauté for 3 minutes on each side over low heat in a small amount of olive oil.

❁ Mix all the salsa ingredients together. Serve the crab cakes hot, with 1 tablespoon of the salsa on the side of each serving.

MAKES 8

Left to right: Painted Desert Coleslaw, Piquant Potato Salad

PIQUANT POTATO SALAD

Avoid the oxidized chili powder found in cellophane packages, which is often stale. Instead, buy chili powder packed in opaque containers without additives or make your own by grinding dried chilies (seeds and stems removed) in a blender and adding fresh-ground cumin or other spices to taste, if you like. Try this flavorful potato salad at your next barbecue or picnic; because the dressing is made without mayonnaise, the salad keeps and travels well.

DRESSING

⅓ cup (3 fl oz/80 ml) olive oil
¼ cup (2 fl oz/60 ml) red wine vinegar
1 tablespoon sugar
1½ teaspoons chili powder
1 teaspoon seasoned salt
¼ teaspoon red hot pepper sauce

4 russet potatoes
1 cup (3½ oz/105 g) thinly sliced red (Spanish) onion
1 cup (6 oz/185 g) corn kernels
½ cup (2 oz/60 g) grated peeled carrot
½ cup (2½ oz/75 g) diced red bell pepper (capsicum)
½ cup (2½ oz/75 g) diced green bell pepper (capsicum)
½ cup (2½ oz/75 g) sliced pitted ripe olives

❀ Whisk all the dressing ingredients together in a small bowl and set aside.
❀ Cook the potatoes in boiling salted water over medium-high heat in a heavy saucepan until tender, about 30 minutes. Drain, peel and cube the potatoes. Put the potatoes in a large bowl and gently toss with the dressing. Cover and chill for 1 hour.
❀ Fold in the remaining ingredients and chill until ready to serve.

SERVES 6

PAINTED DESERT COLESLAW

For a color combination as dramatic as the Painted Desert, use a mixture of red and green cabbage and substitute purple, lavender, orange or white bell peppers when they are in season. Adjust the spiciness of this colorful salad by experimenting with different chili powders; many excellent ones are available in grocery stores and by mail order.

3 cups (9 oz/280 g) shredded cabbage
½ cup (2½ oz/75 g) shredded peeled carrot
1 small yellow bell pepper (capsicum), cored, seeded and diced
1 small red bell pepper (capsicum), cored, seeded and diced
1 small green bell pepper (capsicum), cored, seeded and diced
½ cup (2 oz/60 g) thinly sliced red (Spanish) onion

DRESSING

1 *chili de árbol* (see glossary)
2 tablespoons cider vinegar
1 tablespoon fresh lime juice
2 teaspoons honey
⅓ cup (3 fl oz/80 ml) vegetable oil
salt and freshly ground pepper to taste

❀ Mix together the cabbage, carrot, peppers and onion in a large, nonaluminum bowl.
❀ Toast the *chili de árbol* in a dry skillet, turning once, for 1–2 minutes. Remove the seeds and purée into a powder. Put in a medium bowl and whisk with the remaining dressing ingredients.
❀ In a large bowl, toss cabbage mixture with the dressing.

SERVES 6

CORN NACHOS

Nachos, popular throughout the Southwest, may be as simple as corn chips topped with melted cheese, or an elaborate presentation including chicken or ground beef, refried beans, pickled jalapeños, tomatoes, chilies, guacamole and sour cream. This recipe, which includes corn and red pepper, may be made even spicier by sprinkling pickled jalapeño chilies on top before broiling.

1 tablespoon vegetable oil
½ cup (2½ oz/75 g) finely chopped red bell pepper (capsicum)
⅓ cup (1½ oz/45 g) finely chopped red (Spanish) onion
¾ cup (4 oz/125 g) corn kernels
3 Anaheim chilies, roasted, peeled, cored, seeded and diced (see glossary)
8 oz (250 g) cream cheese at room temperature
1 cup (8 oz/250 g) sour cream
2 teaspoons chili powder
2 teaspoons ground cumin
¼ teaspoon cayenne pepper
salt and freshly ground pepper to taste
10 oz (315 g) white or yellow corn chips, about 72 chips
1 tablespoon sliced pickled jalapeño chilies (optional)

❋ Heat the oil in a large skillet over medium high heat; sauté the bell pepper and red onion until soft, about 3 minutes. Add corn and Anaheim chilies and cook another 2 minutes; set aside.
❋ With an electric mixer, beat together the cream cheese and sour cream in a medium bowl. Add the chili powder, cumin, cayenne, salt and pepper. Fold the sautéed vegetables into the cheese–sour cream mixture.
❋ Spread about ½ tablespoon topping on each corn chip. Sprinkle with jalapeños, if you like. Place on baking sheets and broil about 3 in (7.5 cm) from the heat for 2–3 minutes, or until the cheese melts and the chips begin to brown.

MAKES ABOUT 72

CRAB AND ROASTED PEPPER NACHOS

The rich, creamy mixture used on these nachos is equally delicious on toasted baguette slices or as the filling for a quesadilla. Asadero is a cheese that resembles provolone in flavor and mozzarella in texture. Because it melts easily, it is a perfect cooking cheese.

2 tablespoons unsalted butter
½ cup (2½ oz/75 g) finely chopped onion
1 cup (8 fl oz/250 ml) heavy (double) cream
1 package (3 oz/90 g) cream cheese at room temperature, cut into pieces
¼ cup (1 oz/30 g) grated asadero, provolone or mozzarella cheese
⅛ teaspoon cayenne pepper
salt and freshly ground white pepper to taste
8 oz (250 g) fresh or thawed and well-drained frozen crabmeat
1 red bell pepper (capsicum), roasted, peeled, cored, seeded and diced (see glossary)
2 Anaheim chilies, roasted, peeled, cored, seeded and diced (see glossary)
5 oz (155 g) tortilla chips, about 36 chips

❋ Heat the butter over medium-high heat in a medium skillet. Add the onion and sauté until slightly softened, about 2 minutes. Add the cream, bring to a boil and cook,

stirring occasionally, until the cream is reduced by half. Add the cream cheese and stir until blended. Stir in the asadero cheese, cayenne pepper, salt and pepper. Fold in the crabmeat, pepper and chilies. The mixture can be refrigerated until needed at this point.
❋ Preheat a broiler (griller). Spread each tortilla chip with about 1 tablespoon of the crab-pepper mixture and place on a baking sheet. Broil about 3 in (7.5 cm) from the heat until the nachos are hot and bubbly, 2–3 minutes.

MAKES ABOUT 36

CREAMY CHICKEN NACHOS

Jalapeños are probably the best known hot chilies in the United States. Because they are fiery hot, it is best to add only a portion of the amount called for in any recipe, then to taste for "heat" and add more if desired. Cooked shrimp may be substituted for the chicken in this recipe with equally good results. The creamy topping, which may be made a day ahead, is also delicious spread on toast rounds or flour tortillas and broiled.

1 whole boneless chicken breast, skinned, poached and shredded
8 oz (250 g) cream cheese at room temperature
2 jalapeño chilies, seeded and minced
3 tablespoons minced red (Spanish) onion
2 garlic cloves, minced
1 teaspoon cumin seed, crushed to a coarse powder
1 teaspoon chili powder
1½ cups (6 oz/185 g) shredded Monterey jack cheese
salt and freshly ground pepper to taste
12 oz (375 g) flat tortilla chips (round or triangular), about 100 chips

❋ With an electric mixer, cream together all the ingredients except the tortilla chips until well blended. Refrigerate until ready to use, but bring to room temperature before assembling so that the mixture is spreadable.
❋ Preheat a broiler (griller). Evenly spread each chip with a generous amount of the mixture. Arrange the chips on a baking sheet and broil about 3 in (7.5 cm) away from the heat until puffed and golden.

MAKES 96

Left to right: Creamy Chicken Nachos, Crab and Roasted Pepper Nachos, Corn Nachos

CHICKEN, PEPPER AND AVOCADO TOSTADITAS

Ranchero is a fresh cheese that is lower in fat, sodium and cholesterol than jack or Cheddar cheese, while cotija (ko-tee-hah) is a hard, dry, full-flavored aged cheese; they add a unique taste to this savory chicken mixture. The filling also makes a delicious cheese crisp: Broil a flour tortilla on one side, turn it over, spread the chicken mixture on the unbrowned side, sprinkle cheese over and broil until the cheese is melted, then cut into wedges.

2 tablespoons olive oil
2 tablespoons butter
1 onion, halved and thinly sliced lengthwise
3 garlic cloves, minced
1 tomato, diced
2 tablespoons fresh lime juice
salt to taste

1 whole boneless chicken breast, skinned and diced
1 jalapeño chili, roasted, peeled, cored, seeded and cut into strips (see glossary)
1 red bell pepper (capsicum), roasted, peeled, cored, seeded and cut into strips (see glossary)
1 Anaheim chili, roasted, peeled, cored, seeded and cut into strips (see glossary)
¼ cup (⅓ oz/10 g) minced fresh cilantro (coriander)
1 Haas avocado, peeled, pitted and diced
1 cup (4 oz/125 g) grated ranchero or Monterey jack cheese
½ cup (2½ oz/75 g) crumbled cotija, feta or goat cheese
5 oz (155 g) round tortilla chips, about 36 chips

❁ Heat the olive oil and butter in a large, heavy skillet over medium heat. Add the onion and cook until slightly softened, about 2 minutes; add the garlic, tomato, lime juice and salt; cook, stirring, until the onions are translucent, about 5 more minutes. Add the chicken and continue cooking until chicken is just opaque (do not overcook); add the pepper and chili strips, cilantro and avocado. Remove from heat.

54

1 cup (4 oz/125 g) unbleached all-purpose (plain) flour
1 teaspoon salt
1 cup (8 fl oz/250 ml) beer
5 Anaheim or New Mexico green chilies, roasted, peeled, seeded and cut into ¾-in (2-cm) strips (see glossary)
4 oz (125 g) Monterey jack cheese, cut into ¾-by-½-by-½-in (2-cm-by-12-mm-by-12 mm) pieces and chilled
vegetable oil for frying

❋ In a large bowl, stir together the flour and salt; whisk in the beer until smooth. Allow the batter to rest, covered, for 1 hour at room temperature.

❋ Wrap a chili strip around each piece of cheese and secure with a toothpick. If not frying immediately, refrigerate until ready to use.

❋ Fill a medium, heavy saucepan with oil to a depth of 1 in (2.5 cm). Heat to about 400°F (200°C). Dip the chili-covered cheese pieces in the batter, coating them well, and allow the excess to drip back into the bowl. Drop in the hot oil and cook, turning them once, until they are crisp and golden brown, about 3–5 minutes. Remove from the hot oil with a slotted utensil, drain on paper towels and repeat to cook the remaining rellenos. Remove the toothpicks and serve immediately.

MAKES ABOUT 20

Clockwise from left: Corn Cups with Salsa; Chicken, Pepper and Avocado Tostaditas, Cocktail-Size Chile Rellenos

❋ Preheat a broiler (griller). Combine the cheeses in a small bowl. Spoon 1 tablespoon of chicken mixture on each chip; top with grated cheese and place the tortilla chips on a baking sheet. Broil about 3 in (7.5 cm) from the heat until the cheeses just begin to melt. Transfer to a serving platter and serve immediately.

MAKES 36

SANTA FE, NEW MEXICO

CORN CUPS WITH SALSA

Corn, a symbol of life for many native Americans in the Southwest, lends color, texture and unique taste to this salsa. Mini muffin tins make corn cups just the right size for appetizers, but they also may be made in regular muffin tins and served alongside a grilled entrée.

CORNMEAL PASTRY

6 tablespoons (3 oz/90 g) unsalted butter at room temperature
2 oz (60 g) cream cheese at room temperature
½ cup (2½ oz/75 g) yellow cornmeal
1 cup (5 oz/155 g) unbleached all-purpose (plain) flour
salt to taste

SALSA

5 ripe plum (egg) tomatoes, diced
⅓ cup (1½ oz/45 g) finely chopped red (Spanish) onion
1 red bell pepper (capsicum), cored, seeded and diced
2 jalapeño chilies, seeded and minced
2 tablespoons fresh lemon juice
1 tablespoon fresh lime juice
½ cup (3 oz/90 g) corn kernels
2 tablespoons minced fresh cilantro (coriander)
salt and freshly ground pepper to taste

❋ Preheat an oven to 350°F (180°C). In a medium bowl, with an electric mixer, cream together the butter and cream cheese. Sift together the cornmeal, flour and salt. Stir the dry mixture gradually into the butter-cheese mixture until all of it is incorporated. Knead the dough briefly and divide it into 1-in (2.5-cm) balls. Press each ball into a mini muffin mold, pressing down in the center to fill the mold and form a cup. Bake until light brown and cooked through, about 20 minutes. Remove from the oven; let cool. Remove the cups from the molds.

❋ In a nonaluminum bowl, stir together all the salsa ingredients and adjust the seasoning.

❋ Fill the corn cups with salsa and serve immediately.

MAKES 30

TUCSON, ARIZONA

COCKTAIL-SIZE CHILES RELLENOS

A miniature version of the popular batter-coated, cheese-stuffed green chilies, these are great for cocktail parties. The yeast in the beer helps make a light, airy batter.

CENTRAL HIGHLANDS

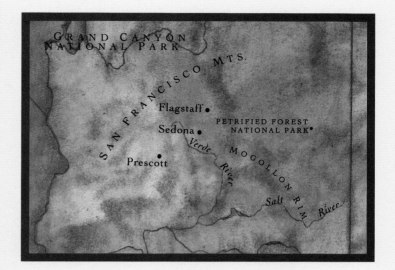

CENTRAL HIGHLANDS

Bordered to the north by the mile-high Colorado Plateau and the steep descent of the Mogollon Rim, and to the south by the vast basin and range deserts, a rugged band of volcanic mountain ranges cuts west to east across the Southwest from central Arizona into western New Mexico. Here the bare bones of the region's geological past are visible, from pastel-colored boulders of volcanic ash in the Datil Mountains to the rust-colored cliff sides of the red rock country around Sedona.

The constantly contrasting landscape of this sparsely populated region inspires awe in visitors driving north on Interstate 17 from Phoenix to Flagstaff, or on the smaller state highways crossing the Arizona–New Mexico border. It is hard to imagine how humans could have survived this beautiful but seemingly threatening land.

But early peoples did survive. The mountain peaks catch the storm clouds, bringing ten to thirty inches of rain each year to water a profusion of edible wild plants. Streams run through the high forests, where game animals live in abundance.

The ancestors of the Mogollon people who lived in this area as many as seven thousand years ago were rudimentary farmers. Archaeological discoveries at

Previous pages: The picturesque Mogollon Rim drops 2000 feet, abruptly marking the edge of the Colorado Plateau which covers much of northern Arizona. Left: A land of tremendous diversity, Arizona encompasses verdant forests and sparkling streams within close proximity of the arid desert; pictured here, the lush landscape of Oak Creek Canyon.

59

In just twenty years, Sedona has grown from a small Arizonan agricultural community to a thriving art center and resort town.

Bat Cave, in the mountains that fringe the former Pleistocene lake bed that is now the San Augustin Plains of western New Mexico, show that they grew small, strawberry-shaped ears of corn as early as 3600 B.C., as well as squashes; beans became a crop by 400 B.C., if not sooner, providing a balanced diet of plant staples that endures in the region to this day.

Wild foods brought considerable variety to that diet, and hunting and gathering probably served to supply the bulk of sustenance during periods when rainfall declined and crops failed. Deposits at Tularosa Cave in the Mogollon Mountains hold remains of some forty different kinds of plants besides the familiar corn, kidney beans and squashes, including piñon nuts, walnuts, acorns, prickly pears, sunflower seeds, Indian rice, wolfberries and mariposa lily bulbs. Also found were the bones of deer, bison, turkeys and muskrats.

The Western and Chiricahua Apache tribes that migrated southward into the region some time after A.D. 1300 brought their hunting and gathering ways with them. Men hunted deer and antelope, a task that became more efficient for them after Spaniards introduced the horse to the Southwest. But even when game was scarce, they shunned the plentiful bear, an animal they considered evil; turkeys, because they fed on snakes and insects; and fish, whose scaly skins brought to mind evil snakes.

Women were left the task of smoke-drying excess meat from the hunt to make jerky. But, more important, from early spring to late autumn, they harvested

The pine-forested Mogollon Rim country of central Arizona is laden with rolling hills, scenic canyons and quiet lakes.

such wild plant life as yucca, agave, mesquite and screw beans, sumac and juniper berries, cactus fruit, strawberries and raspberries, piñon nuts, walnuts, acorns and grapes. In some cases, their gathering involved religious rituals. Elaborate prayers and ceremonies, for example, accompanied the digging, trimming, roasting, pounding, sun-drying and storing of the agave—such an important staple to the Apaches that the Spaniards named the plant *mescal* after the Mescalero branch of the tribe.

The Apaches initially cultivated small crops of corn and melons. Under the influence of neighboring Mexican settlers, those plantings became more diverse, incorporating squashes, beans, chilies, potatoes and onions. But one study of the Western Apaches, published in 1935 by anthropologist Grenville Goodwin, found that all these crops still accounted for no more than 25 percent of the food eaten by a tribe in a given year.

In more recent times, the Southwest's Central Highlands lured European settlers, who brought with them a taste for beef and oysters, wine and whisky. Mines around Magdalena, New Mexico, for example, enjoyed a lead-silver boom between 1880 and 1902, the Magdalena Mountains yielding as much as $9 million worth of ore. At the same time, thanks to one of Arizona's most prolific copper mines, the town of Jerome on the side of Mingus Mountain enjoyed such raucous growth that the closely packed network of twenty-four-hour saloons and bordellos lining its steep streets earned it a reputation as "the wickedest town in America." It went bust after World War II, only to be reborn in the 1960s as the small, charming enclave of artists and craftspeople it is today.

Seekers of a more spiritual sort haunt the highlands. Near Cordes Junction, Arizona, followers of visionary Italian-born architect Paolo Soleri built the futuristic desert commune of Arcosanti, whose cafe and bakery serves wholesome food made from natural ingredients.

Meanwhile, Sedona, in the heart of Arizona's red rock country, is burgeoning under its New Age rubric as one of the planet's key energy centers, a focal point for harmonic convergence and a landing site for UFOs. Mystics, channelers and those hoping for close encounters with extraterrestrials jostle for space with artists who have long been drawn here to capture the beauty of the cliffs and canyons. A happy result of this trendy mayhem is a contemporary approach to dining: even a favorite local Southwestern hangout supplements its standard tacos, enchiladas, tamales and burritos with such dishes as grilled nopal cactus pads on a bed of red chili cream.

But even the most innovative or unusual modern culinary development in Southwestern kitchens nonetheless takes its inspiration from the region's centuries-old food traditions. And in the desire to share sustenance and give people pleasure, Southwesterners still exemplify the same attitude of goodwill expressed in a traditional Apache medicine man's prayer: "I pray, I say, for a long life to live with you where the good people are. . . . Ahead of me is goodness, lead me on."

SOUPS, STEWS AND CHILIS

Soups and stews, staples of early Southwestern cuisine, originated from both Spanish and native American traditions.

SOUPS, STEWS AND CHILIS

The terms *soup* and *stew* can be defined fairly simply: Make a soup's ingredients chunky enough, and simmer it until thick, and it becomes a stew; add sufficient broth to a stew, finely mince or purée its ingredients, and there's soup for you. Yet there is a culinary gray area between soup and stew that remains for the most part delightfully blurred in the Southwest. And the citizenry is happy for it to stay that way, thank you very much.

Take posole as a prime example. The robust bowlful begins with hominy: large kernels of dried corn soaked in lime to remove their hulls and plump them up. Several hours of simmering with a few chunks of pork, dried chilies, onion, garlic, herbs and spices yields an everyday favorite. If more of the pig gets added, the posole becomes a customary New Mexican Christmas and New Year's dish. Substitute lamb for the pork and you have a more typically Navajo recipe. But is posole in any of these forms a soup or a stew? Make your own guess; then pick up any other book or article on Southwestern cooking and you have a roughly fifty-fifty chance of agreeing with the author.

The point is, traditional Southwestern soups and stews exemplify a necessarily rough-and-ready approach to providing human sustenance. Cowboys on the range, pioneers on the trail, native American hunters and early European settlers alike had few options for what they cooked or how they cooked it: Into the pot went their latest catch or scraps of tough and scrawny livestock, along with the odd vegetable, water and whatever seasonings were at hand; out came a one-dish meal, whatever it might be called. Cowboys in particular, from Texas to the Arizona Territory, took particular pride in a concoction involving all the internal organs and sometimes some of the meat from a just-butchered calf or steer. Simmered for five hours or more in a huge cast-iron cauldron, it became a specialty known as Son-of-a-Gun or, less delicately, Son-of-a-Bitch Stew.

It is easy to imagine the dismay such cooking might have caused the uninitiated. Witness the "mixture of meat, chilly verde & onions boiled together" described in the journal sixteen-year-old newlywed Susan Shelby Magoffin kept on her first journey to New Mexico along the Santa Fe Trail in 1846. "There were a few mouthfuls taken," she continues, "for I could not eat a dish so strong, and unaccustomed [sic] to my palate."

Not to say that the émigré's palate could not adjust in time, as Susan Magoffin's did; or that such catch-as-catch-can cooking could not on occasion produce distinctive results. A case in point is the dish many people consider the Southwest's greatest culinary gift to the world: chili.

When most outsiders sing chili's praises, they pay

Previous pages, clockwise from left: Butternut Squash Soup (recipe page 79), Black Bean Soup (recipe page 80), Red Pepper Soup with Poblano Cream (recipe page 66)

64

homage in fact to a specialty of Texas: chili con carne, literally "chili peppers with meat." That term describes a native Texan dish often referred to with typical cowboy terseness as a "bowl o' red": dried red chilies simmered with small cubes of seared beef, some cumin and oregano, salt, garlic, a smattering of other peppers to spice it up a little more and maybe a sprinkling of corn tortilla flour, or masa harina, for thickening. It is easy to imagine the recipe prepared on a trailside chuckwagon, accompanied with a scoop of boiled beans to help soak up and temper the fiery juices.

Staunch traditionalists will swear that true chili begins and ends with such a formula. But a survey of other Southwestern regions tells a different story.

The *chile colorado* (red chili) of New Mexico, for example, stands out as a close cousin of old-fashioned Texas chili. Long, dried red pods are stemmed and seeded, toasted in the oven or over a flame, puréed with broth and simmered with chunks of beef and simple seasonings. The result is generally a thinner, redder, more intense concoction, as much chili peppers as it is meat. And in deference both to the star of the dish and to their Hispanic heritage, New Mexicans call and spell it *chile,* never "chili" as the Texans do.

Even more popular in New Mexico is *chile verde,* green chili. At its simplest, this dish consists of nothing more than freshly picked, fire-roasted New Mexican green chilies, their stems and skins removed, their juicy flesh torn or coarsely chopped and served warm with beans and tortillas. At once green-tasting, sweet and subtly fiery, chilies thus prepared present a quintessential experience of the Southwest. Just as commonly,

Some believe that chili originated in the mid-19th century when Texans combined local ingredients to create a dish easily prepared on the open trail.

you'll find green chilies simmered with pieces of pork to produce a stew with the same moist chili-to-meat balance as its *colorado* cousin. And—horror to Lone Star nationalists—some Texans west of the Rio Grande actually prefer such a pork-and-green-chili stew.

As chili's popularity has grown, so have its variations. Fresh, dried and powdered chilies of all colors, shapes, sizes and intensities may season the stew, singly or in combination. The beans originally served on the side have found their way into the pot, both in Texas and beyond its borders; and not just pinto or kidney beans, but black beans, white beans—beans of every color and creed. Tomatoes may be added to deepen the color and underscore the flavor of the chilies with an edge of sweetness and acidity. Other forms of protein replace the beef or the pork: turkey or chicken, for today's health-conscious cook; all manner of game, for hunter-cooks harkening back to the dish's early pioneer origins; mixtures of two or more kinds of game or domestic meat; meatier varieties of seafood such as tuna or shark; and even beans alone, with no meat at all.

Indeed, every weekend year-round, hundreds of amateur and professional chili chefs show off their own versions of chili in cook-offs throughout the Southwest and throughout the rest of the United States. And no two recipes are ever quite alike.

But when you get right down to the barest of essentials, what they all have in common is chilies. And every recipe induces in its creator a heartwarming and soul-stirring feeling akin to that expressed by Lady Bird Johnson, wife of U.S. president and lifelong Texan Lyndon Baines Johnson, in a letter she wrote to the legendary Dallas chili expert Frank X. Tolbert for publication in his definitive book *A Bowl of Red:*

> My feeling about chili is this—along in November, when the first norther strikes, and the skies are gray, along about five o'clock in the afternoon, I get to thinking how good chili would taste for supper. It always lives up to expectations. In fact, you don't even mind the cold November winds.

Frontiersman and Taos resident Kit Carson certainly would have agreed. His reputed dying words were: "Wish I had time for just one more bowl of chili."

At the first chili stands in early San Antonio, Texas, marketplaces, a "bowl o' red" was served by women known as "chili queens."

SAN ANTONIO, TEXAS

RED PEPPER SOUP WITH POBLANO CREAM

The slightly sweet taste of this soup is complemented by the subtle heat of the poblano cream—a winning combination. Dried rosemary and marjoram can be substituted for fresh, but the result will be slightly less sweet.

SOUP

3 tablespoons olive oil
6 red bell peppers (capsicums), cored, seeded and julienned
6 leeks, white and light green parts only, sliced
3 garlic cloves, minced
4 fresh rosemary sprigs
4 fresh marjoram sprigs
2½ cups (20 fl oz/625 ml) beef stock (see glossary)
salt and freshly ground pepper to taste
1 cup (8 fl oz/250 ml) heavy (double) cream

POBLANO CREAM

½ cup (4 oz/125 g) sour cream
½ cup (4 fl oz/125 ml) heavy (double) cream
1 tablespoon chopped fresh cilantro (coriander)
1 poblano chili, roasted, peeled, cored and seeded
   (see glossary)
salt and freshly ground pepper to taste

❀ To make the soup, heat the oil in a heavy saucepan; add the peppers and cook, stirring, for about 2 minutes or until slightly softened. Add the leeks and garlic; cook another 2 minutes. Add the rosemary and marjoram; cover, reduce heat and cook over low heat for 1 hour, or until the peppers are very soft. Put the mixture in a food processor or blender and purée. Strain the purée back into the saucepan, add the beef stock and season with salt and pepper. Cook for 5 minutes. Add the cream and heat just until hot.

❀ To make the poblano cream, put the sour cream, cream, cilantro and poblano chili in a blender and purée until smooth. Add salt and pepper.

❀ Ladle the soup into 6 bowls. Put the poblano cream into a squeeze-top plastic bottle and decorate the top of the soup.

SERVES 6 *Photograph pages 62–63*

NEW MEXICO

ROASTED CORN SOUP

The subtle flavors of roasted corn and yellow bell pepper add a distinct taste to this toothsome soup. Although it may be made any time with frozen corn, it's best with just-picked yellow or white corn on the cob. For a more refined soup, strain it before adding the half & half.

4 ears (cobs) fresh corn, husked, or 4 cups (24 oz/750 g)
   corn kernels
1 tablespoon olive oil
2 garlic cloves, minced
½ cup (2½ oz/75 g) finely chopped red (Spanish) onion
½ cup (2½ oz/75 g) finely chopped peeled carrot
½ cup (2½ oz/75 g) finely chopped celery
½ teaspoon ground cumin
2 yellow bell peppers (capsicums), roasted, peeled, cored,
   seeded, and diced (see glossary)
1 serrano chili, seeded and minced
4 cups (32 fl oz/1 l) chicken stock (see glossary)

1 cup (8 fl oz/250 ml) half & half (half milk and half cream)
salt and freshly ground pepper to taste

❀ Over an open flame, on a very hot grill, or under a broiler, roast the corn until the kernels are browned and beginning to caramelize. If using whole ears of corn, cut the kernels off the cob after roasting.

❀ In a large saucepan, heat the olive oil; over medium heat, sauté the garlic, onion, carrot and celery until soft, about 5 minutes. Add the corn kernels, cumin and bell pepper and cook, stirring, for a minute or two. Add the serrano chili and the chicken stock, lower heat and simmer for 30 minutes. Transfer to a food processor or blender and purée for 1–2 minutes. Return to the saucepan, add the half & half, season to taste with salt and pepper and heat until warmed through. Divide among 6 bowls and serve immediately.

SERVES 6

Left to right: Tomatillo Soup, Roasted Corn Soup

TOMATILLO SOUP

This versatile soup is good either hot or cold, so it may be served in any season. Available throughout the year in Latino and specialty markets, tomatillos will keep for up to a month if refrigerated in a paper bag.

3 tablespoons olive oil
3 shallots, minced
2 garlic cloves, minced
1 lb (500 g) tomatillos (about 8), husked and diced
3 Anaheim chilies, roasted, peeled, cored, seeded and diced (see glossary)
6 cups (48 fl oz/1.5 l) chicken stock (see glossary)
1 jalapeño chili, seeded and minced

2 tablespoons fresh lime juice
2 tablespoons minced fresh cilantro (coriander)
salt and freshly ground pepper to taste
sour cream thinned with cream and fresh cilantro (coriander) leaves for garnish

❋ In a large saucepan, heat the olive oil over medium heat; add the shallots and garlic and sauté until softened, about 4–5 minutes. Add the tomatillos, Anaheim chilies and chicken stock. Bring to a boil, lower heat and simmer 10–15 minutes, or until the tomatillos are softened. Transfer to a food processor or blender. Purée with the jalapeño, lime juice and cilantro. Add salt and pepper. Divide the soup among 6 bowls, drizzle sour cream on top and garnish with cilantro leaves. Or, refrigerate overnight and serve cold.

SERVES 6

GARLIC SOUP

This creamy combination of onions, garlic, tortillas, chicken stock and cream can be puréed for a more refined soup or left slightly chunky. The garlic supplies plenty of flavor, but for interesting variations, try drizzling the serving with Poblano Cream (recipe on page 66) or Red Chili Sauce (recipe on page 195).

¼ cup (2 oz/60 g) unsalted butter
2 tablespoons olive oil
2 cups (10 oz/315 g) finely chopped onions
26 garlic cloves, minced
1½ flour tortillas, diced
¼ teaspoon dry mustard
½ teaspoon ground cumin

4 cups (32 fl oz/1 l) chicken stock (see glossary)
1 cup (8 fl oz/250 ml) half & half (half milk and half cream)
salt and freshly ground pepper to taste

❁ In a large pot, heat the butter and olive oil over low heat; add the onions and garlic, stir and cover the pot tightly with a lid. Allow the onions and garlic to sweat over very low heat for 1½ hours, or until very soft.

❁ Remove the lid and stir in the diced tortillas, dry mustard and cumin. Cook, stirring, for 10 minutes. Add the stock and bring the mixture to a boil. Stir in the half & half and salt and pepper and simmer over medium-low heat for about 30 minutes. Taste and adjust seasoning.

❁ If desired, transfer soup to a food processor or blender and purée. Serve immediately.

SERVES 6

Garlic Soup

Pumpkin Soup with Lime-Ginger Cream

CENTRAL ARIZONA

PUMPKIN SOUP WITH LIME-GINGER CREAM

Pumpkins have been cultivated for centuries in the Southwest, and native Americans make use of the seeds and blossoms as well as the meat. Serve this easy-to-make soup in a large hollowed-out pumpkin for a buffet or individual miniature ones for a sit-down dinner.

¼ cup (2 oz/60 g) unsalted butter
2 cups (10 oz/315 g) finely chopped onions
½ teaspoon cayenne pepper
1⅓ cups (11 fl oz/330 ml) milk
3 cups (24 fl oz/750 ml) pumpkin purée
6 cups (48 fl oz/1.5 l) chicken stock (see glossary)
salt and freshly ground pepper to taste
¼ cup (2 fl oz/60 ml) fresh lime juice

1 tablespoon grated fresh ginger
½ cup (4 oz/125 g) sour cream
2 tablespoons grated lime zest

✸ In a large skillet, melt the butter over medium heat; add the onions and slowly sauté until translucent. Stir in the cayenne and transfer the mixture to a food processor or blender. Add the milk and pumpkin and process until smooth. Pour the mixture into a saucepan and whisk in the chicken stock. Over medium-high heat, bring the soup to a simmer. Add salt and pepper.

✸ In a small saucepan over medium heat, cook the lime juice and grated ginger together for 2 minutes. Strain into a medium bowl, discard the ginger and whisk the remaining liquid with the sour cream.

✸ Ladle the soup into bowls. Put the lime–sour cream mixture into a squeeze bottle and decorate the bowls of soup by drizzling designs on top. Sprinkle with lime zest.

SERVES 10–12

CHILI BLANCO

White beans and chicken are a winning combination in this white chili. According to culinary expert Jacques Pépin, white beans are usually from the previous year's crop and do not need a long presoaking, and, in fact, will begin to ferment if left to soak too long, thereby causing gastric distress.

2 cups (14 oz/440 g) dried Great Northern white (haricot) beans
3 whole chicken breasts, skinned
3½ cups (28 fl oz/875 ml) water
2 tablespoons olive oil
2 cups (10 oz/315 g) finely chopped onions
4 garlic cloves, minced
6 Anaheim chilies, roasted, peeled, cored, seeded and diced (see glossary)

1 green serrano or jalapeño chili, cored, seeded and minced
2 teaspoons ground cumin
1 tablespoon minced fresh oregano, or 1½ teaspoons dried oregano
¼ teaspoon ground cloves
¼ teaspoon cayenne pepper
3 cups (24 fl oz/750 ml) chicken stock (see glossary)
salt to taste
2 cups (8 oz/250 g) grated Monterey jack cheese
diced tomatoes, grated Monterey jack, chopped green (spring) onions and chopped fresh cilantro (coriander) for garnish

❁ Place the beans in a heavy, large pot and cover with plenty of water. Let soak for 1 hour.
❁ Put the chicken breasts in a large skillet and cover with the 3½ cups (28 fl oz/875 ml) water. Cover the pan, bring to a low simmer and cook for 30 minutes, or until the chicken is opaque throughout. Remove the chicken from the pan,

Clockwise from top left: Black Bean Chili, Chili Blanco, Chili Verde

BLACK BEAN CHILI

A hearty dish such as this needs only a salad and warm tortillas or corn bread to make a delicious and satisfying meal. Black bean chili freezes well and is even better if made a day ahead of time so that the flavors fully develop. Pass bowls of chopped cilantro, sour cream, diced avocado, shredded cheese and chopped onion so guests can garnish as they wish.

1 lb (500 g) dried black (turtle) beans
2 lb (1 kg) boneless pork loin, cut into cubes
4 garlic cloves, minced
2 *chiles de árbol,* toasted, stemmed and seeded
  (see glossary)
3 Anaheim chilies, roasted, peeled, seeded and diced
  (see glossary)
1 tablespoon cumin seed, ground to a coarse powder
1 teaspoon dried oregano
1 tablespoon salt
1 cup (4 oz/125 g) chopped red (Spanish) onion
2 jalapeño chilies, cored, seeded and minced
1 can (28 oz/875 g) crushed tomatoes with juice
1 red bell pepper (capsicum), cored, seeded and diced
1 tablespoon fresh lime juice

❋ Place the beans in a large pot and cover generously with water; soak overnight. Drain the beans and put back in the same pot with the pork, garlic, *chiles de árbol,* Anaheim chilies, cumin, oregano and salt. Cover with water and bring to a boil; cover, reduce heat and cook for 4 hours, adding water if necessary. Add the jalapeños, tomatoes, bell pepper and lime juice and cook, uncovered, for 1 hour, or until thickened.

SERVES 6–8

CHILI VERDE

New Mexicans believe that chili must be undiluted with beans or tomatoes so their recipes often call for little besides meat and New Mexico green chilies. The Anaheim is similar to the New Mexico green chili, although the latter has a sharper flavor. Delicious as a main course served with warm tortillas, chili verde also makes an excellent filling for burros and chimichangas or a sauce for enchiladas and chiles rellenos.

3 tablespoons bacon fat or vegetable oil
1 cup (4 oz/125 g) coarsely chopped onions
2 lb (1 kg) lean pork, cut into ½-in (12-mm) cubes
2 tablespoons flour
½ teaspoon ground cumin
2 garlic cloves, minced
10 New Mexico green or Anaheim chilies, roasted, peeled,
  cored, seeded and diced (see glossary)
3 cups (24 fl oz/750 ml) chicken stock (see glossary) or water
salt and freshly ground pepper to taste

❋ In a large, heavy pot, heat the bacon fat or oil over medium-low heat; sauté the onions until soft, about 5 minutes. Add the pork cubes and cook, stirring, for another 5 minutes, or until the meat loses its pink color. Sprinkle the flour over the pork and onions, raise heat slightly and cook until the pork is browned and the onions are golden. Stir in the cumin, garlic and chilies, mixing well. Slowly add the boiling stock or water and stir until well incorporated. Add salt and pepper. Lower heat and simmer, uncovered, until the meat is tender, about 1½–2 hours. Serve with warm tortillas.

SERVES 6

reserving the cooking liquid, and let cool. When the chicken is cool enough to handle, remove the bones and shred the meat into bite-sized pieces.

❋ Drain the beans, rinse and set aside. Using the same pot, heat the oil over medium heat. Add the onions and cook, stirring, until translucent, about 10 minutes. Add the garlic, chilies, cumin, oregano, cloves and cayenne pepper and cook a few minutes longer. Add the beans, stock and reserved cooking liquid from the chicken breasts; bring to a boil. Cover, reduce heat and simmer, stirring occasionally, until the beans are tender, about 2 hours. Add salt to taste and adjust the seasoning.

❋ Before serving, add the shredded chicken and cheese; stir until the cheese is melted and the chicken is heated through. Garnish, if desired, with diced tomatoes, additional grated cheese, chopped green onions and chopped cilantro.

SERVES 6–8

Orange-Tomato Soup with Melons, Blueberries and Grapes

ORANGE-TOMATO SOUP WITH MELONS, BLUEBERRIES AND GRAPES

A refreshing cooler in the desert heat, this soup is a fruit version of the traditional gazpacho made with vegetables. Served with a hearty bread and a salad, it makes a perfect summer meal, or it may be served anytime as a first course.

1½ cups (12 fl oz/375 ml) tomato purée
2 cups (16 fl oz/500 ml) fresh orange juice
1 teaspoon sugar
2 teaspoons grated orange zest
1 teaspoon grated lime zest
1½ cups (6 oz/185 g) diced cantaloupe (rock melon)
1½ cups (6 oz/185 g) diced honeydew melon
¾ cup (3 oz/90 g) diced apple
¾ cup (3 oz/90 g) blueberries
¾ cup (3 oz/90 g) halved seedless green grapes
1 cup (4 oz/125 g) fresh strawberries, hulled and halved
1 kiwi, peeled and sliced

❋ Put the tomato purée, orange juice, sugar, zests, half of the cantaloupe and half of the honeydew melon in a food processor or blender. Process until smooth.
❋ Pour the tomato mixture into a large nonaluminum bowl. Add remaining cantaloupe and honeydew, apple, blueberries and green grapes. Cover and refrigerate for at least 2 hours or overnight.
❋ Divide the soup among 6 bowls. Garnish with the strawberries and kiwi.

SERVES 6

TORTILLA SOUP

Linda Hopkins, an assistant at Les Gourmettes Cooking School in Phoenix, Arizona, developed this flavorful soup. If you don't have time to make chicken stock, use canned low-salt chicken broth. Red Chili Sauce is a purée of dried red peppers and chicken stock. If a less spicy soup is preferred, delete the red sauce and add an additional 1 cup (8 fl oz/250 ml) chicken stock or broth to the soup.

2 tablespoons corn oil
3 corn tortillas (6 in/15 cm in diameter), cut into 1-in (2.5-cm) pieces
½ cup (2½ oz/75 g) finely chopped onion
3 garlic cloves, minced
1 jalapeño chili, cored, seeded and minced
2 Anaheim chilies, roasted, peeled, cored, seeded and finely chopped (see glossary)
8 plum (egg) tomatoes (about 1 lb/500 g), seeded and diced (see glossary)
2 tablespoons tomato paste
2 teaspoons cumin seed, ground coarsely
¼ teaspoon cayenne pepper
5 cups (40 fl oz/1.2 l) chicken stock (see glossary)

1 cup (8 fl oz/250 ml) Red Chili Sauce (recipe on page 195)
2 whole cooked chicken breasts, shredded
1 ripe avocado, pitted, peeled and diced

GARNISH

½ cup (2 oz/60 g) grated Monterey jack cheese
⅓ cup (¾ oz/20 g) chopped fresh cilantro (coriander)
2 corn tortillas (6 in/15 cm in diameter)

❀ Heat the oil over medium-high heat in a large pot. Add the tortillas, reduce heat and cook until they are golden brown and slightly crisp. Add the onion and cook 3 minutes longer; add the garlic and jalapeño chili and cook another 2 minutes. Add the Anaheim chilies, tomatoes and tomato paste; cook for 10 minutes. Stir in the cumin and cayenne; slowly whisk in the chicken stock and red sauce and simmer the soup for about 20 minutes, or until slightly reduced. Add the shredded chicken and avocado and heat until warmed through.

❀ To make the garnish, preheat an oven to 350°F (180°C). Cut the tortillas into julienne strips. Place the strips on a baking sheet and cook for 10–15 minutes, or until crisp.

❀ To serve, ladle soup into 6 bowls and garnish with the grated cheese, cilantro and baked tortilla strips.

SERVES 6

Tortilla Soup

NAVAJO LAMB STEW

Many Navajos raise sheep on the reservation; traditionally, one measure of a family's wealth has been the number of sheep it owned. This is a typical dish enjoyed by Navajo families during the lambing season. Since lamb is now available year-round in grocery stores, this stew may be made anytime. Serve with biscuits and a green salad.

2 tablespoons vegetable oil (or more if needed)
1½ lb (750 g) lamb (from the leg), cut into cubes
1 cup (5 oz/155 g) finely chopped onions
2 garlic cloves, minced
4 large tomatoes, chopped, or one 16-oz (500-g) can, undrained
1½ cups (6 oz/185 g) corn kernels
1 teaspoon cumin seed, crushed to a coarse powder
1 teaspoon salt
½ teaspoon freshly ground pepper
1 green serrano chili, seeded and minced
1 yellow chili, seeded and minced
1 Anaheim or New Mexico green chili, cored, seeded and finely chopped

❀ Heat the oil in a heavy skillet and sauté the lamb over medium-high heat in small batches to leave enough room between the pieces so that they brown. If necessary, add more oil. Remove browned lamb cubes to a plate and set aside.

❀ Add the onion and garlic to the same pan and cook over medium heat until the onion is translucent. Add all the remaining ingredients, including the browned lamb cubes; cover with water and bring to a boil. Lower the heat and cook at a simmer, covered, for 1½–2 hours, or until the meat is tender.

SERVES 6

BEEF CHILI WITH CACTUS

The first documented evidence of chili dates to 1880, when "bowls of red" were sold in San Antonio's marketplace by "chili queens," but food historians believe concoctions of meat and chilies were known to the Aztecs, Incas and Mayas before Columbus arrived in the New World. Today, competition for the best chili recipe is fierce at contests throughout the Southwest. New Mexicans don't include beans in their chili, while Arizonan and Texan aficionados serve them alongside chili, if at all.

4 tablespoons (2 fl oz/60 ml) vegetable oil
2 lb (1 kg) round steak, cut into ¼-in (6-mm) cubes
1 cup (4 oz/125 g) chopped onions
1 cup (5 oz/155 g) chopped green bell pepper (capsicum)
2 garlic cloves, chopped
1 tablespoon ground cumin
½ teaspoon cayenne pepper
¼ teaspoon dried oregano
1 teaspoon dried hot red pepper flakes
1 poblano chili, roasted, peeled, cored, seeded and diced (see glossary)
2 Anaheim chilies, roasted, peeled, cored, seeded and diced (see glossary)
2 serrano chilies, cored, seeded and diced
1 can (28 oz/875 g) tomatoes
1 cup (8 fl oz/250 ml) tomato sauce (puréed tomatoes)
1 cup (8 fl oz/250 ml) beer
½ cup (4 oz/125 g) nopalitos (julienned cactus pads), chopped
salt and freshly ground pepper to taste

¼ cup (1 oz/30 g) masa harina (see glossary)
sour cream, shredded cheese and chopped green (spring) onions for garnish

❀ In a large skillet, heat half of the vegetable oil over medium-high heat. Add half of the steak cubes and brown them; remove and set aside. Repeat with the remaining steak. To the same skillet, add the remaining vegetable oil and sauté the onions and bell pepper until lightly browned, about 10 minutes. Add the garlic, cumin, cayenne pepper, oregano and dried red pepper flakes. Cook, stirring, for 2 minutes, or until the flavors are well blended.

❀ Put the browned meat and onion mixture in a large pot. Add the chilies, tomatoes, tomato sauce, beer and nopalitos. Cook, uncovered, over low heat for 1 hour.

❀ Sprinkle the masa harina over the chili and stir until thoroughly mixed. Add salt and pepper. Cover the pot and simmer gently for 3 hours.

❀ Divide the chili among 6 bowls; pass the sour cream, shredded cheese and chopped green onions for garnish.

SERVES 6

Clockwise from top: Elk Chili, Navajo Lamb Stew, Beef Chili with Cactus

ELK CHILI

Elk inhabit the mountainous regions of Colorado, and native Americans have been making use of their meat, hides and antlers for centuries. A great recipe for hunters, this chili may also be made with ground venison, veal, beef or pork. Delicious on its own, it's also thick enough to use as a sandwich, burrito or taco filling.

2 tablespoons vegetable oil
2 cups (8 oz/250 g) chopped onions
2 red bell peppers (capsicums), cored, seeded
  and diced
2 New Mexico green or Anaheim chilies, cored,
  seeded and diced
4 garlic cloves
2 lb (1 kg) ground elk
2 dried chiltepín chilies, crushed
4 cups (24 oz/750 g) coarsely chopped ripe tomatoes
1 teaspoon ground cumin
1 teaspoon dried oregano
1 teaspoon cayenne pepper
salt and freshly ground pepper to taste
2 tablespoons flour
¼ cup (1 oz/30 g) cornmeal
½ cup (4 fl oz/125 ml) water
grated Cheddar or Monterey jack cheese and finely
  chopped green (spring) onions for garnish

❀ In a large, heavy saucepan, heat the oil over medium heat. Add the onions, bell peppers and green chilies and cook until the onions are soft, about 5 minutes. Add the garlic and meat and cook, stirring, until the meat is browned. Stir in the chiltepín, tomatoes and spices and bring to a boil. Reduce heat to low and simmer for 1 hour, stirring occasionally.
❀ Mix together the flour, cornmeal and water and stir into the meat mixture. Cook over low heat for 1 hour. Ladle into bowls and garnish with grated cheese and chopped green onions.

SERVES 6

GAZPACHO

Gazpacho is a summertime favorite in the Southwest as well as in Spain, the country that gave us this cold, spicy vegetable soup. Served with crusty bread and a salad, it is a refreshing meal that makes hot weather more bearable.

3½ cups (28 fl oz/875 ml) tomato juice
1½ lb (750 g) (about 4 medium) ripe tomatoes, diced
1 cup (5 oz/155 g) finely chopped cucumber
½ cup (2½ oz/75 g) finely chopped red (Spanish) onion
½ cup (2½ oz/75 g) finely chopped celery
¼ cup (1 oz/30 g) finely chopped green bell pepper (capsicum)
2 tablespoons minced fresh Italian (flat-leaf) parsley
3 garlic cloves, minced
1 jalapeño chili, seeded and minced
2 tablespoons red wine vinegar
2 tablespoons fresh lime juice
2 tablespoons olive oil
1 teaspoon ground cumin
½ teaspoon red hot pepper sauce
salt and freshly ground pepper to taste
¼ cup (⅓ oz/10 g) finely chopped fresh cilantro (coriander)
1 cup (3 oz/90 g) garlic croutons
½ cup (2½ oz/75 g) chopped black olives

SANTA FE, NEW MEXICO

CHILLED TOMATO SOUP GARNISHED WITH SHREDDED CABBAGE

Deborah Madison, author of The Greens Cookbook *and* The Savory Way, *offers this refreshing summer soup that marries the flavors of tomato, lime and cilantro.*

4 cups (32 fl oz/1 l) chilled tomato juice
½ cup (⅔ oz/20 g) fresh cilantro (coriander) leaves, minced
1 garlic clove, minced
2 green (spring) onions, finely chopped
1 teaspoon minced jalapeño chili (or more to taste)
¼ teaspoon ground cumin
¼ cup (2 fl oz/60 ml) fresh lime juice
salt to taste
1 avocado, peeled, pitted and diced

GARNISH

2 tablespoons fresh cilantro (coriander) leaves
6 tablespoons (1 oz/30 g) shredded Napa cabbage leaves

❁ Pour the chilled tomato juice into a large bowl and stir in the cilantro, garlic, green onions, jalapeño, cumin and lime juice. Season to taste, adding salt and more lime juice, if necessary; stir in the avocado. Chill.

❁ Divide the soup among 6 chilled bowls. Garnish each serving with 1 teaspoon cilantro leaves and 1 tablespoon shredded Napa cabbage leaves.

SERVES 6

SEDONA, ARIZONA

COLD APPLE SOUP

Apple orchards dot the landscape in picturesque Sedona. Served with Apple Cider Sorbet (recipe on page 229), this soup is perfect for a hot day.

4 tart apples, such as Granny Smith, peeled, cored and quartered
1 cup (8 fl oz/250 ml) dry white wine
2 cinnamon sticks
3 slices fresh ginger
5 tablespoons sugar
1 tablespoon Calvados or applejack
¼ cup (2 oz/60 g) sour cream
1 cup (8 fl oz/250 ml) beef stock (see glossary)
1 cup (8 fl oz/250 ml) heavy (double) cream
2 tablespoons fresh lemon juice
¼ teaspoon salt

GARNISH

½ cup (2½ oz/75 g) finely julienned apple tossed with
    2 tablespoons fresh lemon juice for garnish

❁ Place the quartered apples, wine, cinnamon sticks, ginger, and sugar in a heavy saucepan. Over medium-high heat, bring to a boil. Cover, lower heat to medium and simmer for 10 minutes. Let cool; discard the cinnamon sticks and ginger.

❁ Place the cooked apples and the liquid in which they were cooked into a food processor or blender. Add the Calvados or applejack and sour cream; process until smooth. With the machine running, add the beef stock, then the cream, in a slow steady stream. Add the lemon juice and salt. Cover and refrigerate until chilled thoroughly.

❁ Divide the soup among 6 chilled bowls and garnish with julienned apple.

SERVES 6

Clockwise from left: Chilled Tomato Soup Garnished with Shredded Cabbage, Gazpacho, Cold Apple Soup

❁ In a food processor or blender, put 1 cup (8 fl oz/250 ml) tomato juice, half of the tomatoes, ½ cup (2½ oz/75 g) of the cucumber, ¼ cup (1 oz/30 g) red onion, ¼ cup (1 oz/30 g) celery, 2 tablespoons green pepper, parsley, garlic, jalapeño, vinegar, lime juice, olive oil, cumin and hot pepper sauce. Process or blend until almost smooth. Pour into a large bowl and add the remaining tomato juice and vegetables. Add salt and pepper. Cover and chill for several hours or overnight so that the flavors blend and the soup is cold.

❁ Divide soup among 6 chilled bowls; pass the cilantro, croutons and olives as optional garnish.

SERVES 6

POSOLE

Posole, a traditional dish in New Mexico, is a rustic stew made of hominy, pork, dried New Mexico red chili pods and spices. Served by the Pueblo people on feast days and New Year's Day, it is often accompanied with Red Chili Sauce and bread or tortillas. In Latino markets, hominy (limed whole corn) is usually available dried or canned. If using dried, soak it overnight in water. Canned hominy should be drained and rinsed before using.

1½ cups (8 oz/250 g) dried hominy, soaked overnight in water and drained, or two 16-oz/500-g cans hominy, rinsed and drained (about 3 cups)
1½ lb (750 g) lean boneless pork, cut into ½-in (5-cm) cubes
2 dried New Mexico red chilies, stems and seeds removed, torn into pieces
2 cups (10 oz/315 g) finely chopped onions

3 garlic cloves, minced
2 teaspoons minced fresh oregano, or 1 teaspoon dried oregano
1 teaspoon cumin seed, crushed
6 cups (48 fl oz/1.5 l) water or more as needed
salt to taste
Red Chili Sauce (recipe on page 195) or cored, seeded and minced jalapeño chilies for garnish

❁ In a large pot, combine all the ingredients except the salt and the red chili sauce or jalapeños. Bring to a boil over medium-high heat; lower heat and simmer, uncovered, for 2–3 hours, or until the meat is tender and the hominy kernels have burst and are swelled and tender. The stew should have plenty of liquid, so add more water if necessary throughout the cooking time.
❁ Divide the hominy among 6 bowls and pass the chili sauce or jalapeños.

SERVES 6

Left to right: Green Chili Soup, Posole

6 Anaheim or New Mexico green chilies, roasted, peeled,
  cored, seeded and diced (see glossary)
1 jalapeño chili, seeded and minced
1 red bell pepper (capsicum), roasted, peeled, cored, seeded
  and diced (see glossary)
2 large ripe tomatoes, diced
1 tablespoon minced fresh cilantro (coriander)
salt and freshly ground pepper to taste
grated Cheddar or Monterey jack cheese for
  garnish (optional)

❁ Heat a large, heavy skillet over medium-high heat; add the
bacon and cook until crisp. Remove the bacon with a slotted
spoon, drain on paper towels, crumble, and reserve. Add the
chicken and pork cubes to the hot bacon fat and sauté until
brown, about 5 minutes. Drain and set aside.

❁ In a large, heavy pot, melt the butter; add the onion and
sauté until softened. Stir in the flour and cook for 2–3
minutes, stirring constantly; add crushed *chiles de árbol,*
cumin and garlic and continue cooking, stirring, for another
minute. Slowly add the warm chicken stock, whisking until
the mixture is smooth and thickened. Add the chilies, bell
pepper, tomatoes, cilantro, bacon, pork and chicken to the
soup; add salt and pepper. Lower the heat and simmer for
10 minutes, or until flavors are blended and soup is hot.
Divide into 6 bowls, garnish with grated cheese, if desired,
and serve with warm tortillas.

SERVES 6

T A O S ,   N E W   M E X I C O

BUTTERNUT SQUASH SOUP

*This buttery-tasting soup is perfect for chasing away the doldrums
on a cold, blustery day. The taste can be varied by adding different
types of cheeses and nuts, depending on personal preference.*

4 tablespoons (2 oz/60 g) unsalted butter
½ cup (2½ oz/75 g) finely chopped onion
1 teaspoon salt
1½ lb (750 g) butternut squash, peeled, scraped clean of
  strings and diced into ½-in (12-mm) pieces
2 cloves
3½ cups (28 fl oz/875 ml) chicken stock (see glossary)
½ cup (4 fl oz/125 ml) heavy (double) cream (optional)
½ cup (2½ oz/75 g) blue cheese, finely diced
1 tablespoon minced fresh sage, or 1 teaspoon dried sage
freshly ground pepper to taste
2 tablespoons minced fresh parsley, preferably
  Italian (flat-leaf)

❁ Melt 1 tablespoon of the butter in a large, heavy saucepan.
Add the onion and cook over moderately low heat until
translucent. Add the salt, squash and cloves; cover and
continue cooking until the squash is tender, about 15 minutes. Uncover, add the stock and cook another 15 minutes.
Add the cream, if desired, and bring the mixture to a boil.

❁ In a small saucepan, cook the remaining 3 tablespoons
butter over medium-high heat until it turns brown. Remove
from heat immediately and add the browned butter to the
soup mixture.

❁ Drain the squash, reserving the liquid. Remove the cloves
and discard. Place the squash in a food processor or blender
and purée. Place the purée and liquid in the original pan and
stir thoroughly. Add the cheese and sage and stir over low
heat until the cheese is melted. Add salt and pepper to taste.
Divide into 6 bowls and sprinkle each bowl with
chopped parsley.

SERVES 6   *Photograph pages 62–63*

A L B U Q U E R Q U E ,   N E W   M E X I C O

GREEN CHILI SOUP

*This spicy soup is a perfect remedy for a cold or whatever ails.
Homemade chicken stock rather than canned will make it even better. Serve this with warm corn tortillas.*

3 slices smoked bacon
1 whole chicken breast, boned, skinned and cut into
  ½-in (12-mm) cubes
6 oz (185 g) boneless pork, cut into ½-in (12-mm) cubes
¼ cup (2 oz/60 g) unsalted butter
1 cup (5 oz/155 g) finely chopped onion
⅓ cup (2 oz/60 g) unbleached all-purpose (plain) flour
2 *chiles de árbol,* toasted, stemmed, seeded and crushed
  (see glossary)
1 teaspoon ground cumin
1 garlic clove, minced
6 cups (48 fl oz/1.5 l) chicken stock (see glossary)

CHILI SIN CARNE

A traditionalist would not consider this a true chili since it has no meat, but this flavorful combination of beans, peppers, tomatoes and zucchini is as filling and flavorful as any chili con carne. Serve with corn bread or tortillas, or ladle on top of cooked rice or baked potatoes. Epazote, commonly known as wormseed, or Mexican tea, is a Mexican herb that is used when cooking black beans to add a unique flavor and to reduce the beans' gassy effect. It grows wild in many parts of the United States, but is obtained easily in Latino markets.

1 tablespoon vegetable oil
1½ cups (7½ oz/230 g) finely chopped red (Spanish) onion
3 cloves garlic, minced
1 red bell pepper (capsicum), cored, seeded and
  finely chopped
1 green bell pepper (capsicum), cored, seeded and
  finely chopped
1 jalapeño chili, seeded and finely chopped
1 cup (5 oz/155 g) peeled diced carrot
1½ cups (9 oz/280 g) diced tomatoes
¾ cup (6 fl oz/180 ml) tomato juice
1 teaspoon ground cumin
¼ teaspoon cayenne pepper
1 teaspoon minced fresh epazote, or ½ teaspoon dried
  epazote (optional)
1 teaspoon dried oregano
1 guajillo chili, toasted, stemmed, seeded and crushed
  (see glossary)
salt and freshly ground pepper to taste
1 cup (8 oz/250 g) cooked black beans
1 cup (8 oz/250 g) cooked kidney beans
1 cup (8 oz/250 g) cooked pinto beans
1 cup (8 fl oz/250 ml) dry red wine
1 cup (5 oz/155 g) diced zucchini (courgette)
grated Cheddar cheese and chopped green (spring) onions
  for garnish

❀ In a large saucepan, heat the oil over medium heat. Add the onions, garlic, bell peppers and jalapeño and sauté until the onion is translucent, about 5 minutes.
❀ Add the carrot, tomatoes, tomato juice, cumin, cayenne, epazote, oregano, guajillo chili and salt and pepper. Bring to a simmer and cook, stirring occasionally, for 15 minutes.
❀ Add the black, kidney and pinto beans to the onion-pepper mixture. Stir in the red wine and simmer, uncovered, for 45–60 minutes. Add the zucchini and cook until tender, about another 10 minutes.
❀ Divide the chili among 6 bowls and top with grated cheese and onions.

SERVES 6

BLACK BEAN SOUP

Black bean soup is one of the most popular of Southwestern soups. This slightly sweet version is the creation of Lenard Rubin, a chef at 8700 in Scottsdale. Servings may be garnished a number of ways, but Chef Rubin suggests a dollop of sour cream and sprinklings of diced red onions and chopped cilantro.

1 tablespoon corn oil
8 slices smoked bacon, finely julienned
2 onions, finely chopped
2 carrots, finely chopped
2 stalks celery, finely chopped
2 garlic cloves, minced

1 lb (500 g) dried black (turtle) beans, washed and soaked in
  water overnight
8 cups (64 fl oz/2 l) chicken stock (see glossary)
1 red bell pepper (capsicum), cored, seeded and finely diced
1 green bell pepper (capsicum), cored, seeded and
  finely diced
1 yellow bell pepper (capsicum), cored, seeded and
  finely diced
¼ cup (2 fl oz/60 ml) sherry vinegar
3 tablespoons Grand Marnier
3 tablespoons soy sauce
2 tablespoons honey

Chili sin Carne

2 tablespoons molasses
½ cup (4 oz/125 g) canned diced green chilies
¼ cup (⅓ oz/10 g) chopped fresh cilantro (coriander)
¼ cup (¾ oz/20 g) chopped green (spring) onions
1 teaspoon dried oregano
1 teaspoon dried thyme
1 teaspoon ground cumin
1 teaspoon chili powder
¼ cup (2 fl oz/60 ml) fresh lemon juice
¼ cup (2 fl oz/60 ml) fresh lime juice
sour cream, diced red (Spanish) onions and chopped fresh
   cilantro (coriander) for garnish

❀ Heat the oil in a large, heavy pot. Add the bacon and cook until crisp. Add the chopped onions, carrots, celery and garlic to the crisped bacon and cook until soft. Add the black beans and stock to the saucepan, cover and bring to a boil. Lower heat and simmer for about 2 hours, or until the beans are tender but not mushy.

❀ Remove one third of the soup from the pot and purée it in a blender or food processor; pour the purée into the pot.

❀ Add all the remaining ingredients to the soup and simmer for 1 more hour. Divide among 8 bowls and top with sour cream, onions and cilantro.

SERVES 8

Photograph pages 62–63

Colorado Plateau

COLORADO PLATEAU

The Four Corners, where Arizona, New Mexico, Colorado and Utah meet at perfect right angles near the eastern end of the mile-high Colorado Plateau, may be the world's best example of unimaginative political boundary-drawing. To be sure, a certain novelty exists in being able not only to see but actually to occupy four different states by standing on a single spot. But the two intersecting dotted lines on the map hardly begin to hint at the wondrous geological region that surrounds the Four Corners.

Less than twenty-five miles to the south-southeast, majestic Ship Rock rises like a great rusted sailing vessel from the high-desert plain. A journey 120 miles to the north-northwest brings the visitor to Arches National Park, where water and wind have carved fantastic soaring arches and towers of red sandstone over a period of some 150 million years. Thirty miles east-northeast, and seventy miles south-southwest of the Four Corners, respectively, the dizzyingly sheer cliff sides of Mesa Verde and Canyon de Chelly shelter the ruins of an ancient civilization. Farther southwest sweep the canyons and mesas of the Painted Desert, whose myriad pastel hues—seemingly applied with a

Previous pages: The awe-inspiring Grand Canyon can be appreciated in sheer numbers alone: stretching 277 miles across northern Arizona, it measures up to ten miles wide and one mile deep. Left: The Anasazi built cliff dwellings 2,000 feet above the valley floor at Colorado's Mesa Verde in the thirteenth century; one hundred years later, they inexplicably abandoned their fortresses, leaving behind jewelry, mugs, weapons and pots of corn.

watercolor brush—may also be found in the ancient trees-turned-to-stone of the Petrified Forest. Sixty miles due west along the Arizona-Utah border rise the colossal monoliths of Monument Valley. Bryce Canyon's delicate filigree of eroded limestone spires awaits some 170 miles to the west-northwest. And that same distance to the west-southwest leads to the greatest natural wonder in North America, and perhaps the world: the awesome abyss of the Grand Canyon, carved by the Colorado River over the past 350 million years.

To call the Colorado Plateau a magical landscape understates the point. How fitting that, starting as many as twelve thousand years ago and lasting well into the present millennium, it was occupied by an equally magical people, the direct ancestors of many of the tribes who still occupy the region. They are referred to today as the Anasazi, the Ancient Ones, and legend has it that they were led to this beautiful but largely barren land by the promise of sustenance: game for hunting, plants for gathering, rich soil for growing crops, and ample water.

Game and plants there were, to be sure. Archaeologists have found the bones of deer, antelope, elk, mountain sheep, turkey and rabbit at Anasazi sites, and the Ancient Ones probably also ate small rodents, birds and fish. Their wild harvest included piñon nuts, acorns, walnuts, juniper berries, agave, prickly pears, Indian rice grass, various roots and tubers, and leafy greens.

But the Anasazi's agriculture showed their true ingenuity. Like other Southwestern peoples, by the middle of the first millennium A.D. they were raising corn, squashes and beans, which together provided the foundation of a healthy, well-balanced diet. To tap water that lay deep in the sandy soil, they systematically developed cultigens of corn whose seeds could be planted more than a foot deep, producing ears almost as big as those grown today. And their growing methods showed extraordinary efficiency, with squash, corn and beans often planted in the same hole. First the squash would germinate, its low-lying leaves providing cool, water-conserving ground cover. Next the corn would shoot up, and its sturdy stalk would provide a pole around which the bean plant—which germinated last—could twine.

The Anasazi also showed tremendous invention in the way they cooked, though they were not the only Southwestern peoples to do so. Originally, they simmered soups or stews in tightly woven baskets, adding stones from a fire to heat the liquid. Before the sixth century A.D., however, they had developed the art of pottery making, yielding vessels that could cook directly over a fire—and, in the process, establishing a craft that still yields some of the Southwest's most exquisite handiworks.

A poignant reminder of the spiritual importance with which the Anasazi endowed food was found in a

Volcanic eruptions formed the La Sal Mountain range of southern Utah about 30 million years ago; streams and glaciers later carved the stunning canyons and ridges that we admire today.

The Fremont River Valley lies in southern Utah, a land of expansive vistas, pristine meadows, dense forests and sparkling streams.

87

gravesite at Canyon de Chelly. The regally dressed body of an old man lay with a single ear of corn placed on its chest. Five pottery jars and four baskets surrounding the corpse contained piñon nuts, beans, salt and husked, shelled and ground corn.

Around the eighth century A.D., the Anasazis began to evolve into the numerous Pueblo tribes that today live in the Colorado Plateau, the New Mexican High Country and the Rio Grande Rift. Chief among these, and occupying the largest land area, are the Hopis and Zunis of northeastern Arizona and northwestern New Mexico. Though the two tribes exhibit some distinctive cultural differences, they share similar spiritual approaches to food and the natural world from which it comes. For example, before going on a hunt—today more of a ceremonial act than one essential to survival—tribesmen pray to the spirits of the animal world for permission to catch them; though deer, antelope and mountain sheep usually agree, wily and skittish rabbits are notoriously less accommodating.

Kachinas, well known to modern enthusiasts for the hand-carved effigies called kachina dolls, are the tribes' messengers to the spirit world. In a regular annual calendar of dances and ceremonies, initiates of the kachina cult dress and perform as, and thus become, these messengers. Each kachina represents a different element of the physical world—including corn, squashes, chilies, game animals, rain and the earth itself—and embodies humankind's hopes for a bounteous blessing from the spirit world.

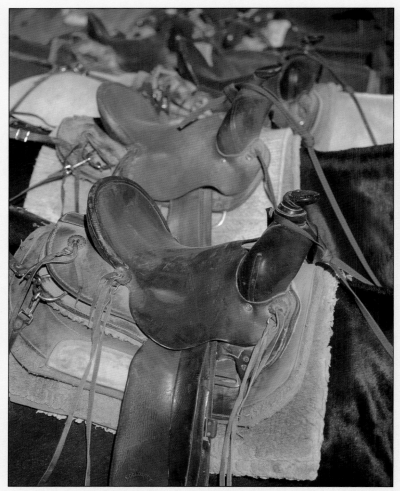

Sure-footed mules have been carrying visitors in and out of the Grand Canyon for over a century.

The Colorado and Green rivers flow through the heart of Utah's vast Canyonland National Park.

Arizona's Canyon de Chelly has sheltered native Americans
since the Anasazi developed communities there 2,000 years ago.

One of the most unusual landscapes on the continent, Arizona's Petrified Forest is comprised of fragments of fossilized trees that lived nearly 222 million years ago.

Daily ritual still revolves around cooking, and in no case more so than in the preparation of corn. In her richly informative book *Hopi Cookery,* native-born Creek Indian and adopted Hopi, Juanita Tiger Kavena, details some of the charming traditions that went into the making of the tribe's more than thirty different corn dishes:

> Corn grinding often turned into a social occasion, when a group of girls gathered to grind while an uncle or grandfather sang. The girls would grind to the rhythm of the song. A small window was often located next to the grinding stones and provided a safe way for a boy to court a girl while she was grinding. If the maiden was interested in the young man, they would visit through the window. But, if she wanted to discourage him, she would fling cornmeal at him.

One dish still made daily from ground corn is the crisp scrolls of tissue-thin blue cornbread known as *piki,* a preparation steeped in tradition. The fluid batter is smeared by hand onto the smooth surface of a fire-heated stone devoted to *piki* alone, then gingerly peeled off, briefly flipped and quickly rolled and folded—a process neatly described by the name given to the bread in the San Ildefonso pueblo: *bowahejajui,* meaning "put it on, take it off."

With the coming of Spanish and Anglo settlers, the Pueblo diet expanded to embrace new foods and new ways of growing and preparing them. This interaction also profoundly affected the Navajos who began to make a homeland among the Pueblos in the Four Corners area some time between the eleventh and sixteenth centuries A.D. From the Spaniards, they learned to raise sheep and to cultivate and tend fruit orchards, particularly peach. Wheat also became a staple, most notable today in the puffy rounds of yeast- or soda-leavened Navajo fry bread one finds throughout the Southwest and particularly at tribal celebrations.

Legal conflicts and controversies over the land of the Colorado Plateau continue today between the Hopis and the Navajos—a situation that must also be judged in light of centuries of subjugation of these two tribes at the hands of the Spanish, Mexicans and Anglos. Regardless of any of these or other hardships, however, one can only say of all these people, as Juanita Tiger Kavena says of the Hopis, that they have "not only endured but fashioned a fruitful existence in a harsh environment."

The All Indian Days Pow Wow, held every June in Flagstaff, Arizona, invites native Americans from all over the U.S. to exhibit arts and crafts and participate in a three-day dance competition.

MEAT, FISH, POULTRY, GAME AND EGGS

From the days of the early pioneers, Texans have been cattlemen and ranchers.

MEAT, FISH, POULTRY, GAME AND EGGS

Ramble down any back road in the Texas Hill Country and sooner rather than later a seductive perfume will tantalize you. Borne by the breeze, the aromas of wood smoke, meat and marinades will lead you to barbecue.

The mouthwatering smell might emanate from the back of a butcher shop or a general store, from the front parlor of a saloon or from a humble shack. All of these places sell Southwestern barbecue, as native Texans, New Mexicans and Arizonans have cooked it for centuries.

In the most traditional sense of the word, *barbecue* refers to closed-pit cooking. This calls for a pit to be dug for a fire built of mesquite, hickory, pecan or other fragrant woods. The meat is then wrapped in wet burlap, placed on the coals and covered with earth to cook and smoke ever so slowly. For a really big feast, a whole gutted animal might be cooked with its hide left on to shorten preparation time and to seal in the meat's juices.

Today, a structure of brick usually replaces the earthen pit, accommodating smaller but still generous cuts of beef, pork, mutton, and goat—as well as the many plump sausages popularized in west Texas by the Germans, Czechs and Poles who emigrated here during the first half of the nineteenth century. In springtime, kid—known by the Mexican term *cabrito*—and lamb get the smoky, slow-cooking treatment, resulting in meat of indescribable succulence and sweetness.

Smaller-scale barbecuing may be the norm nowadays, but large communal events still occur, not just on the big ranches but also in isolated villages. "The slaughtering of a pig specially fed for the occasion was usually referred to as *la matanza del cochino* or *del puerco,* depending on the region," writes Arthur L. Campa in *Hispanic Culture in the Southwest.* "In New Mexico and west Texas slaughtering took place in the fall. Friends and neighbors were invited after the 'preliminaries' were over." At day's end, all the guests carried home their portion of meat or some of the crisply fried, puffy strips of pig skin known as chicharrones, a popular snack throughout the region.

Though barbecuing may be the best-known form of cooking meat in these parts, it shares today's spotlight with other methods. The grill and griddle in particular produce an abundance of seared specialties that are instantly identifiable as Southwestern, most notably a contemporary favorite known as fajitas.

Strictly speaking, the Spanish word *fajita* means a little skirt or belt, fancifully describing the beef skirt steak, cut from the diaphragm muscle. A cheap and tough cut not deemed suitable for sale to the public, the meat was a favorite of northern Mexican ranchers, who would marinate and quickly grill it, then slice it thinly

Previous pages, clockwise from left: Grilled Rabbit with Achiote Paste (recipe page 118), Lime-Tequila Grilled Chicken (recipe page 97), Barbecued Cabrito (recipe page 108), Marinated Grilled Leg of Lamb (recipe page 105)

94

to bestow a semblance of tenderness before wrapping the meat in flour tortillas to be eaten. In the late 1960s, Austin butcher Sonny Falcon began to serve his own version of fajitas at weekend fairs across the countryside, earning himself the nickname "Fajita King." Within a decade, fajitas were popular throughout the Southwest and in fun, fashionable restaurants nationwide; and the term was liberally extended to cover anything quickly seared, thinly cut and tortilla-wrapped, be it prime steak, boneless and skinless chicken breasts, butterflied shrimp or even a vegetarian mélange.

The popularity of fajitas demonstrates another significant aspect of protein consumption in the Southwest: when there's little meat to put on the table, some sort of tortilla wrapper and inexpensive garnish can transform a few scraps into a filling meal. Fold that meat inside a fresh, warm corn tortilla, add some salsa and it becomes a taco. Roll up the meat with cheese and seasonings inside a corn tortilla and bake it with a chili-laced sauce, and you have a modern-day version of the traditional enchilada. Snugly enclose beef, pork or chicken with a smear of beans inside a flour tortilla and a burrito, or burro, appears, its name vividly illustrating the fact that the large, sturdy wrapper can carry as much cargo as a pack animal. Frying that same package until crisply browned produces one of Tucson's greatest culinary contributions, the chimichanga, a lively sounding term that some etymologists claim means "toasted monkey" and others primly declare an untranslatable expletive.

Tortillas also play the role of flavorful filler at breakfast and brunch in many of the Southwest's egg dishes. Plopped atop soft fried tortillas, napped with a spicy sauce and crowned with melted cheese, sunny-side-up eggs metamorphose into ranch-style huevos rancheros. Breakfast burritos may be stuffed with scrambled eggs and spicy chorizo sausage; a dollop of sour cream might finish them off in Arizona, while in New Mexico the state's signature red or green chili sauces will be ladled over them, singly or in a combination sometimes referred to as "Christmas-style."

With all the attention that naturally gets paid to foods provided by animals of the barnyard or the open

Taking a break from the rigors of life on the range, cowboys satisfy their hearty appetites with good old-fashioned Texas barbecue.

The lakes of the Southwest team with freshwater fish; here, fishermen in southeastern Utah cast their hooks through the ice.

range, it is easy to forget the role game continues to play in a region originally populated by hunter-gatherers. And it's also easy to overlook fish in states whose mention instantly brings to mind vast expanses of desert and rocky bluffs.

Game animals continue to thrive throughout the Southwest, attracting hunters drawn by sport alone or by the need to put meat on the table. The mountains shelter deer, elk, bear and wild turkey, which are hunted from late fall to early winter. In autumn, ducks and geese fill the skies above the Colorado and Rio Grande basins; grouse, quail and dove play hide-and-seek in the tall grasses; rabbits skitter about everywhere.

Some seafood, of course, comes to the two southernmost corners of the Southwest from the Gulfs of Mexico and California; and fish such as salmon arrive fresh via air freight on the tables of restaurants and homes in Phoenix, Santa Fe and other enclaves. But the region's mountain streams and lakes also hold a year-round treasure there for the taking, a tantalizing roll call of trouts: browns and rainbows, cutthroats and brooks. Though the Navajos have long regarded the fish as spirits not to be tampered with, many people prize them as one of nature's greatest gifts to the region. Take, for example, the rhapsodic reminiscence of Santa Fe–born California chef John Sedlar in his book *Modern Southwest Cuisine*:

> When I was very young, my dad took me trout fishing in the icy waters of the Pecos River, high in the Sangre de Cristo Mountains. The crisp air, the deer and the small rabbits we saw, the scent of the aspen trees—all created an unforgettable picture in my memory. And fresh brook trout cooked over an open fire became one of my ideals of perfect, simple cooking.

FAJITAS

Now popular throughout the Southwest, fajitas have their roots in Texas and originally were made only with skirt steak. The name means "little belts," because after marinating and grilling, the steak is cut across the grain into strips. The strips are then rolled in flour tortillas, along with condiments such as salsa, cheese, tomatoes and guacamole. In most restaurants today, fajitas are made with either chicken, steak or shrimp and are delivered to the table on very hot skillets.

MARINADE

¼ cup (2 fl oz/60 ml) fresh lime juice
1 jalapeño chili, seeded and diced
1 teaspoon cumin seed, crushed
2 garlic cloves, minced
2 tablespoons vegetable oil
½ cup (4 fl oz/125 ml) beer

1 skirt, flank or top sirloin steak, about 1½ lb (750 g)
salt and freshly ground pepper to taste
12 flour tortillas (8 in/20 cm in diameter)
2 tablespoons vegetable oil
1 red bell pepper (capsicum), cored, seeded and julienned
1 yellow bell pepper (capsicum), cored, seeded and julienned
1 green bell pepper (capsicum), cored, seeded and julienned
1 cup (3½ oz/105 g) thinly sliced red (Spanish) onions
Guacamole (recipe on page 191), shredded jack or Cheddar cheese, salsa and diced tomatoes for garnish

❋ Mix all the marinade ingredients together and pour over the steak in a nonaluminum shallow dish. Marinate at room temperature for 2 hours or cover and marinate overnight in the refrigerator, turning several times.
❋ Preheat an oven to 350°F (180°C). Light a fire in a charcoal grill. Wrap the flour tortillas tightly in aluminum foil and place in the preheated oven. Heat for 15–20 minutes, or until very warm and flexible.
❋ Remove the steaks from the marinade and season to taste with salt and pepper. Grill the steak over medium coals 10–15 minutes; turn and cook another 10–15 minutes. Remove from heat and slice diagonally across the grain into thin strips. Keep warm.
❋ Heat a heavy skillet over high heat; add the oil, then the pepper strips and onions. Sauté until vegetables are tender and slightly caramelized, about 5 minutes.
❋ Add the strips of meat to the skillet of vegetables. Serve with warm tortillas, guacamole, shredded cheese, salsa and diced tomatoes.

MAKES 12

TACO SALAD

A staple among most home cooks in Arizona, this hearty salad is a perfect main course for a hot summer night. For a dramatic presentation, serve it in a large flour tortilla that has been deep-fried in a bowl shape. Or, serve without the shell and add crisp tortilla chips to the salad for extra crunch and flavor.

vegetable oil for frying
6 flour tortillas (10 in/25 cm in diameter)
1 lb (500 g) ground beef
1 cup (5 oz/155 g) chopped onions
1 garlic clove, minced
1 teaspoon cayenne pepper
1 teaspoon chili powder
½ teaspoon ground cumin

1 cup (8 fl oz/250 ml) cooked pinto beans
2 New Mexico green or Anaheim chilies, roasted, peeled, seeded and diced (see glossary)
1 cup (6 oz/185 g) chopped tomatoes
¼ cup (1 oz/30 g) sliced pitted ripe olives
3 green (spring) onions, finely chopped
1 cup (4 oz/125 g) grated Cheddar cheese
1 avocado, peeled, pitted and diced
4 cups (4 oz/125 g) shredded lettuce
6 deep-fried tortilla shells (instructions follow), or 2 cups (4 oz/125 g) slightly crushed tortilla chips

❋ In a deep, heavy saucepan, over high heat, heat the oil to 375°F (190°C) or until a strip of tortilla browns in 60 seconds when dropped in the oil. Place 1 flour tortilla into the oil by pushing down on its center with a large ladle. Hold the tortilla in the oil with the ladle until it takes the shape of a bowl and continue to cook until brown and crisp. Remove from the oil and drain on paper towels. Repeat with the remaining tortillas.
❋ In a large skillet, sauté the ground beef over medium-high heat until almost browned; drain off the fat. Stir in the onions, garlic, cayenne, chili powder and cumin and continue to cook for another 2 minutes. Add the beans and diced chilies and cook until the meat is completely browned, about 1 minute. Let cool slightly.
❋ Put the ground beef mixture into a large bowl and add the tomato, olives, green onions, cheese, avocado and lettuce. Toss well and turn into the prepared tortilla shells, or toss with tortilla chips and spoon onto 6 plates.

SERVES 6

RIO VERDE CHICKEN ENCHILADAS

One of Arizona's oldest and most influential families, the Goldwaters have contributed in countless ways to the state's history. This wonderful main course is the creation of Joanne Goldwater, owner of Goldwater's Foods. Meant to be made with her Rio Verde tomatillo salsa, which is available throughout the country in specialty shops, it is just as good using Tomatillo Salsa. These enchiladas are also good made with spinach in place of chicken.

2 whole boneless chicken breasts, skinned, poached and shredded
1 cup (4 oz/125 g) chopped onions
3 tablespoons grated Parmesan cheese
1 cup (4 oz/125 g) shredded Monterey jack cheese
vegetable oil for softening tortillas
12 corn tortillas (6 in/15 cm in diameter)
1 cup (8 fl oz/250 ml) Tomatillo Salsa (recipe on page 200)
2 cups (16 fl oz/500 ml) heavy (double) cream or milk
4 eggs
2 cups (8 oz/250 g) shredded Cheddar cheese
Guacamole (recipe on page 191), sour cream, shredded lettuce, chopped tomatoes and chopped black olives for garnish

❋ Preheat an oven to 350°F (180°C). Combine the chicken, onions and Parmesan and jack cheeses.
❋ Heat about ¼ in (6 mm) of oil in a small skillet. Dip each tortilla into the oil for 5 seconds per side; drain on paper towels.
❋ Place 3–4 tablespoons chicken mixture in each tortilla and roll the tortilla up; place seam-side down in a baking dish large enough to hold 12 enchiladas. Repeat until all the filling is used.

*Clockwise from bottom left: Fajitas, Taco Salad,
Rio Verde Chicken Enchiladas*

❁ Blend the salsa, cream or milk, and eggs; pour over the tortillas. Sprinkle the Cheddar cheese over the enchiladas and bake for 30 minutes.

❁ Garnish with guacamole, sour cream, shredded lettuce, chopped tomatoes and black olives arranged in colorful rows over the enchiladas.

MAKES 12

SAN ANTONIO, TEXAS

LIME-TEQUILA GRILLED CHICKEN

This easy-to-make, low-calorie, low-cholesterol main course may be varied by offering it with different salsas or sauces.

MARINADE

⅔ cup (5 fl oz/160 ml) olive oil
½ cup (4 fl oz/125 ml) fresh lime juice

1 jalapeño chili, seeded and minced
¼ cup (2 fl oz/60 ml) tequila
2 tablespoons Triple Sec
¼ cup (⅓ oz/10 g) minced fresh cilantro
  (coriander)

---

6 skinned and boned half chicken breasts
Green Chili Salsa (recipe on page 199), Pumpkin Seed Salsa
  (recipe on page 201) or Red Pepper Sauce (recipe on
  page 190)

❁ Mix all the marinade ingredients together and pour into a nonaluminum shallow pan. Add the chicken and coat thoroughly with the marinade. Cover and refrigerate for 4 hours, turning the chicken several times.

❁ Light a fire in a charcoal grill or preheat a broiler (griller). Remove the chicken from the refrigerator 30 minutes before cooking.

❁ Cook the chicken for about 4 minutes on each side on a grill or 4 in (10 cm) from the heating element of a broiler (griller). Serve with salsa.

SERVES 6   *Photograph pages 92–93*

Braised Pot Roast with Orange Prickly Pear Sauce

BRAISED POT ROAST WITH ORANGE PRICKLY PEAR SAUCE

The fruit of the prickly pear (called tunas*), which is about the size of an egg, is actually a berry. Soft and spongy, it smells like watermelon, and the vibrant red color pulp is quite sweet. This recipe can be adapted to any cut of meat that is good braised, and if prickly pears are not available, substitute blueberries. Serve with potatoes so the extra sauce does not go to waste.*

MARINADE

2 cups (16 fl oz/500 ml) Merlot or other dry red wine
½ cup (4 fl oz/125 ml) fresh orange juice
2 tablespoons olive oil
1 teaspoon salt
½ teaspoon freshly ground pepper
½ cup (2½ oz/75 g) diced peeled carrots
½ cup (2 oz/60 g) diced onions

1 boneless pot roast (2–2½ lb/1–1.2 kg)
2–3 tablespoons unbleached all-purpose (plain) flour
2 tablespoons olive oil
6 prickly pears, peeled, puréed and strained
¼ cup (⅓ oz/10 g) chopped fresh parsley

1½ cups (12 fl oz/375 ml) chicken stock (see glossary)
¼ cup (1 oz/30 g) julienned orange zest, boiled in water for 10 minutes and drained

❈ Mix all the marinade ingredients together in a nonaluminum bowl; add the pot roast, cover and refrigerate overnight.
❈ Drain the meat and pat it dry. Strain the vegetables, reserving the marinade. Coat the meat with the flour, shaking off the excess. In a large, heavy pot, heat the oil. Add the floured roast and brown on all sides over medium heat. Remove the meat from the pan and add the drained vegetables; sauté until tender, about 8–10 minutes. Put the meat back in the pot on top of the vegetables; add the reserved marinade, prickly pear purée, parsley and chicken stock. Mix well and season with salt and pepper. Bring to a boil, lower heat to a simmer and cook until the meat is tender, about 2 hours. Skim off any fat that rises to the surface.
❈ Remove the meat from the liquid and keep warm. With a slotted spoon, remove the vegetables from the liquid and purée them in a food processor or blender; return to the liquid in the pot. Add the orange zest and cook over medium heat until sauce is slightly thickened, about 10 minutes. Reheat the meat in the sauce, cut into 6 portions and serve with a generous amount of the sauce.

SERVES 6

P H O E N I X ,   A R I Z O N A

STUFFED BEEF TENDERLOIN WITH ANCHO CHILI SAUCE

Frequently mislabeled as pasillas, ancho chilies are dried poblanos and are the sweetest of the dried chilies. Soaked until soft and puréed with fresh poblanos, they make a slightly fruity sauce that goes well with stuffed meat. New York strip steak may be substituted if beef tenderloin is not in your budget. Bake extra heads of garlic and spread the softened cloves along with goat cheese on crisp French bread as a garnish.

six 1-in (2.5-cm) thick filet mignon steaks (about
  4–6 oz/125–185 g each)
2 heads garlic
1 tablespoon olive oil
1 tablespoon minced fresh oregano
salt and freshly ground pepper to taste
2 Anaheim chilies, roasted, peeled, cored, seeded and sliced
  (see glossary)

ANCHO CHILI SAUCE

3 ancho chilies
3 poblano chilies, roasted, peeled, and seeded

salt and freshly ground pepper to taste
¼ cup (2 fl oz/60 ml) heavy (double) cream

❂ Preheat an oven to 350°F (180°C). Horizontally slice a pocket in the steaks; set aside.
❂ Liberally rub the heads of garlic with the olive oil; wrap the garlic in aluminum foil and bake in the oven for 1 hour, or until the garlic is soft.
❂ Light a fire in a charcoal grill. Make a paste of the puréed garlic, oregano, and salt and pepper. Rub the inside of the steak pockets generously with the garlic mixture. Place a piece of green chili inside each pocket; press to seal. Season the steaks with salt and pepper and grill over hot coals until medium rare, about 4–5 minutes per side.
❂ To make the sauce, place the ancho chilies in a bowl and cover with very hot water; let soak for 45 minutes. Reserve ½ cup (4 fl oz/125 ml) water in which chilies were soaked; place ancho and poblano chilies in a blender with the reserved soaking water and purée until smooth. Strain into a small saucepan and add salt and pepper and cream. Heat and adjust the seasonings.
❂ Place 1 steak on each of 6 plates and spoon 1–2 tablespoons sauce on top of each one.

SERVES 6

Stuffed Beef Tenderloin with Ancho Chili Sauce

BEEF MACHACA CHIMICHANGAS

An Arizona specialty, chimichangas are burritos that are usually filled with shredded chicken or beef, machaca or green chili sauce and then deep-fried and served with guacamole, sour cream and sometimes a sauce. Machaca is a stewlike filling that is also delicious in tacos, enchiladas or burritos.

MACHACA

2 tablespoons vegetable oil
1 boneless chuck roast, about 3 lb (1.5 kg)
salt and freshly ground pepper to taste
1½ cups (12 fl oz/375 ml) water
1 large onion, quartered
5 garlic cloves, crushed
2 tablespoons lard (or vegetable oil)
1 cup (6 oz/185 g) chopped tomatoes
½ cup (1½ oz/45 g) finely chopped green (spring) onions
1 cup (5 oz/155 g) diced cooked potatoes
¼ cup (⅓ oz/10 g) chopped fresh cilantro (coriander)

12 flour tortillas (8 in/20 cm in diameter)
vegetable oil for frying
Green Chili Sauce (recipe on page 195), Guacamole (recipe on page 191), sour cream, shredded lettuce and grated cheese for garnish

❋ To make the machaca, preheat an oven to 350°F (180°C). In a large, heavy skillet, heat the vegetable oil. Salt and pepper the chuck roast and brown on all sides in the hot oil. Transfer the roast to a baking dish. Pour the water into the hot skillet and cook over medium heat, stirring to dislodge any brown bits from the bottom of the pan. Pour the pan liquid into the baking pan with the roast; add the onion and garlic. Bake until the meat shreds easily, about 2 hours. Remove the roast from the oven and let cool. Shred the cooled meat and set aside. Pour the pan drippings into a glass measuring cup and skim off any fat; set aside.
❋ In a large skillet, melt the lard or heat the oil over medium heat; add the shredded meat to the pan and cook, stirring, for about 5 minutes. Add 1 cup (8 fl oz/250 ml) of the reserved pan drippings, tomatoes, onions, potatoes and cilantro. Cover, lower heat and simmer for 30 minutes.
❋ To make the chimichangas, put ⅓ cup (3 oz/90 g) machaca into the center of each tortilla and roll as for a burrito; secure with a toothpick. Add the oil to a large saucepan to a depth of 3 in (7.5 cm); over high heat bring to a temperature of 365°F (185°C), or until a cube of bread browns in 60 seconds. Fry the chimichangas, 2 or 3 at a time, until golden; drain on paper towels, remove the toothpicks and keep warm. Serve the chimichangas warm, garnished with green chili sauce, guacamole, sour cream, shredded lettuce and grated cheese.

MAKES 12

SPICY FLANK STEAK

This marinade is good on other cuts of beef or lamb. The longer the meat is left in the marinade, the spicier it will taste, and the flavor will permeate more quickly at room temperature than in the refrigerator.

MARINADE

¼ cup (2 fl oz/60 ml) olive oil
¼ cup (⅓ oz/10 g) minced fresh cilantro (coriander)
4 garlic cloves, minced
2 teaspoons salt

2 teaspoons ground cumin
1 teaspoon ground coriander
1 teaspoon cayenne pepper
1 teaspoon freshly ground pepper

1 flank steak, about 1½ lb (750 g)

❋ Mix all the marinade ingredients together and spread the mixture over both sides of the flank steak. Marinate for at least 30 minutes or up to 2 hours at room temperature or 24 hours in the refrigerator (cover if refrigerated); remove from the refrigerator 30 minutes before cooking. Grill over hot coals or broil under a preheated broiler for about 5 minutes per side. Slice diagonally across the grain and serve immediately.

SERVES 6

Clockwise from left: Spicy Flank Steak, Chalupa,
Beef Machaca Chimichangas

CHALUPA

Chalupa *means "little boat" and refers to boat-shaped pieces of*
tortilla dough that are cooked and filled with a shredded meat fill-
ing. This chalupa filling is also terrific in burritos or chimichangas,
or it may be served in individual bowls with tortilla chips, grated
cheese, shredded lettuce, diced tomatoes and chopped onions.

1 lb (500 g) dried pinto beans
3 lb (1.5 kg) pork loin roast
2 garlic cloves, minced
6 Anaheim chilies, roasted, peeled, cored, seeded and
  chopped (see glossary)

1 guajillo chili, toasted, stemmed and seeded (see glossary)
1 tablespoon ground cumin seed
1 teaspoon dried oregano
1 tablespoon salt

❀ Put the beans in a large pot and cover with water. Over
high heat, bring to a boil and cook for 5 minutes. Remove
the pot from the heat, cover and let stand 1 hour. Add the
remaining ingredients to the pot and cover with water.
❀ Cook, covered, over medium-low heat for 6 hours,
adding water as necessary. Remove the pork roast from the
pot and discard all bones. Break up the meat and return it
to the pot. Cook, uncovered, for 1 hour, or until the mixture is thick.

SERVES 8–10

NEW MEXICO

STUFFED ROASTED QUAIL

Coveys of quail are a common sight in the desert, even in areas where homes have been built. Most cooks prefer to purchase quail partially deboned at their local butcher shop or specialty foods store. These small birds yield little meat, so a hearty stuffing makes them stretch further. Six pheasants or game hens may be used in the place of the quail, but they will need to be cooked about 15 minutes longer.

12 partially boned quail, rinsed and dried
6 cups (2 lb/1 kg) Blue Corn Chorizo Stuffing (recipe on
   page 136)
salt and freshly ground pepper to taste
2 tablespoons unsalted butter
1 tablespoon olive oil
½ cup (4 fl oz/125 ml) Madeira or red wine

❊ Preheat an oven to 350°F (180°C). Stuff each quail with about ½ cup (3 oz/90 g) stuffing and truss with cotton string; sprinkle with salt and pepper. In a large skillet over medium-high heat, melt the butter and oil together; when hot, add the quail, breast side down. Turn the quail to brown on all sides. If the pan is not large enough to brown all the quail at once, brown them in batches, transferring them to a baking pan as they are finished.
❊ Pour off any fat left in the skillet and return the pan to high heat. Add the wine and cook while stirring to scrape up any browned bits on the bottom of the pan. Strain the wine mixture over the quail in the baking dish; bake for 30–40 minutes, or until the quail are browned and their juices run clear when a thigh is pierced with a knife.

SERVES 6   *Photograph page 4*

LAS CRUCES, NEW MEXICO

CREAMY CHILI EGG CASSEROLE

A delicious brunch dish, this casserole may be made heartier by layering cooked shrimp or diced poached chicken with the chilies and grated cheeses. The recipe may be scaled up or down easily, depending on the size of the crowd.

4 New Mexico green or Anaheim chilies, roasted, peeled,
   seeded and chopped (see glossary)
1½ cups (12 oz/375 g) grated Cheddar cheese
1½ cups (12 oz/375 g) grated Monterey jack cheese
6 eggs
⅔ cup (5 oz/155 g) milk
1 teaspoon salt
1 teaspoon sugar
freshly ground pepper to taste
2 tablespoons unbleached all-purpose (plain) flour
4 oz (125 g) cream cheese, cut into ½-in (12-mm) pieces, at
   room temperature

❊ Preheat an oven to 325°F (165°C). Butter an 8-in (20-cm) square baking pan. Evenly distribute the chilies in the bottom of the prepared pan. Combine the grated cheeses and reserve ½ cup (2 oz/60 g) to sprinkle on top of the casserole. Spoon the remaining grated cheese over the chilies.
❊ In a medium bowl, beat together the eggs, milk, salt, sugar, pepper and flour. Add the cream cheese and beat until incorporated. Pour over the chilies and cheese. Bake for 40–45 minutes, or until the eggs are cooked and the cheeses are melted. Let cool slightly and spoon onto serving plates.

SERVES 4–6

TUCSON, ARIZONA

BREAKFAST BURRITOS

Chorizo is a reddish brown sausage made of coarsely ground pork seasoned with spices and chilies and available in many grocery stores. The casing should be removed from the sausage before cooking it over low heat. These burritos are delicious for brunch, although they are good anytime.

8 oz (250 g) chorizo (Spanish sausage), casing
   removed, crumbled
1 cup (5 oz/155 g) finely chopped onion
2 jalapeño chilies, cored, seeded and minced
1 tablespoon butter

Left to right: Breakfast Burritos, Creamy Chili Egg Casserole

12 eggs
¼ cup (2 fl oz/60 ml) milk
salt and freshly ground pepper to taste
4 cups (32 fl oz/1 l) Ranchero Sauce (recipe on page 190)
1½ cups (12 oz/375 g) grated Monterey jack cheese
6 flour tortillas (8 in/20 cm in diameter)
sour cream and shredded lettuce for garnish

❋ Preheat an oven to 350°F (180°C). Lightly oil a 7½-by-11½-in (18-by-28-cm) baking pan.
❋ In a large skillet over low heat, brown the chorizo with the onion and jalapeños. Drain well on paper towels; set aside.
❋ Melt the butter in a large skillet over medium heat. In a large bowl, whisk together the eggs, milk, salt and pepper. Pour the eggs into the hot skillet and cook, stirring, until the eggs are firm but not dry. Fold the reserved chorizo mixture and 2 cups (16 fl oz/500 ml) of the ranchero sauce into the eggs.
❋ Divide the egg-chorizo mixture among the tortillas, top each with ¼ cup (1 oz/30 g) cheese, and roll up. Place the rolled tortillas in the prepared baking dish; pour the remaining sauce over the burritos and bake for 15–20 minutes, or until they are warmed through and the cheese is melted. Serve individually with a dollop of sour cream on top and shredded lettuce on the side.

MAKES 6

Clockwise from left: Tacos de Pescado, Indian Tacos, Picadillo Tacos

SOUTHWEST TEXAS

PICADILLO TACOS

Tacos with almost every filling imaginable are popular throughout the Southwest and Mexico. This spicy ground beef filling is especially good with corn tortillas. Picadillo in Spanish-speaking countries is the name of a traditional meat and vegetable dish; here it is adapted as a taco filling.

½ cup (4 fl oz/125 ml) vegetable oil
12 corn tortillas (6 in/15 cm in diameter)
2 tablespoons olive oil
1 cup (5 oz/155 g) finely chopped onions
½ cup (2½ oz/75 g) green bell pepper (capsicum), diced
3 garlic cloves, minced
1 lb (500 g) lean ground beef
1 lb (500 g) plum (egg) tomatoes, diced
⅔ cup (3½ oz/105 g) chopped pimiento-stuffed green olives
½ cup (3 oz/90 g) corn kernels
⅓ cup (2 oz/60 g) raisins
2 tablespoons packed brown sugar
1 tablespoon distilled white vinegar

¼ teaspoon ground cinnamon
⅛ teaspoon ground cloves
salt and freshly ground pepper to taste
shredded lettuce and grated Cheddar or Monterey jack
  cheese for garnish

❀ In a medium skillet, heat the vegetable oil over medium-high heat. Using tongs, dip each tortilla in the hot oil for about 10–15 seconds on each side, or until softened. Shape into a folded shell and cook until crisp. Drain on paper towels and keep warm; repeat with the remaining tortillas.
❀ In a large skillet, heat the olive oil over medium heat; add the onions and sauté until softened, about 5 minutes. Add the green pepper and garlic and cook, stirring, for another 3 minutes. Add the ground beef and continue cooking until the meat is cooked through and no longer pink. Stir in all the remaining ingredients except the lettuce and cheese and cook, stirring, until the mixture is dry, about 10 minutes. Fill each taco shell with about ⅓ cup (3 oz/90 g) filling and top with shredded lettuce and grated cheese. Serve immediately.

MAKES 12

SOUTHWEST

Tacos de Pescado

Modern transportation brings fresh fish to the metropolitan areas of the Southwest daily, so easy-to-prepare fish tacos are a popular dish. They are especially good made with flour tortillas hot off the skillet.

6 flour tortillas (8 in/20 cm in diameter) (recipe on page 137)
1 lb (500 g) firm white-fleshed fish such as snapper, rockfish or sea bass
2 tablespoons fresh lemon juice
salt and freshly ground pepper to taste
2 garlic cloves, minced
1 tablespoon vegetable oil
Guacamole (recipe on page 191), sour cream and shredded lettuce for garnish

❈ If using packaged tortillas, wrap them tightly with aluminum foil and place in a preheated 350°F (180°C) oven for 15–20 minutes, or until warmed through. If making tortillas from scratch, grill them in a hot skillet just before cooking the fish; keep warm.
❈ Rinse the fish with cold water and pat dry. Rub 1 tablespoon of the lemon juice over the surface of the fish; sprinkle with salt, pepper and minced garlic. Heat a large cast-iron skillet over high heat until almost smoking, about 7 minutes; add the vegetable oil, then the fish. Cook for 2–3 minutes on each side, or until golden. Sprinkle the fish with the second tablespoon of lemon juice, then shred or dice it and place in the center of the warm flour tortillas. Fold the tortillas in half and place on hot serving plates. Garnish with guacamole, sour cream and shredded lettuce.

MAKES 6

NAVAJO NATION

Indian Tacos

Most native Americans of the Southwest eat some version of these tacos. A favorite treat when skiing at Sunrise Resort on the White Mountain Apache Reservation in northern Arizona is the Apache Taco, fry bread topped with chili con carne, lettuce, tomatoes and cheese. The lamb topping here would typically be found on the Navajo Reservation, where sheep are prevalent. If desired, beef may be substituted for lamb in this recipe. It is best to make the stew before frying the bread so the bread is hot and crisp.

2 teaspoons cayenne pepper
1 teaspoon ground white pepper
2 teaspoons paprika
1 teaspoon salt
1 teaspoon crumbled dried thyme
1¼ teaspoons ground cumin
1½ lb (750 g) lamb, cubed
2 tablespoons vegetable oil
2 cups (8 oz/250 g) chopped onions
¼ cup (2 oz/60 g) unsalted butter, or 3 tablespoons oil
4 Anaheim chilies, roasted, peeled, cored, seeded and diced (see glossary)
2 garlic cloves, minced
1 red bell pepper (capsicum), cored, seeded and diced
2 poblano chilies, cored, seeded and diced
2 tablespoons unbleached all-purpose (plain) flour
1 cup (8 fl oz/250 ml) chicken stock (see glossary)
shredded lettuce, chopped tomatoes, grated cheese and salsa for garnish

1 recipe Indian Fry Bread (recipe on page 132)

❈ In a small bowl, combine the cayenne, white pepper, paprika, salt, thyme and cumin. Place the lamb in another bowl and sprinkle 1 tablespoon of the spice mixture over the cubes. With your hands, work the spice mixture into the lamb cubes.
❈ Heat the oil in a large skillet until very hot. Add the onions and 1 tablespoon of the spice mix and cook over medium-high heat for about 5 minutes. Add the butter or oil; when hot, add the lamb and cook, stirring occasionally, until the lamb is browned, about 10 minutes. Stir in the Anaheim chilies, garlic, bell pepper, poblano chilies and remaining seasoning mix and cook for another 2 minutes. Add the flour to the lamb mixture and cook, stirring constantly, for 3 minutes. Slowly add the chicken stock, stirring well to combine, and bring to a boil. Lower heat; cook for another 15 minutes, or until the flavors are well blended and the sauce is thick.
❈ Cook the fry bread and drain on paper towels. Place a piece of fry bread on each of 6 plates. Spoon the lamb topping evenly on top of the fry bread and garnish with shredded lettuce, chopped tomatoes, grated cheese and salsa. Serve at once.

SERVES 6

VALLEY OF THE SUN, ARIZONA

Marinated Grilled Leg of Lamb

Because this dish is best marinated for at least 24 hours, it is a perfect do-ahead dish for entertaining. It is delicious served with Green Chili Sauce, especially if mint is substituted for cilantro in that recipe. For best results, grill over mesquite.

MARINADE

½ cup (4 fl oz/125 ml) olive oil
⅓ cup (3 fl oz/80 ml) fresh orange juice
2 teaspoons finely grated orange zest
1 tablespoon Grand Marnier
1½ teaspoons minced fresh thyme, or ½ teaspoon crumbled dried thyme
1 teaspoon cumin seed, crushed to a coarse powder
1 tablespoon minced fresh cilantro (coriander)
salt and freshly ground pepper to taste

1 leg of lamb (about 5 lb/2.5 kg) boned, butterflied and trimmed of all fat
1½ cups (12 fl oz/500 ml) Green Chili Sauce (recipe on page 195)

❈ Combine all the marinade ingredients in a large nonaluminum baking pan. Add the lamb, cover and refrigerate overnight or for as long as 2 days, turning the lamb occasionally.
❈ Light a fire in a charcoal grill. Remove the lamb from the refrigerator and let sit at room temperature while the coals are heating. Grill over hot coals, about 3 in (7.5 cm) from the heat, basting frequently with the marinade and turning once, for about 20 minutes, or until the lamb is medium rare (135°F/60°C internal temperature).
❈ Slice the lamb across the grain and serve with green chili sauce.

SERVES 6   *Photograph pages 92–93*

Left to right: Shellfish Tamales with Ancho Cream, Baked Southwest Chicken with Jack Cheese and Peppers

PHOENIX, ARIZONA

BAKED SOUTHWEST CHICKEN WITH JACK CHEESE AND PEPPERS

Serve this dish as an elegant main course, or leave the breasts whole and serve them at room temperature for a festive picnic dish.

3 tablespoons Southwest Seasoning Mix (recipe on page 196)
3 tablespoons dry bread crumbs
6 boneless half chicken breasts, skinned
12 thin slices (about 6 oz/185 g) Monterey jack cheese, each about 2 by 3 in (5 by 7.5 cm)
1 red bell pepper (capsicum), cored, seeded and cut into ¼-by-3-in (6-mm-by-7.5-cm) strips
1 yellow bell pepper (capsicum), cored, seeded and cut into ¼-by-3-in (6-mm-by-7.5-cm) strips
1½ teaspoons chili powder
2 tablespoons minced fresh cilantro (coriander)
salt and freshly ground pepper to taste
1 avocado, peeled, pitted, diced and tossed with 1 tablespoon lime juice, for garnish
1 ripe tomato, seeded and diced, for garnish
Red Pepper Sauce (recipe on page 190), optional

❀ Preheat an oven to 375°F (190°C). Lightly oil a baking dish large enough to hold the chicken breasts in a single layer. In a small bowl, stir together the seasoning mix and the bread crumbs; set aside.
❀ Cut a pocket along the length of each chicken breast and, keeping one edge attached, fold back the top of the pocket. Line each pocket with a slice of cheese and top with rows of red, then yellow bell peppers. Sprinkle ¼ teaspoon chili powder, 1 teaspoon cilantro, salt and pepper over each last row of peppers and top with a second slice of cheese. Fold the top back over the filling and secure with toothpicks.
❀ Coat both sides of each stuffed chicken breast with the seasoned bread crumb mixture. Place the breasts in the prepared baking pan; cover and bake for 10 minutes. Remove the cover and bake another 10 minutes. Transfer the breasts to a cutting board, remove the toothpicks and slice the

breasts diagonally into ½-in (12-mm) slices. Fan the slices on warm plates, sprinkle the diced avocado and tomato over the slices and serve immediately. Serve with red bell pepper sauce if desired.

SERVES 6

ROCKY MOUNTAINS

VENISON SALAMI

Deer are abundant in the higher elevations of the Southwest and this recipe for salami, supplied by Todd Fenzl, the manager of a wildlife refuge in Idaho, is the ideal way for hunters to make use of extra ground venison.

2 lb (1 kg) ground venison
1 tablespoon curing salt
1 teaspoon mustard seed
4 garlic cloves, minced
1 teaspoon dried hot red pepper flakes
1 teaspoon chili powder
1 teaspoon freshly ground pepper

❀ In a large bowl, mix together the meat, salt, mustard seed, garlic, pepper flakes, chili powder, and pepper. Cover and refrigerate for 3–4 days, stirring the mixture at least once a day.
❀ Shape the meat into 2 logs about 1 lb (500 g) each and about 2 in (5 cm) in diameter. Place the rolls in a smoker with mesquite, hickory or cherry wood chips at 120°F (50°C) for 4 hours, turning for uniform smoke. Then place in a 160°F (70°C) oven for 4 hours, turning occasionally, to finish drying. Or, to cook in a grill: Soak mesquite wood chips in water overnight. Place the chips in an aluminum pan on the grill along with the salami. Cook over low coals for 4–5 hours, adding water to the wood chips as necessary to create low smoke. If not using a smoker or a grill, place the rolls in a 160°F (70°C) oven for 6 hours; the salami will not have the same smoky taste, however.
❀ Remove the rolls from the oven, let cool, wrap in plastic and refrigerate. When ready to serve, cut into slices ¼ in (6 mm) thick.

MAKES 2 LOGS (ABOUT 1 LB/500 G EACH)

DALLAS, TEXAS

SHELLFISH TAMALES WITH ANCHO CREAM

Considered fiesta food in Mexico since pre-Hispanic times, tamales are always a welcome addition to a meal. This version, using shrimp and scallops, is the creation of Stephan Pyles, one of the fathers of modern Southwest cuisine.

1 small (6 oz/185 g) sweet potato, peeled and cut into ¼-in (6-mm) dice (about 1½ cups)
4½ cups (36 fl oz/1.1 l) chicken stock (see glossary)
½ teaspoon salt
1 tablespoon pure maple syrup
½ cup (4 oz/125 g) plus 2 tablespoons vegetable shortening (vegetable lard) at room temperature
2 cups (10 oz/315 g) masa harina (see glossary)
½ cup (2½ oz/75 g) cornmeal
1 teaspoon baking powder
¼ teaspoon cayenne pepper

¼ teaspoon ground cumin
2 teaspoons salt
1½ cups (12 fl oz/375 ml) warm (110°F/40°C) water
18 corn husks soaked in water for 30 minutes
4 cups (32 fl oz/1 l) heavy (double) cream
3 tablespoons clarified butter or corn oil
3 ancho chilies, cored and seeded
1 lb (500 g) shrimp (prawns), peeled, deveined and diced
½ cup (3 oz/90 g) corn kernels
8 oz (250 g) bay scallops
3 tablespoons diced red bell pepper (capsicum)
3 tablespoons diced yellow bell pepper (capsicum)
3 tablespoons diced green bell pepper (capsicum)
1 tablespoon chopped fresh basil
1 tablespoon chopped fresh cilantro (coriander)
salt to taste
8 fresh cilantro (coriander) sprigs for garnish

❋ Place the diced sweet potato in a medium saucepan and cover with the chicken stock. Add the salt and maple syrup; bring to a boil. Reduce heat, simmer for 4 minutes and strain the diced sweet potato, reserving the stock. Plunge half the diced sweet potato into ice water; when chilled, strain again and set aside. Purée the other half of the diced sweet potato in a blender or food processor; set aside.

❋ In the bowl of an electric mixer, whisk the vegetable shortening until light and fluffy, scraping down the sides of the bowl as necessary. In another bowl, combine the masa harina, cornmeal, baking powder, cayenne, cumin and salt, then gradually pour in the warm water and mix to form a soft dough. Whisk the dough into the shortening; add the sweet potato purée and gradually add ½ cup (4 fl oz/125 ml) of the reserved potato cooking liquid. Mix for 1 minute more.

❋ Drain the corn husks and pat dry. Tear sixteen ⅛-in (3-mm) wide strips from 2 of the husks for tying the tamales.

Place 2 husks together with the large ends overlapping by 2 in (5 cm). Repeat with the remaining husks. Divide the tamale dough evenly among the 8 double husks; spread over the center, leaving 1 in (2.5 cm) at each end of corn husk uncovered. Roll the corn husks so that the dough filling is completely enclosed. Twist and tie each end with the strips already torn off.

❋ Steam the tamales in a conventional steamer or in a strainer set over a saucepan and covered with a tight-fitting lid; it is important that little or no steam escapes. Steam for 30–35 minutes; the water should always be lightly boiling. The tamales are done when the dough comes away easily from the husks.

❋ Meanwhile, prepare the ancho cream and shellfish. Cut 1 of the anchos into julienne and set aside. Soak the other 2 ancho chilies in very hot water until softened, about 20 minutes. Remove from the water and purée in a food processor or blender. Strain into a bowl and set aside. In a medium saucepan, boil the cream to reduce it to 2 cups (16 fl oz/500 ml). In a separate saucepan, boil the remaining reserved potato cooking liquid to reduce it to 1 cup (8 fl oz/250 ml). In a sauté pan, heat the clarified butter or corn oil over medium heat until lightly smoking. Add the shrimp, julienned ancho and corn; sauté for 1 minute. Add the scallops, peppers, ancho purée, basil, cilantro, reduced cream, reserved sweet potatoes and reduced cooking stock. Bring to a boil, reduce heat and simmer for 1 minute. Add salt.

❋ When the tamales are cooked, slice them from end to end with a knife. Push the ends gently together, as for a baked potato. Transfer to serving plates, pour the shellfish mixture over, and spoon the remaining shellfish and sauce around the tamales. Garnish with cilantro sprigs.

MAKES 8

Venison Salami

BARBECUED CABRITO

Cabrito, or baby goat, is often barbecued in West Texas and served with Red Chili Sauce (recipe on page 195), fresh flour tortillas, beans and coleslaw. This recipe is from Elin Jeffords, a food writer and restaurant consultant who lived in West Texas before moving to Arizona. Goat is available from meat markets if ordered ahead of time, particularly in the spring. Use this same recipe for cooking javelina; just be certain the musk sac has been removed.

2 cups (16 fl oz/500 ml) fresh lime juice
1 cup (8 fl oz/250 ml) vegetable oil
10 garlic cloves, crushed
½ cup (3 oz/90 g) mild chili powder
1 tablespoon ground cumin
salt and freshly ground pepper to taste
1 baby goat, butterflied (about 10 lb/5 kg)

❀ Dig a pit slightly larger than the goat. Line it with gravel. Build a fire at the bottom of the pit using hardwood. When the fire is hot, put a grate over the top and place a drip pan on the grate to catch the juices.

❀ Combine the first 6 ingredients and brush over the goat. Impale the goat on a spit and cook about 20 in (50 cm) above the fire. Brush the goat every 15 minutes with the marinade and pan drippings. Cook until the flesh pulls easily away from the bones and the skin is brown and crackly, about 3 hours. Remove from the spit and cut into serving pieces.

❀ Alternatively, cook the marinated goat in a covered grill, directly on the cooking rack, with a drip pan underneath, turning the goat every 30 minutes and basting it every 15 minutes, until done (see above).

SERVES 8   *Photograph pages 92–93*

1 tablespoon balsamic vinegar
2 tablespoons raspberry vinegar
1 teaspoon freshly ground pepper
5 juniper berries, crushed
1 bay leaf, crumbled
1 rosemary sprig
1 tablespoon chopped fresh tarragon
1 teaspoon chopped fresh sage

1 buffalo sirloin steak, 2-in (5-cm) thick (about 2 lb/1 kg)
salsa or Ancho Chili Sauce (recipe on page 99)

❋ To make the marinade, preheat an oven to 350° F (180° C). Liberally rub the head of garlic with olive oil; wrap the garlic in aluminum foil and bake in the oven for 1 hour, or until the garlic is soft. Combine all the ingredients and the softened garlic in a shallow nonaluminum dish. Place the buffalo steak in the marinade, coat completely, cover and refrigerate overnight, turning occasionally.
❋ Remove the steaks from the refrigerator 30 minutes before cooking.
❋ Light a fire in a charcoal grill or preheat a broiler (griller). Cook the steaks 4–6 in (10–13 cm) from heat for 5–6 minutes on each side, or until medium rare. Slice and serve with salsa or ancho sauce.

SERVES 6

Left to right: Marinated Buffalo Steak, Barbecued Spareribs

S O U T H E R N   C O L O R A D O
MARINATED BUFFALO STEAK

Lower in fat and cholesterol and sweeter in flavor than most cuts of beef, buffalo (technically, the American bison) can be used in almost any recipe calling for beef. Because buffalo has less fat, its meat is darker in color and should be cooked only rare to medium at low heat for less time than for beef. Farm-raised American bison is available from butchers and by mail order, and it comes in cuts similar to those for beef.

MARINADE

1 small head garlic
¼ cup (2 fl oz/60 ml) orange juice
1 tablespoon grated orange zest
½ cup (4 fl oz/125 ml) dry red wine
½ cup (4 fl oz/125 ml) olive oil
¼ cup (1 oz/30 g) chopped red (Spanish) onion

T E X A S   H I L L   C O U N T R Y
BARBECUED SPARERIBS

In Texas, almost any type of meat is barbecued, including whole goats and heads of cows, but beef, pork and game spareribs are the most popular. Barbecuing requires low heat, and the sauce should be added toward the end of the cooking time so the sugar in it does not burn.

SAUCE

2 tablespoons vegetable oil
1 cup (5 oz/155 g) finely chopped onions
2 garlic cloves, minced
2 jalapeño chilies, seeded and minced
1 cup (8 fl oz/250 ml) tomato sauce (puréed tomatoes)
½ cup (4 fl oz/125 ml) cider vinegar
2 teaspoons paprika
1 tablespoon dry mustard
2 tablespoons packed brown sugar
salt and freshly ground pepper to taste

4 lb (2 kg) spareribs (beef, pork, venison or elk)

❋ To make the sauce, heat oil in a medium skillet over medium-high heat; sauté the onions, garlic and jalapeños until the onions are soft and translucent, 3–5 minutes. Place in a blender and purée; transfer to a saucepan.
❋ Add the remaining sauce ingredients to the saucepan containing the onion mixture. Bring to a boil over high heat, lower heat and simmer, covered, for about 30 minutes.
❋ Light a fire in a charcoal grill or preheat an oven to 325°F (165°C). Grill the ribs about 4–6 in (10–15 cm) from the coals until browned, about 30–45 minutes, or bake them in a roasting pan for 45 minutes. If roasting in an oven, drain the fat from the roasting pan, raise the oven temperature to 375°F (190°C), cover the ribs with sauce and bake 30 minutes longer. If grilling, baste the ribs with sauce and cook an additional 30 minutes, basting every 10 minutes. Cut into individual ribs and serve.

SERVES 6

SOUR CREAM TURKEY ENCHILADAS

A perfect way to use leftover turkey, these creamy enchiladas can be made a few hours ahead of time, covered, refrigerated and baked just before serving. To cut down on fat, brush the tortillas with water and heat them on a dry griddle or in a large dry skillet.

1½ tablespoons unsalted butter
1½ tablespoons unbleached all-purpose (plain) flour
1½ cups (12 fl oz/375 ml) chicken stock (see glossary)
¼ teaspoon red hot pepper sauce
salt and freshly ground pepper to taste
1½ cups (12 oz/375 g) sour cream
3 cups (18 oz/560 g) shredded cooked turkey breast
    (1 turkey breast, poached, or leftover turkey breast)
2 Anaheim chilies, roasted, peeled, cored, seeded and diced
    (see glossary)
2 cups (8 oz/250 g) grated Manchego or white
    Cheddar cheese
½ cup (4 oz/125 g) finely chopped green (spring) onions
vegetable oil for frying
12 corn tortillas (6 in/15 cm in diameter)
1 cup (4 oz/125 g) grated Monterey jack cheese

❋ Heat the butter in a medium, heavy saucepan. Add the flour and cook, stirring constantly, for 3 minutes. Gradually add the chicken stock and continue stirring until the sauce is smooth and thick. Add the hot pepper sauce, salt and pepper. Add the sour cream and mix until smooth. Divide the sauce in half. Add the shredded turkey and chilies to one half; stir until incorporated. Reserve the other half of the sauce. Mix together the Manchego or Cheddar cheese and onions.
❋ To cook the enchiladas, preheat oven to 350°F (180°C). Fill the bottom of a small skillet with ¼ in (6 mm) of oil and heat the oil until almost smoking. Dip a corn tortilla into the hot oil for a few seconds until soft; drain on a paper towel. Put 1 tablespoon filling and 1 tablespoon sauce on the edge of the tortilla and roll the tortilla up. Put the filled enchilada in a 13-by-9-in (32.5-by-23-cm) baking dish. Repeat with the remaining tortillas. Pour the reserved sauce over the enchiladas; sprinkle Monterey jack cheese on top and bake for 20 minutes, or until the cheese is melted and the enchiladas are warmed through.

MAKES 12

SMOKED WILD TURKEY

In pre-Columbian times, the only domesticated food animal in the New World was the turkey. Wild ones still roam on Arizona's Mogollon Rim and, once a year, in the late fall, hunters draw from a lottery to obtain a permit to shoot one. Usually not much heavier than ten pounds, a wild turkey has more flavor than a farm-raised one, especially when smoked. Mitch Sivertson, a stockbroker in Phoenix, has brought home a wild turkey each year for the last five years, and his wife Michelle shares her recipe for smoking them to perfection.

1 teaspoon ground dried sage
1 teaspoon freshly ground pepper
1 wild or domestic turkey, about 10–12 lb (5–6 kg)
¼ cup (2 fl oz/60 ml) olive oil
⅓ cup (2.5 fl oz/75 ml) fresh lemon juice
1 tablespoon Worcestershire sauce
¼ cup (2 fl oz/60 ml) dry white wine, plus more for water pan
2 tablespoons unsalted butter, melted
1 teaspoon salt

1 teaspoon chopped fresh marjoram, or ½ teaspoon
    dried marjoram

❋ Rub ground sage and freshly ground pepper all over the turkey.
❋ Combine all of the remaining ingredients in a small bowl and brush or rub the mixture over the outside and inside of the turkey. If any of the mixture is left over, add it to the water pan of the smoker.
❋ Heat a smoker to its highest setting using charcoal or mesquite wood. Fill the water pan of the smoker with half water and half dry white wine. Place the turkey in the smoker and smoke according to manufacturer's directions for about 8 hours, or until a meat thermometer inserted in a thigh reaches 180°F (80°C); add liquid to dripping pan as necessary.
❋ Alternatively, to cook on a covered grill, make an indirect fire using mesquite charcoal or mesquite wood chips soaked in water overnight and added to lighted coals. Over medium-hot coals, cook the turkey, covered, over a drip pan filled with half water and half dry white wine for 2–3 hours or until a meat thermometer inserted in a thigh reaches 180°F (80°C); add liquid to dripping pan as necessary.
❋ To make the gravy, pour the liquid from the drip pan into a large glass measuring cup. Spoon 3 tablespoons of the fat at the top of the cup into a skillet. Pour off the remaining fat. Heat the fat in the skillet and stir in 3 tablespoons flour; cook and stir for 2–3 minutes. Whisk in the liquid from the measuring cup and cook over medium heat until thickened; add chicken stock as necessary to make a smooth gravy.

SERVES 6–8

ROASTED TURKEY TOSTADA SALAD WITH CRANBERRY SALSA

Celebrate Thanksgiving year round with this imaginative salad from Stephan Pyles, chef-owner of Baby Routh in Dallas and author of The New Texas Cuisine. *If possible, use caciotta, an Italian cheese made by Paula Lambert's Mozzarella Company in Dallas. What a terrific way to use leftover turkey!*

CRANBERRY SALSA

1 cup (4 oz/125 g) cranberries
2 tablespoons orange juice
⅓ cup (3 oz/90 g) sugar
2 medium red bell peppers (capsicums), roasted, peeled,
    seeded and diced (see glossary)
3 tablespoons chopped fresh cilantro (coriander)
2 tablespoons pecans, toasted and chopped (see glossary)
1 teaspoon grated lime zest
1 tablespoon grated orange zest
salt to taste

6 corn tortillas (6 in/15 cm in diameter)
vegetable oil for frying
2 cups (12 oz/375 g) diced roasted turkey
½ cup (2½ oz/75 g) finely chopped onion
1 small tomato, peeled, seeded and chopped
    (see glossary)
¼ cup (1 oz/30 g) pecans, toasted (see glossary)
1 avocado, peeled, pitted and sliced
¼ cup (1 oz/30 g) pitted black olives

BUTTERMILK DRESSING

½ cup (4 fl oz/125 ml) buttermilk
½ cup (4 fl oz/125 ml) mayonnaise
1 shallot, minced
1 clove garlic, minced

Clockwise from bottom left: Sour Cream Turkey Enchiladas, Smoked Wild Turkey, Roasted Turkey Tostada Salad with Cranberry Salsa

2 teaspoons fresh lime juice
1 tablespoon fresh basil, minced
¼ teaspoon hot pepper sauce
salt and freshly ground pepper to taste

¾ cup (3 oz/90 g) grated caciotta or Monterey jack cheese
1 head romaine lettuce, shredded
1 head radicchio or red cabbage, shredded
½ cup (4 fl oz/125 ml) Cilantro Citrus Vinaigrette (recipe on page 198)
¼ cup (2 oz/60 g) sour cream
12 pickled jalapeño chilies, sliced, for garnish (optional)

❂ To make the salsa, in a food processor or blender, blend the cranberries, orange juice and sugar for 30–45 seconds. Transfer to a bowl and add the peppers, cilantro, pecans and zests; season with salt and set aside.
❂ Preheat a broiler (griller). Pour oil into a large skillet or pan to a depth of 1 in (2.5 cm). Heat over medium-high heat until lightly smoking and fry 4 of the tortillas (in batches if necessary) until crisp, about 2 minutes, keeping them as flat as possible by holding them down with 2 spatulas. Remove the tortillas from the pan, drain on paper towels and sprinkle with

salt; transfer to a baking sheet. Cut the remaining 2 tortillas into strips ⅛ in (3 mm) wide and fry until crisp. Remove from the pan, drain on paper towels and sprinkle with salt.
❂ In a large bowl, combine the turkey, onion, tomato, pecans, avocado and olives.
❂ To make the buttermilk dressing, in a medium bowl, whisk together all ingredients. Add the dressing to the turkey mixture and toss until thoroughly combined.
❂ Divide the turkey mixture into 4 equal portions and place on top of the 4 fried tortillas. Sprinkle the cheese over the turkey mixture and place the tostadas under the broiler (griller). Broil for about 1 minute, or just until the cheese melts. Transfer the tostadas to heated plates.
❂ In a mixing bowl, toss the shredded lettuce and radicchio or cabbage with the vinaigrette. Place the tossed greens around the tostadas on the plates and sprinkle with the reserved tortilla strips. Place 1 tablespoon of sour cream in the center of each tostada and top with a dollop of cranberry salsa. Place the remaining salsa in a serving bowl to be passed at the table. Sprinkle the optional sliced jalapeños over the tostadas and lettuces and serve immediately.

SERVES 4

111

Left to right: Salmon Cooked Camp Fire Style with Chipotle Vinaigrette,
Gulf Red Snapper with Rocky Point Shrimp

SALMON COOKED CAMP FIRE STYLE WITH CHIPOTLE VINAIGRETTE

Robert McGrath, the talented former chef of the Four Seasons and Sierra in Houston and the Scottsdale Princess, developed this recipe using a stove-top smoker for which he holds a patent. A smoker can easily be created by using a rack that fits inside a heavy-bottomed covered pan. Place the fish on the rack and the wood chips on the pan bottom, cover tightly and cook slowly over very low heat.

¾ cup (4 oz/125 g) seeded, quartered and sliced cucumber
¾ cup (4 oz/125 g) quartered, cored and sliced pear
⅓ cup (1 oz/30 g) peeled and finely julienned jícama
⅓ cup (3 fl oz/80 ml) fresh lemon juice

2¼ lb (1.1 kg) salmon fillet, cut into 12 crosswise strips
salt and freshly ground pepper to taste

CHIPOTLE VINAIGRETTE

1 canned chipotle chili and 2 teaspoons adobo sauce (see glossary)
3 tablespoons chopped fresh cilantro (coriander)
2 teaspoons minced garlic
2 teaspoons minced shallot
⅓ cup (3 fl oz/80 ml) seasoned rice vinegar

½ cup (4 fl oz/125 ml) corn oil
1 tablespoon fresh lemon juice

⅓ cup (1 oz/30 g) finely julienned pickled beets
6 fresh cilantro (coriander) sprigs for garnish

❋ Toss the cucumber, pear and jícama in the lemon juice; set aside.
❋ Weave the salmon strips on wooden skewers that have been soaked in water for 30 minutes. Salt and pepper the salmon skewers and place in a stove-top smoker or in a covered grill with hickory sawdust or finely ground chips sprinkled over the coals. If using a smoker, cook over medium-high heat for 3–4 minutes, then reduce the heat to medium-low for 8–9 minutes. Be careful not to cook the salmon too fast or the smoke may give it a bitter flavor. If using a covered grill, cook the salmon over hot coals for about 4 minutes on each side, or until firm to the touch.
❋ To make the vinaigrette, purée the chili, cilantro, garlic, shallot and vinegar in a food processor or blender. With the machine running, add the corn oil slowly, then the lemon juice.
❋ Just before serving, add the pickled beets to the cucumber, pear and jícama. Nap the bottom half of each of 6 plates with 2 tablespoons chipotle vinaigrette. Place the cucumber mixture on the top left of the plate and place the salmon skewers on top of the cucumber mixture. Garnish with fresh cilantro sprigs.

SERVES 6

GULF RED SNAPPER WITH ROCKY POINT SHRIMP

The historic Wrigley Mansion, which perches prominently over the Arizona Biltmore Resort in central Phoenix, is now a private dining club. Its imaginative chef, Cary Neff, created this dish of snapper fillets topped with slices of shrimp- and goat cheese–stuffed chilies. Neff garnishes each plate with a tomato-piñon salsa, but any tomato-based salsa works well.

8 red snapper fillets (6 oz/185 g each)
¼ cup (2 fl oz/60 ml) olive oil
2 tablespoons chopped shallots
1 lb (500 g) shrimp (prawns), peeled, deveined and diced
2 cups (6 oz/185 g) sliced stemmed shiitake mushrooms
½ cup (4 oz/125 g) sun-dried tomatoes in oil, drained
2 tablespoons tequila
2 cups (10 oz/315 g) crumbled mild fresh goat cheese
1 tablespoon minced fresh oregano
8 red Anaheim chilies, roasted, peeled, cored and seeded
 (see glossary)

CILANTRO OIL

3 bunches fresh cilantro (coriander), stemmed
¼ cup (2 fl oz/60 ml) olive oil
⅛ teaspoon fresh lime juice
salt and freshly ground pepper to taste

salsa for garnish
fresh cilantro (coriander) sprigs for garnish

❈ Remove the skin and any bones from the snapper fillets. Place a layer of plastic wrap on both sides of each fillet and pound with the flat side of a meat mallet until each forms a ¼-in-thick (6-mm) circular portion. Set aside.
❈ In a large skillet, heat the olive oil over medium heat; add shallots and shrimp and sauté for 2 minutes. Add the shiitake mushrooms and sun-dried tomatoes; sauté another 2 minutes. Remove from heat and add the tequila. Ignite the tequila by tilting the pan toward the flame, then stir until the flame goes out. Empty the mixture into a bowl and stir in the goat cheese and oregano. Transfer to a pastry bag and pipe into the Anaheim peppers. Wrap each pepper with foil; set aside.

❈ To make the cilantro oil, put the cilantro into a juice extractor or blender and purée. Slowly add the olive oil, then the lime juice. Season to taste and place in a squirt bottle.
❈ To cook, preheat a broiler (griller). Place each foil-wrapped chili under the broiler 3–4 in (7.5–10 cm) from the heat for 7 minutes, turning halfway through. Place each snapper fillet on a 6-by-6-in (15-by-15-cm) piece of aluminum foil lightly greased with olive oil. Broil the snapper 3–4 in (7.5–10 cm) from the heat for 3 minutes and transfer immediately to serving plates. Squirt a few teaspoons of cilantro oil over each piece of snapper. Unwrap the chilies and cut each into 4 diagonal slices. Place 4 slices of stuffed chili on each piece of snapper. Spoon salsa around the border of each serving plate and garnish with cilantro sprigs.

SERVES 8

MARINATED AHI TUNA

A perfect entrée for entertaining, the tuna is cooked on the grill just before serving; the marinade may be made well ahead of time.

½ cup (4 fl oz/125 ml) seasoned rice vinegar
4 green (spring) onions, finely chopped
2 teaspoons Dijon-style mustard
½ teaspoon crushed dried red pepper
3 tablespoons olive oil

6 Ahi tuna steaks (about 1 in/2.5 cm thick and 6 oz/
 185 g each)
Pineapple Salsa (recipe on page 201)

❈ In a shallow nonaluminum bowl, combine the vinegar, onions, mustard and pepper. Whisk in the olive oil, a little at a time, until well incorporated. Coat the tuna with the marinade and marinate for 1–4 hours, refrigerated, turning occasionally.
❈ Light a fire in a charcoal grill or preheat a broiler (griller). Remove the tuna from the refrigerator 30 minutes before cooking. Broil or grill the tuna 4–6 in (10–15 cm) from the broiler or very hot coals, 4–5 minutes per side for rare to medium rare doneness. Serve immediately with pineapple salsa.

SERVES 6

Marinated Ahi Tuna served with Pineapple Salsa (recipe on page 201)

Clockwise from top left: Huevos Rancheros, Torta Mexicana, Eggs and Tortillas in Tomatillo Sauce

EGGS AND TORTILLAS IN TOMATILLO SAUCE

One of the "fathers" of modern Southwest cooking, Robert Del Grande and his wife Mimi have made their restaurant, Cafe Annie in Houston, Texas, a mecca for food-lovers. This creation of Robert's is perfect for a hearty breakfast, buffet brunch or light supper.

TOMATILLO SAUCE

24 tomatillos, husked and stemmed
8 serrano chilies, seeded and chopped
1 cup (4 oz/125 g) coarsely chopped white onions
4 garlic cloves, peeled

2 cups (2 oz/60 g) loosely packed fresh cilantro
  (coriander) leaves
2 tablespoons fresh lime juice
2 teaspoons kosher salt
pinch of freshly ground pepper

peanut oil for frying
12 corn tortillas (6 in/15 cm in diameter), cut into quarters
12 eggs
¼ cup (2 fl oz/60 ml) heavy (double) cream or milk
2 tablespoons butter
2 cups (8 oz/250 g) grated Monterey jack cheese
1 cup (4 oz/125 g) grated cotija or Parmesan cheese

❀ To make the sauce, combine the tomatillos, serrano chilies, onions and garlic in a saucepan. Add enough water to cover. Bring to a boil, then simmer for about 10 minutes,

114

or until the tomatillos are tender. Drain and transfer the vegetables to a blender. Add the cilantro, lime juice, salt and pepper. Blend for 15–30 seconds to make a coarse purée; do not overblend. If the salsa is very tart, add a pinch of sugar; set aside.

❀ Preheat an oven to 300°F (150°C).

❀ To a medium skillet, add peanut oil to a depth of ¼ in (6 mm). Heat the oil until very hot and lightly fry the tortilla quarters in batches for 2–3 seconds per side, or until soft; do not let the tortillas become crisp. Drain on paper towels and set aside.

❀ Break the eggs into a large bowl and mix in the cream or milk. Heat a medium saucepan over medium-low heat and melt the butter in it. Add the eggs and cook them, stirring, until softly scrambled; do not overcook the eggs.

❀ Lightly butter a 9-in (23-cm) square or 7½-by-11½-in (19.5-by-29.5-cm) casserole dish. Line the bottom of the casserole with a single layer of the fried tortillas. Spoon one third of the tomatillo sauce over the chips. Spoon one half of the scrambled eggs over the sauce. Sprinkle one third of the grated cheese over the eggs. Cover the cheese layer with another layer of fried tortillas, then sauce, remaining eggs and another third of the cheese. Finish the casserole with another layer of tortillas, tomatillo sauce and grated cheese. Bake until heated through, about 45 minutes.

❀ To serve, spoon the hot casserole onto dinner plates and serve with grated cheese and any remaining sauce.

SERVES 6–8

Torta Mexicana

This colorful, layered dish is perfect for brunch and can be assembled a few hours ahead and baked just before guests arrive. It's easy to scale up or down, depending on the depth of the springform pan.

2 tablespoons melted butter

SAUSAGE LAYER

12 oz (375 g) spicy breakfast sausage or chorizo
   (Spanish sausage)
6 large green (spring) onions, finely chopped
2 garlic cloves, minced
2 jalapeño chilies, cored, seeded and minced

EGG LAYER

1 cup (4 oz/125 g) dry bread crumbs
3 green (spring) onions, finely chopped
½ cup (¾ oz/20 g) minced fresh cilantro (coriander)
½ cup (4 fl oz/125 ml) milk
12 eggs
½ teaspoon salt
freshly ground pepper to taste
½ teaspoon chili powder
2 tablespoons unsalted butter
1 cup (4 oz/125 g) grated Monterey jack cheese
1 cup (4 oz/125 g) grated Cheddar cheese

2 flour tortillas (9 in/23 cm in diameter)
3 red bell peppers (capsicums), roasted, peeled, cored,
   seeded and halved (see glossary)
4 Anaheim chilies, roasted, peeled, cored, seeded and
   halved (see glossary)
½ cup (2 oz/60 g) grated Monterey jack cheese
½ cup (2 oz/60 g) grated Cheddar cheese

❀ Preheat an oven to 400°F (200°C) and place the oven rack in the center of the oven. Brush some of the melted butter

along the bottom and sides of a 9-in (23-cm) springform pan. Reserve the rest of the butter for the tortillas.

❀ To make the sausage layer, cook the sausage or chorizo in a heavy skillet over medium-high heat until browned, crumble with a fork. Drain off excess fat. Add the green onions, garlic and jalapeños and continue cooking for about 2 minutes, or until heated through; set aside.

❀ To make the egg layer, mix together the bread crumbs, green onions and cilantro in a small bowl and add the milk. Let soak until the liquid is absorbed, then squeeze out all the moisture. Whip the eggs, salt, pepper and chili powder together. Melt the butter in a large, heavy skillet over medium-low heat. Add the egg mixture and cook, stirring continually, just until the eggs are no longer runny. Remove from heat, add the soaked crumbs and cheeses and mix thoroughly.

❀ To cook, butter 1 flour tortilla on both sides with the reserved melted butter. Place the tortilla in the bottom of the buttered springform pan. Cover the tortilla with half of the sausage mixture, then half of the egg mixture. Layer the red pepper evenly over the egg mixture. Brush both sides of the second tortilla with the remaining melted butter and place the tortilla on top of the egg mixture. Spread the second half of the sausage mixture on top of the tortilla; top with the remaining egg mixture. Layer the Anaheim chilies over the eggs and evenly sprinkle the cheeses on top.

❀ Bake for 30 minutes and let rest for 15 minutes. Carefully run a thin knife blade around the side of the pan and remove the side. Transfer the torta to a serving dish and cut into wedges.

SERVES 8–10

Huevos Rancheros

Perfect for a hearty breakfast or a light supper, huevos rancheros are prepared differently in various parts of the Southwest. Some versions require frying the eggs in oil, while others dictate poaching them in red chili sauce. All interpretations, however, include tortillas, eggs and sauce or salsa.

1 tablespoon vinegar
12 large eggs
1½ cups (12 fl oz/375 ml) Ranchero Sauce (recipe on
   page 190)
vegetable oil for frying
6 corn or flour tortillas (6 or 8 in/15 or 20 cm in diameter)
1 cup (4 oz/125 g) grated ranchero or Monterey jack cheese

❀ Fill a large saucepan or skillet with water and bring to a boil. Add the vinegar and crack the eggs one at a time into the boiling water, in batches if necessary; lower heat and simmer the eggs for 3 minutes, or until poached to the desired doneness. Drain on paper towels.

❀ Heat the ranchero sauce in a saucepan over low heat. Preheat a broiler (griller). If using corn tortillas, heat ½ in (12 mm) of vegetable oil in a skillet over high heat. Fry the tortillas one at a time for a few seconds on each side, until soft. Remove and drain on paper towels. If using flour tortillas, wrap them in aluminum foil and place them in a preheated 350°F (180°C) oven for 15–20 minutes, or until heated through.

❀ Place 2 poached eggs on each tortilla; top with ¼ cup (2 fl oz/60 ml) ranchero sauce and sprinkle with 2 tablespoons grated cheese. Transfer to a baking sheet and broil 3 in (7.5 cm) from heat until the cheese is melted. Serve immediately.

SERVES 6

TEXAS

PORK TENDERLOIN WITH CRANBERRY-CHIPOTLE SAUCE

Chipotles are smoke-dried jalapeños. Often they may be found canned in a red adobo sauce in specialty markets. This sauce also complements game, duck and other cuts of pork. If fresh cranberries are not in season, frozen ones may be substituted.

1 tablespoon unsalted butter
1 tablespoon olive oil
1½ lb (750 g) pork tenderloin
salt and freshly ground pepper to taste

CRANBERRY-CHIPOTLE SAUCE

2 tablespoons minced shallots
2 garlic cloves, minced
2 cups (6 oz/185 g) fresh or thawed frozen cranberries
3 tablespoons sugar
1 cup (8 fl oz/250 ml) dry red wine
2½ cups (20 fl oz/ 625 ml) chicken stock (see glossary)
1 canned chipotle chili in adobo sauce, puréed (see glossary)
1 teaspoon minced fresh sage, or ½ teaspoon crumbled dried sage
3 tablespoons unsalted butter at room temperature
salt and freshly ground pepper to taste

❋ Preheat an oven to 375°F (190°C). In a large skillet over medium heat, melt the butter and olive oil. Season the pork with salt and pepper and brown the meat on all sides. Remove the meat to a rack set on a baking pan and cook until it reaches an internal temperature of 150°F (65°C), about 40 minutes. Reserve the skillet and drippings.

❋ To make the sauce, sauté the shallots and garlic in the reserved drippings for about 30 seconds. Add the cranberries and sugar and cook, stirring, another 30 seconds. Add the red wine, scraping up any browned bits on the bottom of the pan; boil the mixture over high heat until about ¾ cup (6 fl oz/180 ml) of liquid remains. Add the chicken stock, chipotle purée and sage. Boil over high heat until about 2 cups (16 fl oz/500 ml) of liquid remain. Strain the mixture into a clean saucepan and bring to a boil. Whisk in the butter, add salt and pepper and keep warm.

❋ When the pork is done, remove it from the oven, cover it loosely with aluminum foil and let it sit for 10 minutes. Transfer to a cutting board and cut into ½-in (12-mm) thick slices. Place a few slices on each of 6 plates and spoon the sauce over.

SERVES 6

SANTA FE, NEW MEXICO

PORK TENDERLOIN STUFFED WITH SERRANO, CHEESE AND PIÑONS

The piñon, New Mexico's state tree, grows wild throughout the Southwest and has always been important to native Americans. The nuts of the piñon are scarce because many are devoured by deer, turkeys, boars, birds and rodents. Used in this succulent dish, which may be assembled a day ahead, piñons add a unique taste and added texture.

2 garlic cloves, minced
¼ cup (¾ oz/20 g) finely chopped green (spring) onions
1 tablespoon minced fresh cilantro (coriander)
1 serrano chili, cored, seeded and minced
1 tablespoon grated fresh ginger
2 tablespoons fresh lime juice
2 tablespoons olive oil
salt and freshly ground pepper to taste
2 pork tenderloins, about 12 oz (375 g) each
½ cup (2 oz/60 g) grated jalapeño jack cheese
¼ cup (1½ oz/45 g) piñon (pine) nuts, toasted (see glossary)

❋ In a nonaluminum bowl, whisk together the garlic, green onions, cilantro, chili, ginger and lime juice. Slowly whisk in the olive oil and salt and pepper. Spread half of the mixture on a flat side of one of the pork tenderloins. Sprinkle the cheese and pine nuts over the marinade mixture. Fit the second tenderloin over the first, matching the thin ends to the thick to make an even cylinder; tie securely with cotton string. Spread the remaining marinade over the outside of the tenderloins. Place in a nonaluminum dish; cover and refrigerate several hours or overnight.

❋ Preheat an oven to 400°F (200°C). Cook the tenderloins on a rack in a baking sheet until they reach an internal temperature of 150°F (65°C), about 40–50 minutes. Remove from the oven, cover loosely with aluminum foil and let sit for 10 minutes. Remove the string and cut into slices, reserving any juices to spoon on top.

SERVES 6

Left to right: Pork Tenderloin with Cranberry-Chipotle Sauce, Pork Tenderloin Stuffed with Serrano, Cheese and Piñons

QUAIL SALAD WITH TOASTED PUMPKIN SEEDS

Main-dish salads are popular during the heat of Southwest summers, and this one combines a delightful variety of textures and flavors. Since the quail is marinated a day ahead, this is an easy dish for entertaining.

½ cup (4 fl oz/125 ml) Cilantro Citrus Vinaigrette (recipe on page 198), omitting the achiote seeds, if desired
6 partially boned quail

DRESSING

3 tablespoons fresh orange juice
1 shallot, minced
1 garlic clove, minced
½ cup (4 fl oz/125 ml) hazelnut oil
salt and freshly ground pepper to taste

2 tablespoons unsalted butter
4 oz (125 g) fresh shiitake mushrooms, stemmed and sliced
3-oz (90-g) log pepper-coated goat cheese
6 cups (6 oz/185 g) torn mixed lettuces

1 small head radicchio, torn into pieces
½ cup (4 oz/125 g) unsalted shelled pumpkin seeds (pepitas), toasted (see glossary)

❀ Pour the vinaigrette into a nonaluminum container, add the quail, cover and marinate overnight in the refrigerator, turning the quail several times.
❀ Light a fire in a charcoal grill. Remove the quail from the refrigerator 30 minutes before cooking.
❀ To make the salad dressing, combine the orange juice, shallot and garlic in a small bowl; whisk the oil in a little at a time until well incorporated. Add salt and pepper, set aside.
❀ Preheat a broiler (griller). Meanwhile, grill the quail over hot coals for 3–4 minutes on each side, or until the quail is no longer springy to the touch and the juices run clear.
❀ Heat the butter in small skillet and sauté the mushroom slices until browned and softened, about 3–5 minutes.
❀ Cut the goat cheese into ½-in (12-mm) slices and place under broiler until warm and bubbly, about 1–2 minutes.
❀ Place the lettuces and radicchio in a large bowl; toss with the salad dressing and divide among 6 large plates. Sprinkle the mushrooms and pumpkin seeds over each plate of lettuce and top with a quail and a slice of goat cheese. Serve immediately.

SERVES 6   *Photograph page 4*

MARINATED TROUT

The streams of New Mexico, northern Arizona and Colorado provide mouth-watering trout, and this easy recipe enhances their natural flavor.

4 trout (about 1 lb/500 g each)
½ cup (4 fl oz/125 ml) vegetable oil
¼ cup (2 fl oz/60 ml) fresh lemon juice
3 tablespoons fresh lime juice
½ cup (4 fl oz/125 ml) dry white wine
1 tablespoon minced fresh cilantro (coriander)
½ teaspoon dried hot red pepper flakes
½ teaspoon dry mustard
1 teaspoon freshly ground pepper

❋ Wash the trout in cold water and drain on paper towels. Combine all the remaining ingredients in a shallow non-aluminum dish.
❋ Place the trout in the mixture and marinate at room temperature, turning occasionally, for 1 hour.
❋ Light a fire in a charcoal grill or preheat a broiler (griller). Grill the trout over medium-hot coals, for 7–10 minutes; baste with marinade, turn and grill an additional 5–7 minutes. Or, broil about 3 in (7.5 cm) from the heat, for 7–10 minutes, basting with marinade once, turn and broil an additional 5–7 minutes. Serve immediately.

SERVES 4

PECAN HONEY–COATED TROUT

Trout is abundant in mountain streams throughout the Southwest. The crunchy topping in this recipe seals in the juices, keeping the flesh moist, and trout prepared this way may be either grilled or pan fried.

MARINADE

¼ cup (2 fl oz/60 ml) Dijon mustard
1 tablespoon honey
1 tablespoon light molasses
2 garlic cloves, minced

¾ cup (4 oz/125 g) pecans, toasted (see glossary)
¼ cup (½ oz/15 g) fresh bread crumbs
1 teaspoon chili powder

6 trout, butterflied
2 tablespoons olive oil (optional)

❋ Combine the marinade ingredients and set aside. In a food processor or blender, blend the pecans, bread crumbs and chili powder until finely ground. Transfer to a plate or shallow dish.
❋ Open the trout and lay them flat in a nonaluminum container; remove any tiny bones. Spread the marinade evenly over the flesh. Let sit at room temperature for about 30 minutes.
❋ Light a fire in a charcoal grill or heat the olive oil in a heavy skillet over medium-high heat. Coat the fleshy side of the fish with the topping mixture. Grill or sauté, skin-side down, for about 4 minutes. Turn and cook until the coated side of the fish is browned, about 2 minutes. Serve immediately.

SERVES 6

GRILLED RABBIT WITH ACHIOTE PASTE

Achiote are the tiny red seeds of the tropical annatto tree and are often used as a coloring agent, especially in Cheddar-like cheeses. In the Yucatán peninsula of Mexico, they are often ground with garlic, chilies, and spices for adobos, or seasoning pastes. The recipe for this achiote paste is from Charles Wiley, executive chef of the Boulders in Carefree, Arizona. The deep red earthy color of the paste is similar to that of the spectacular red rocks found in northern Arizona and southern Utah.

ACHIOTE PASTE

3 dried ancho chilies
1 garlic clove

Top to bottom: Marinated Trout, Pecan Honey–coated Trout

¼ teaspoon ground allspice
½ teaspoon cumin seeds, toasted and crushed (see glossary)
1 teaspoon achiote (annatto) seeds (available in Latino and
   specialty foods shops)
1 teaspoon olive oil
2 tablespoons white wine vinegar
¼ cup (2 fl oz/60 ml) orange juice
½ teaspoon salt

2 rabbits, cut into serving pieces
¾ cup (6 fl oz/185 ml) chicken stock (see glossary)
½ cup (4 fl oz/125 ml) heavy (double) cream
salt and freshly ground pepper to taste

❀ To make the paste, toast the ancho chilies in a heavy skillet over medium-high heat for 2–3 minutes, or until they release some oil and a toasted fragrance. Let cool slightly, then core, seed and tear into strips. Place the strips in a blender with the remaining achiote paste ingredients and purée until smooth. Cover and refrigerate for at least 24 hours to allow the flavors to blend.

❀ Reserve 2 tablespoons of the achiote paste for the sauce. Brush the remaining paste over the rabbit pieces and marinate at room temperature for 1 hour or in the refrigerator for up to 3 hours.

❀ Light a fire in a charcoal grill. Remove the excess marinade from the rabbit and grill over hot coals, turning once, for a total of 8–10 minutes. The loin pieces will be done before the legs, which should take another 5–7 minutes.

❀ To make the sauce, heat the chicken stock over high heat in a medium saucepan. Whisk in the cream and the reserved achiote paste. Cook to reduce to about ¾ cup (6 fl oz/185 ml). Adjust the seasoning with salt and pepper.

❀ Divide the rabbit among 6 serving plates and spoon the sauce over.

SERVES 6   *Photograph pages 92–93*

119

DUCK BREASTS WITH JUNIPER BERRIES IN RED WINE SAUCE

Whole dried juniper berries are crushed to release their unusual essence into this richly colored wine sauce. This dish also makes a lovely salad; place the fanned duck breast over a bed of baby lettuces and drizzle the sauce over all.

6 boneless half duck breasts (6 oz/185 g each) with skin
salt and freshly ground pepper to taste
2 shallots, minced
½ cup (4 fl oz/125 ml) raspberry vinegar
2 teaspoons sugar
10 juniper berries, crushed
¾ cup (6 fl oz/180 ml) dry red wine
1 teaspoon cornstarch (corn flour)
½ cup (4 fl oz/125 ml) duck or chicken stock (see glossary)
1 tablespoon unsalted butter (optional)

❀ Cut the skin off the duck breasts. Salt and pepper the breasts and set aside. Put the duck skin in a large skillet over medium-high heat and cook to render 2 tablespoons of fat from the skin. Remove the skin from the skillet and add the duck breasts. Cook the duck breasts until they are springy to the touch, or about 3–4 minutes on each side. Remove the breasts from the skillet and keep warm.
❀ Add the minced shallots to the same skillet and cook over medium heat until they begin to brown, about 2 minutes. Add the vinegar, sugar and juniper berries, stirring to remove any brown bits from the bottom of the pan. Raise heat and bring the mixture to a boil; cook until it is reduced to a glaze. Add the wine and continue cooking over high heat until reduced to about ⅓ cup (2½ fl oz/75 ml). Stir the cornstarch into the stock and add to the skillet. Lower heat and cook, stirring, until the sauce has thickened. Remove from heat and whisk in butter, if desired. Season with salt and pepper.
❀ Cut the duck breasts into long thin slices and fan out on 6 heated plates. Spoon the sauce over and serve immediately.

SERVES 6 *Photograph page 4*

WARM CHICKEN SALAD WITH GOAT CHEESE, PEPPERS AND ROASTED CORN

A perfect main-dish salad for a warm evening or a luncheon, this combination of flavors reflects the best of the Southwest. The dried chili used in the dressing, chiltepín, is a small, spherical, fiery devil that grows wild in Sonora, Mexico and southern Arizona. Powerful enough to cause sneezing when powdered and inhaled, native Americans sometimes use these chilies as an aid in childbirth.

DRESSING

1 chiltepín or other dried small red chili, crushed
1 tablespoon fresh lime juice
1 tablespoon white wine vinegar
½ cup (4 fl oz/125 ml) extra-virgin olive oil
salt and freshly ground pepper to taste

6 skinned and boned half chicken breasts
6 oz (185 g) mild fresh goat cheese
salt and freshly ground pepper to taste

4 large ears (cobs) corn, husked and roasted over charcoal or under a broiler (griller)
2 poblano chilies, roasted, peeled, cored, seeded and cut into 2-by-¼-in (5-cm-by-6-mm) strips (see glossary)
2 red bell peppers (capsicums), roasted, peeled, cored, seeded and cut into 2-by-¼-in (5-cm-by-6-mm) strips (see glossary)
3 green (spring) onions, finely chopped
6 corn tortillas (6 in/15 cm in diameter), cut into 2-by-¼-in (5-cm-by-6-mm) strips
vegetable oil for frying
12 cups (12 oz/375 g) assorted lettuces
2 avocados, peeled, pitted and diced

Warm Chicken Salad with Goat Cheese, Peppers and Roasted Corn

❁ In a nonaluminum bowl, whisk together the chiltepín, lime juice and vinegar; slowly whisk in the oil. Taste and, if too hot, strain the dressing through a fine sieve into a clean bowl to remove the chiltepín (the longer it soaks in the dressing, the hotter the dressing will become). Add salt and pepper; set aside.

❁ Light a fire in a charcoal grill. Cut a pocket in each half breast and spread the goat cheese inside the pocket; press the meat together to seal in the cheese. Sprinkle the chicken with salt and pepper and grill for about 4 minutes per side, or until opaque throughout. Set aside and keep warm.

❁ Cut the roasted corn off the cobs and place in a medium bowl. Toss with the chilies, peppers, green onions and

¼ cup (2 fl oz/60 ml) of the dressing; set aside. Pour vegetable oil into a small skillet to a depth of 1 in (2.5 cm). Heat until hot but not smoking. Add the tortilla strips and fry until golden brown, about 1–2 minutes; drain on paper towels.

❁ In a large bowl, toss the lettuce with ¼ cup (2 fl oz/60 ml) dressing and divide among 6 large plates. Arrange some of the corn, pepper and onion mixture over each plate of lettuce. Slice each chicken breast diagonally across the grain into ½-in (2.5-cm) thick slices and arrange over the vegetable mixture. Sprinkle the fried tortilla strips and diced avocado over all and serve immediately, passing any remaining dressing.

SERVES 6

RIO GRANDE BASIN

RIO GRANDE BASIN

Below Santa Fe, New Mexico, the southern trails of the Rocky Mountains begin to open. As they approach Albuquerque, the mountain chains spread to form a series of broad, peak-fringed basins through which the Rio Grande—born in a narrow rift in the mountains of southern Colorado—winds its way toward the border at El Paso.

In prehistoric times, this region was settled largely by the Mogollon people, who also dwelled in the Central Highlands *(see pages 56–61)*. The most notable subgroup of that culture were the people of the Mimbres area in southwestern New Mexico. Starting around the eleventh century A.D., the Mimbres people developed an elaborate array of black-and-white decorated pottery for cooking and storage. Found intact in archaeological sites, these pots are one of the greatest artistic legacies of the region and also provide a visual record of the Mimbres people's tribal legends, the foods they ate and the animals they hunted or caught—including jackrabbits, mountain sheep and fish.

Hunter-gatherer Apache tribes—the Chiricahuas and the Mescaleros—migrated into the Rio Grande Basin

Previous pages: The "sand" in the shimmering dunes of the White Sands National Monument in New Mexico is actually fine gypsum eroded from the San Andres Mountains. Left: The Mogollon, who inhabited the Gila Cliff Dwellings in New Mexico in the mid-thirteenth century, were primarily farmers, raising squash, corn and beans, and supplementing their diet with berries, nuts and an occasional deer or rabbit.

125

after the fourteenth century A.D. They found the region a beneficent place to live, its soil enriched over the centuries by the flooding of the river, and the river itself providing a reliable source of water.

Just south of the present-day site of Albuquerque, the people of Isleta Pueblo had dug simple ditches leading from the Rio Grande to irrigate their rich land well before the arrival of the Spaniards in the sixteenth century. Fish from the river, as well as game animals, supplemented their diet of corn, beans and squashes.

Following European contact, the Isletas and other tribes of the region broadened their diet substantially. Sheep and cattle found good grazing on the grassy slopes fringing the basin—though overgrazing has left those areas barren today save for the pervasive, inedible creosote bush. The area around Albuquerque, founded in 1706 and now the capital of New Mexico, was in the mid-nineteenth century the largest sheep-ranching region in the state.

Wheat, peaches, plums and apricots added further variety to the cooking of central and southern New Mexico. Today, wheat production exceeds that of corn in the state, though you'd never know it from the hands-down preference for corn tortillas over flour. Around Las Cruces, pecans are now a significant cash crop. Apples grow in the Mimbres Valley, and so do grapes that yield connoisseur-quality wines.

And then there are chiles: the New Mexican (and Spanish) spelling of the Americanized *chilies*. It's hard to believe that these hallmarks of the region's cuisine did not become a staple here until just a few hundred years ago. But archaeological studies have found no trace of the spicy peppers predating the arrival of Spaniards carrying them from Mexico. Chilies were adopted by New Mexicans with a fervor, however, especially the long green chili known as the New Mexico green and, in its autumnal ripened form, the New Mexico red.

Regional versions of the New Mexico chili have developed as a result of decades of dedicated cultivation, each kind varying in color, texture, heat and sweetness according to the soil, climate and growing methods of origin. The town of Hatch, on the banks of the Rio Grande in the southern part of the state, celebrates its annual harvest with a Chile Festival on Labor Day weekend and declares itself the "Chile Capital of the World," throwing down the gauntlet to such northern competitors as Chimayo and Española. Such healthy competition has helped thrust New Mexico into first place among chili-growing states, ahead of California, Texas and Arizona.

In Albuquerque, the New Mexican love of chilies has been immortalized since 1989 in the annual mid-February National Fiery Foods Show, organized by the

San Felipe de Neri Church in Old Town, Albuquerque, New Mexico, has not missed a Sunday sermon in 278 years.

Laguna Pueblo, built in 1699, is the newest and one of the largest pueblos in New Mexico. Almost 5,000 members live in the seven villages that make up the reservation.

husband-and-wife team of Dave DeWitt and Mary Jane Wilan, creators of the high-spirited yet serious-minded *Chile Pepper Magazine,* a publication based in that city. Staged primarily for producers of chili-spiced commercial food products, this convention also draws an ever-larger, increasingly ravenous crowd of so-called "chili heads" from around the world, to try everything from a wide array of salsas to such seeming oddities as beer, pecan brittle and chocolates—all flavored with chilies.

Meanwhile, Las Cruces, the state's second-largest city, has long since elevated chilies to nothing less than high science. Since 1907, horticulturists at the New Mexico College of Agriculture and Mechanical Arts—now New Mexico State University—have worked to develop new, reliable and consistent strains of chilies. Given such unimaginative laboratory names as New Mexico No. 9, New Mexico No. 6, and the now wide-spread New Mexico No. 6-4, these chilies have revolutionized agriculture in the state. The legendary former leader of the program was the late Roy Nakayama, Ph.D., whom Jean Andrews, in her definitive book *Peppers,* described as "The darling of the pod set . . . an unassuming horticulture professor, long green/red chili breeder, and World War

II hero of Japanese descent from New Mexico . . . , who is reputed to be the 'Hottest Pod in the West.'" Strains developed by Dr. Nakayama now account for approximately 80 percent of the state's current commercial chili production. He also helped the average consumer by developing a simple numerical rating for the heat of chilies, ranging from a 1 for the relatively mild No. 6, through a 4 for hotter varieties of the broad-shouldered poblano chili and a 7 for the familiar spicy-hot jalapeño, to a 10 for the beyond-incendiary habanero.

It is hard for the uninitiated to understand the devotion of the people of New Mexico to this simple vegetable-fruit. But after a little exposure to the local cuisine, the chili novice may begin to understand the combination of pride, dedication, affection and respect New Mexicans feel for their chilies and chili cuisine. Twenty-five years ago, that feeling was summed up in a letter Albuquerque resident Arch Napier wrote to *Life* magazine, calling its editors to task for failing New Mexico and its chili in an article they ran on Texas chili con carne: "When New Mexico chili cuisine is discussed in our newspapers," he informed the New York-based periodical, "it is usually carried on the Art and Music pages."

TORTILLAS, BREADS AND PASTAS

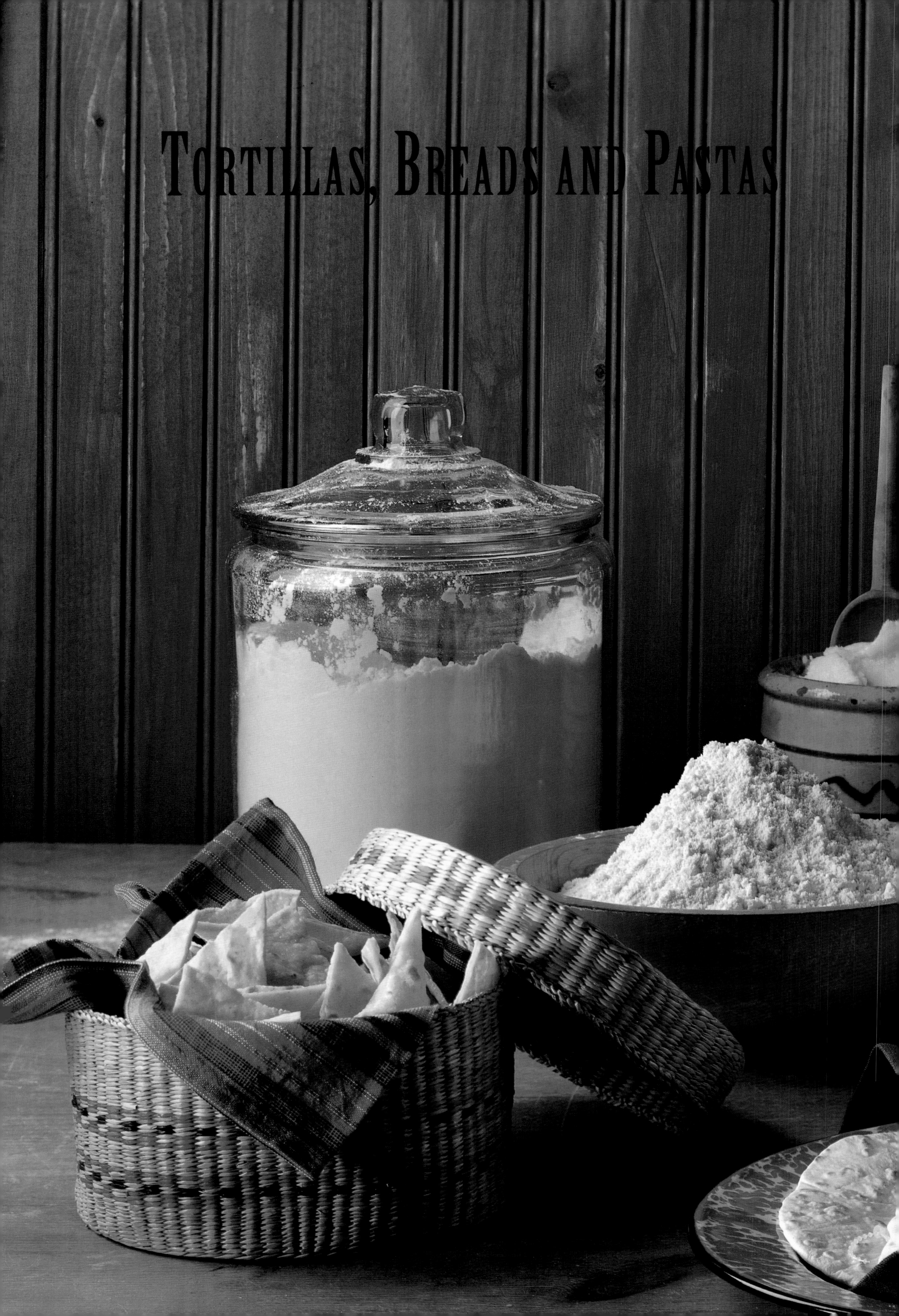

The word tamale *refers to anything wrapped and cooked in a corn husk.*

TORTILLAS, BREADS AND PASTAS

El pan partido Dios lo aumenta, goes an old Spanish proverb of the Southwest: "God blesses the bread that is shared."

Sharing bread remains fundamental to Southwestern hospitality. Hosts or hostesses would no sooner stint on the tortillas, tamales, biscuits, muffins, scones, fry bread, pancakes or sopaipillas than they would turn out the lights and lock the door the moment before guests arrived.

As in many places throughout the world, bread is the staff of life in the Southwest, and that life-giving food takes many and varied forms here. Most widespread in traditional Hispanic kitchens are tortillas. Seldom now does one hear the *pat-pat-pat* of a woman rhythmically slapping a ball of cornmeal masa back and forth between her palms to form a disk of unleavened bread—except in the occasional restaurant where handmade tortillas are a featured attraction. But that doesn't mean there's a scarcity of fresh tortillas. Today, however, a home cook who bothers to make tortillas is more inclined to use a cast-iron tortilla press to form the dough into a perfect circle. Or the bread's more likely to emerge from the conveyor belt of a small automated factory, where locals queue up to buy stacks of both corn and flour tortillas still hot inside their plastic wrappers.

The variety of tortillas on display in such an establishment suggests the wide range of uses to which they are put. Corn tortillas five to six inches in diameter are eaten as bread at table, or are dipped in chili sauce and stacked with or rolled around cheese to make the region's many different forms of enchiladas—literally, "chilied" tortillas. A New Mexican tortilla factory also offers the option of slate-colored tortillas made from blue corn. Crisply fried corn tortilla wedges in airtight plastic bags are used for dipping or snacking. Flour tortillas come in a range of sizes, from fairly thin circles six to eight inches in diameter for enfolding fajitas, to thicker rounds a foot or more across, big and sturdy enough to securely enclose a burrito of gargantuan proportions.

Good ethnic markets throughout the Southwest offer another ready-made, homestyle specialty: the tamale. But no self-respecting cook of Hispanic origin would dream of buying them—especially come December, when an abundance of tamales is essential to the Christmas feast. The word *tamale* comes from the Nahuatl *nextamalli,* for the soft Aztec bread made from *nixtamal,* lime-treated corn hominy. And it describes something very similar to that bread served in the halls of Montezuma half a millennium ago: a soft, rich cornmeal dough, wrapped in dried corn husks and steamed to make a large, tender, immensely satisfying sort of dumpling.

That describes the simplest tamales of the Southwest. But cooks also elaborate them with all

Previous pages, left to right: Tortilla Chips (recipe page 132), Flour Tortillas (recipe page 137), Corn Tortillas (recipe page 132)

130

kinds of fillings and flavorings: pork, beef, chicken, turkey, cheese; strips of roasted chili; almonds, piñon nuts, raisins, orange zest, herbs and spices.

And contemporary Southwestern chefs venture farther afield, lightening tamale dough with beaten egg whites to achieve a soufflélike consistency, and combining it with mousses of seafood or vegetable, strips of sun-dried tomato, niçoise-style olives and other ingredients as wide-ranging as human imagination and good taste might embrace. Ironically, their most lavish and outrageous creations pale next to the incredible offerings sold in the street markets of sixteenth-century Mexico, as described by Fray Bernardino de Sahagún in his *General History of the Things of New Spain:*

> . . . salted wide tamales, pointed tamales, white tamales, tamales with beans forming a seashell on top; . . . crumbled, pounded tamales; spotted tamales; white fruit tamales, red fruit tamales, turkey egg tamales; . . . tamales of tender maize, tamales of green maize, adobe-shaped tamales, braised ones; honey tamales, beeswax tamales, . . . gourd tamales, . . . maize flower tamales.

Other Southwestern breads seem equally steeped in Hispanic or native American tradition, even though their history goes back only as far as the introduction of wheat flour by Spanish settlers. Sopaipillas, a New Mexican specialty, are puffy little hand-sized, deep-fried triangles or squares of leavened wheat dough. Though slightly sweetened and resembling a sort of Southwestern doughnut or the Mexican *buñuelo,* they are commonly served as an accompaniment to savory foods; their airy pockets also are stuffed with meat or refried beans. Dipping them in honey or a cinnamon-spiced sugar syrup transforms sopaipillas into a simple dessert.

Similar in concept but larger in size is fry bread, a specialty so closely identified with the Navajo nation that few people realize that just a few centuries ago the

Native Americans use a flat stone called a metate *for grinding grains.*

Beehive-shaped ovens called hornos, *which replicate a centuries-old Spanish design, are still used by Pueblo Indians.*

tribe neither had wheat nor cooked anything by frying. Be that as it may, the large, puffy circles of soft, crisp-edged, soda-leavened bread—at once reminiscent of tortillas, pita breads and the tandoori oven–baked nan of the Indian subcontinent—are sold at fairs and festivals everywhere, often identified by other tribal names or just generically called "Indian" fry bread. Spread with refried beans and topped with ground beef, cheese, lettuce and other garnishes, fry bread becomes—no big surprise—an "Indian taco."

Anglo settlers brought to the region their own favorite bread recipes, which over the years have taken on a decidedly Southwestern demeanor. Pancakes can only get better when embellished with piñon nuts. Scones, those much-beloved quick breads of English teatime, pack a hidden wallop when fresh jalapeño peppers are mixed into their dough. And an ordinary blueberry muffin gains new distinction when cornmeal is included in the batter and the muffin is baked in a corn husk, tamale-style.

Even pasta, a distant cousin to bread, becomes dramatically transformed when it migrates from a traditional Italian kitchen to a modern Southwestern one. Mashed avocado enriches fresh fettuccine noodles and graces them with a soft green hue, while smokey chipotle chilies add a fiery mien to fresh pasta ribbons. Neither would be likely to win approval from a native-born resident of Parma or Palermo. But, as another old Spanish proverb of the Southwest says, *A cada tierra, su uso:* "To each land, its customs."

Or, in other words, "When in Phoenix, do as the Phoenicians do!"

CORN TORTILLAS

Masa harina, the base of corn tortillas, is made from lime-soaked dried corn, which is called hominy in North America. Traditionally, the dough is cooked on a very hot comal (a griddle especially for tortillas), but a heavy cast-iron skillet works just as well. Although these may seem like a lot of work, since tortillas are readily available in markets everywhere, they are well worth the effort.

1½ cups (15 oz/470 g) masa harina (see glossary)
2 teaspoons salt
2 teaspoons lard or vegetable shortening (vegetable lard)
1¼ cups (10 fl oz/315 ml) water

❀ In a medium bowl, stir together the masa harina and salt. In a small saucepan over high heat, bring the lard or shortening and water to a boil and stir until melted. Pour this liquid into the masa harina and blend well with a fork or pastry blender. Knead on a lightly floured board until smooth, about 5 minutes.
❀ Divide the dough into 12 pieces and roll each into a ball about 1 in (2.5 cm) in diameter. Roll out the dough between pieces of parchment or waxed paper until the dough is paper thin and about 6 in (15 cm) in diameter.
❀ Heat a large cast-iron or other heavy skillet over high heat until very hot. Remove a circle of dough from the paper and place it in the hot skillet. Cook until brown on 1 side, about 30 seconds, turn and brown the other side; keep warm in a cloth towel. Repeat until all the tortillas are made.

MAKES 12   *Photograph pages 128–129*

TORTILLA CHIPS

vegetable oil for frying
12 corn tortillas (6 in/15 cm in diameter)

❀ Cut each tortilla into 8 wedges; set aside. Pour oil into a large, heavy saucepan or skillet to a depth of 1 in (2.5 cm). Over medium-high heat, heat to a temperature of 375°F (190°C), or until a tortilla chip browns in 60 seconds.
❀ Drop the tortilla wedges into the hot oil in batches and cook for 1–2 minutes, or until they turn golden. Drain on paper towels. Let cool and store in airtight containers.

MAKES 96   *Photograph pages 128–129*

INDIAN FRY BREAD

A staple of the family meal on the Navajo Reservation, fry bread is also a treat at native American festivals throughout the Southwest. Served with honey or confectioners' sugar, fry bread is a snack; topped with chilies, stews, or cheeses and vegetables it becomes a meal in itself.

3 cups (12 oz/375 g) sifted unbleached all-purpose (plain) flour
1 tablespoon baking powder
½ teaspoon salt
1 cup (8 fl oz/250 ml) lukewarm water
8 cups (64 fl oz/2 l) lard or vegetable oil
honey, sifted confectioners' (icing) sugar or Indian Taco meat mixture (recipe on page 105)

❀ Mix together the flour, baking powder and salt in a large bowl. Slowly add the water until the dough is soft but not sticky. Turn out onto a lightly floured board and knead gently. Cover with a cloth and let stand about 15 minutes.
❀ In a large, heavy pot or deep-fryer, heat the oil to 375°F (190°C), or until a small piece of dough browns in 60 seconds. Divide the dough into 12 pieces and, with a rolling pin, flatten each piece into a disc about ¼ in (6 mm) thick. With a fork, pierce each round several times (this allows the dough to puff when it is cooked in the oil).
❀ Drop the rounds into the hot oil and cook until bubbles appear on the top side; turn over and fry until both sides are golden brown. Drain on paper towels and serve hot. Dust with confectioners' sugar or top with honey or meat mixture.

MAKES 12

Top to bottom: Indian Fry Bread, Stacked Enchiladas Verdes

NEW MEXICO

STACKED ENCHILADAS VERDES

In New Mexico, enchiladas are traditionally stacked rather than rolled, and they are often topped with a poached or fried egg. This version uses green sauce rather than the more familiar red one. Vary this delicious specialty by layering shredded cooked chicken, beef or pork with the cheese and onions.

vegetable oil for frying
12 corn tortillas (6 in/15 cm in diameter)
1½ cups (12 fl oz/375 ml) Green Chili Sauce (recipe on page 195)
2 cups (8 oz/250 g) grated Monterey jack or Cheddar cheese
¾ cup (4 oz/125 g) finely chopped onion

❀ Preheat an oven to 350°F (180°C). Pour vegetable oil into a medium, heavy skillet to a depth of ½ in (12 mm); heat the oil over medium-high heat to 375°F (190°C), or until a strip of tortilla browns in 60 seconds. Soften the tortillas, one at a time, for about 5 seconds per side in the hot oil and drain on paper towels.
❀ Heat the green chili sauce in a shallow pan and dip each softened tortilla into the sauce. Place 1 coated tortilla on an ovenproof plate and top with 1 tablespoon green chili sauce, 2 tablespoons grated cheese and 1 tablespoon chopped onion; repeat twice so that 1 serving contains 3 layered tortillas. Repeat with the remaining ingredients to make 4 tortilla stacks. Bake the stacks for 3–5 minutes, or until the cheese melts.

SERVES 4

133

GREEN CORN TAMALES

Tamales are a traditional Christmas dish in the Southwest, but they are popular any time of year. The fillings may be varied, but the basic technique of using masa and corn husks is always the same. This favorite version is the creation of Norman Fierros, who is known in Phoenix for his fabulous "nueva Mexicana" cuisine.

3 cups (15 oz/470 g) stone-ground masa harina
  (see glossary)
½ teaspoon baking powder
1½ teaspoons salt

1 tablespoon sugar
2 cups (16 oz/500 g) lard or vegetable shortening (vegetable
  lard) at room temperature
2½ cups (15 oz/470 g) white corn kernels, puréed
4 Anaheim chilies, roasted, peeled, seeded and cut into
  strips (see glossary)
2 cups (8 oz/250 g) grated Cheddar cheese
20 corn husks, soaked in hot water for 20 minutes, then
  individually washed

❀ In a large bowl, combine the masa, baking powder, salt and sugar. In the bowl of an electric mixer, beat the lard or shortening until light and fluffy. Add the dry ingredients 1 cup (8 fl oz/250 ml) at a time until fully incorporated

134

Left to right: Green Corn Tamales, Red Tamales

strip of corn husk. Repeat to make 16 tamales. To seal, tear extra corn husks into strips about ½ in (12 mm) wide and use them to tie each end of the tamale, or simply wrap them burrito style in baking parchment.

❀ Steam the tamales as soon as they are made to ensure freshness; they may also be frozen. Steam fresh tamales in a steamer for 20 minutes and frozen tamales 30–40 minutes.

MAKES 16

RED TAMALES

Red tamales are a Christmas tradition in the Southwest and Mexico. Masa harina is available in Latino markets. Masa is made from dried corn kernels cooked in lime water and soaked overnight. The wet corn is then ground into masa and the dough is used to make corn tortillas.

FILLING

2 lb (1 kg) lean beef or pork, cubed
3 garlic cloves, minced
2 tablespoons lard or vegetable shortening (vegetable lard)
2 tablespoons all-purpose (plain) flour
1 cup (8 fl oz/250 ml) Red Chili Sauce (recipe on page 195)
1 cup (8 fl oz/250 ml) reserved broth
salt and freshly ground pepper to taste

MASA

1½ cups (12 oz/375 g) lard or vegetable shortening (vegetable lard)
3½ cups (17½ oz/540 g) masa harina (see glossary)
½ cup (4 fl oz/125 ml) red chili mixture reserved from filling, above
¾ cup (6 fl oz/180 ml) reserved broth or more as needed
salt to taste

25 corn husks, soaked in hot water for 30 minutes
additional red chili sauce for topping (optional)

❀ To make the filling, in a large, heavy saucepan over medium heat, place the beef or pork and add water to cover. Add 1 of the garlic cloves and bring to a boil. Reduce heat and cook, stirring occasionally, for 1–2 hours, or until the meat is tender. Drain and let the meat cool; reserve the broth.

❀ In a large skillet, melt the lard or shortening; add the remaining 2 garlic cloves and cook until slightly browned; add the flour and cook, stirring, for 2–3 minutes, or until lightly browned. Stir in the red chili sauce and the reserved broth; simmer for 10 minutes. Remove ½ cup (4 fl oz/ 125 ml) of the liquid and set aside. Shred the meat and add to the simmering liquid; cook over low heat for 5 minutes. Add salt and pepper and let cool.

❀ To make the masa, in the bowl of an electric mixer, cream the lard or shortening until light and fluffy, about 5 minutes. Add the masa harina and reserved red chili mixture from the filling. Add the reserved broth. If too dry to spread, add additional broth until the mixture is of spreading consistency. Add salt to taste.

❀ Open the soaked corn husks, rinse and drain on paper towels. Spread about 2 tablespoons of masa over the bottom half of each corn husk. Top with 1½ tablespoons of meat mixture. Fold the sides of the husk toward the center, one side at a time. Fold the bottom of the husk up and the top down, tying with a strip of soaked corn husk. Continue until all the filling and masa are used. If not cooking immediately, freeze individually and, when frozen, place in freezer bags.

❀ Cook the tamales in a steamer for 25–35 minutes, or until the masa is firm and the filling is heated through. Serve with additional red chili sauce, if desired.

MAKES ABOUT 24

and all lumps of masa are gone. Mix in the puréed white corn until evenly distributed.

❀ Tear each of 4 of the corn husks into 8 strips ½ in (12 mm) wide and set them aside. Place a softened corn husk in the palm of your hand, point up. Using a rubber spatula, gently spread about 4–5 tablespoons of masa mixture as evenly as possible across the center of the husk. Place the chili strips down the center of the masa and top with 1 tablespoon of shredded cheese. Pick up the long sides of the husk with your fingertips and bring them together above the center of the filling. Pinch the sides of the husk together so the masa encircles the filling; fold the excess husk to one side or the other. Tie each end with a

135

PECAN SOURDOUGH WAFFLES WITH PECAN-HONEY BUTTER

In place of yeast, early settlers used a sourdough starter made of flour and water and allowed to ferment in wooden kegs or porcelain crocks. Because the sourdough starter in this recipe must be made 2 to 3 days ahead of time, this dish needs some forethought. It's well worth the effort, however, and the starter will keep indefinitely, refrigerated, as long as it is replenished each time it is used. These savory waffles are a natural with pecan-honey butter (recipe follows), but they're also good as a base for a creamy entrée or a seafood salad.

SOURDOUGH STARTER

2 cups (10 oz/315 g) unbleached all-purpose (plain) flour
2 tablespoons sugar
1 package active dry yeast
2 cups (16 fl oz/500 ml) warm water
½ teaspoon salt

WAFFLES

1½ cups (7½ oz/235 g) unbleached all-purpose (plain) flour
2 teaspoons baking powder
¼ teaspoon baking soda (bicarbonate of soda)
½ teaspoon salt
1 tablespoon sugar
1 teaspoon dried sage
½ teaspoon cayenne pepper
1 cup (8 oz/250 g) sourdough starter
2 eggs, lightly beaten
¼ cup (4 fl oz/125 ml) vegetable oil
1½ cups (12 fl oz/375 ml) milk
1 cup (4 oz/125 g) pecans, toasted and finely chopped
  (see glossary)
pecan-honey butter (recipe follows) or warm maple syrup

❀ Two to 3 days before making the pancakes, make the sourdough starter. Mix all the starter ingredients together in a large bowl; loosely cover and refrigerate for 2–3 days, stirring occasionally. Remove 1 cup (8 oz/250 g) starter and replenish with 1 cup (5 oz/155 g) flour and 1 cup (8 fl oz/250 ml) water to keep the starter going for future use.
❀ To make the waffles, stir the flour, baking powder and baking soda, salt, sugar, sage and cayenne pepper together in a large bowl. In another bowl, whisk together the sourdough starter, eggs, oil and milk. Pour the wet ingredients into the dry and mix thoroughly; fold in the pecans.
❀ Heat a waffle iron to high heat. Brush with oil; when hot, pour ⅓ cup (3 fl oz/80 ml) of the batter into the waffle iron. Cook until the waffles are light brown on both sides, about 3–5 minutes per side. Serve with pecan honey butter or warm maple syrup.

SERVES 8

PECAN-HONEY BUTTER

Delicious on pancakes, waffles or muffins, this butter is perfect with pecan sourdough waffles (preceding recipe). It will keep for up to 1 week, covered, in the refrigerator.

⅓ cup (1 oz/30 g) pecans, toasted (see glossary)
½ cup (4 oz/125 g) unsalted butter, cut into pieces
½ cup (6 oz/185 g) honey

Put the pecans in a food processor or blender with the butter and the honey; purée until smooth. Refrigerate until needed; bring to room temperature before serving.

MAKES ¾ CUP (9 OZ/280 G)

PUMPKIN-APPLE MUFFINS

Although they may be made year-round with canned pumpkin, these muffins are a delightful way to welcome fall by using fresh pumpkin and just-picked apples. Perfect for breakfast or brunch, they may be made in mini muffin tins to serve a large crowd; cut the baking time by 5 minutes for the smaller muffins.

STREUSEL TOPPING

3 tablespoons unbleached all-purpose (plain) flour
¼ cup (2 oz/60 g) sugar
½ teaspoon ground cinnamon
2 tablespoons cold unsalted butter

Left to right: Pecan Sourdough Waffles with Pecan-Honey Butter, Pumpkin-Apple Muffins

MUFFINS

2½ cups (12½ oz/390 g) unbleached all-purpose (plain) flour
2 cups (16 oz/500 g) sugar
1 teaspoon ground cinnamon
1 teaspoon ground ginger
½ teaspoon ground cloves
½ teaspoon ground nutmeg
1 teaspoon baking soda (bicarbonate of soda)
½ teaspoon salt
2 eggs, lightly beaten
1 cup (12 oz/375 g) pumpkin purée
½ cup (4 fl oz/125 ml) vegetable oil
2 cups (8 oz/250 g) finely chopped peeled apples

❀ Preheat an oven to 350°F (180°C). Butter 18 muffin cups (3 in/7.5 cm in diameter) or line them with muffin papers.
❀ To make the topping, in a small bowl, stir together the flour, sugar and cinnamon. With a fork or pastry blender, cut in the butter until the mixture resembles coarse meal. Set aside.
❀ To make the muffins, mix together the flour, sugar, spices, soda and salt in a large bowl. In a medium bowl, whisk together the eggs, pumpkin and oil; add to the dry ingredients and stir just until the dry ingredients are moist. Stir in the apples. Fill each muffin cup two thirds full; sprinkle about 1½ teaspoons of topping onto each muffin.
❀ Bake for 35–40 minutes, or until a toothpick inserted into the center comes out clean.

MAKES 18

139

VALLEY OF THE SUN, ARIZONA

ORANGE-DATE MUFFINS

This muffin recipe reaps the benefit of two of the most successfully transplanted types of trees in Arizona: orange and date palm. Many Valley of the Sun homeowners have both kinds growing in their yards, and citrus and date farms dot the outlying areas. These moist muffins freeze well, but they are best when warm from the oven.

1 cup (5 oz/155 g) whole-wheat flour
1 cup (5 oz/155 g) unbleached all-purpose (plain) flour
2 teaspoons baking powder
1 teaspoon baking soda (bicarbonate of soda)
½ teaspoon salt
1 egg
½ cup (3½ oz/105 g) packed brown sugar
⅔ cup (5 fl oz/160 ml) buttermilk
¼ cup (2 oz/60 g) unsalted butter, melted and cooled
¼ cup (2 fl oz/60 ml) orange juice
1 orange
½ cup (3 oz/90 g) chopped pitted dates

TOPPING

1 tablespoon granulated sugar
½ teaspoon ground cinnamon

❈ Preheat an oven to 400°F (200°C). Prepare 12 muffin cups (3 in/7.5 cm in diameter) by buttering them well or lining them with paper muffin liners. Sift the flours, baking powder, baking soda and salt into a large bowl. In a medium bowl with an electric mixer, beat the egg and brown sugar together; add the buttermilk, melted butter and orange juice.

❈ Grate the zest of the orange, being careful only to use the orange outer layer (the white part is bitter). Peel and segment the orange, discarding the white membrane, and chop the orange segments into ¼-in (6-mm) pieces. Add to the egg-sugar mixture along with the dates.

❈ Fold the wet mixture into the dry and quickly combine the two, stirring just until mixed. Divide among the prepared muffin cups, filling each cup ¾ full.

❈ To make the topping, in a small bowl, stir together the sugar and cinnamon. Sprinkle the mixture evenly on top of the muffins. Bake for 15 minutes, or until a toothpick inserted into the center of a muffin comes out clean.

MAKES 12

Left to right: Blueberry Corn Muffins in Corn Husks, Orange-Date Muffins

BLUEBERRY CORN MUFFINS IN CORN HUSKS

Using corn husks instead of paper liners adds a festive Southwestern touch to these muffins. They may be made year-round using frozen blueberries, but be sure not to thaw the berries or the juices will run and discolor the dough. If using fresh berries, reduce the cooking time slightly.

4 corn husks, soaked in hot water for 20 minutes and torn into ½-by-6-in (12-mm-by-15-cm) strips
2 eggs
¾ cup (6 fl oz/180 ml) buttermilk
¼ cup (2 fl oz/60 ml) corn oil
¾ cup (60 oz/185 g) packed brown sugar
½ cup (2½ oz/75 g) cornmeal
1 cup (5 oz/155 g) unbleached all-purpose (plain) flour
2 teaspoons baking powder
½ teaspoon baking soda (bicarbonate of soda)
¼ teaspoon salt
1½ cups (6 oz/185 g) blueberries, fresh or frozen (unthawed)

❋ Preheat an oven to 400°F (200°C). Generously butter 12 muffin cups (3 in/7.5 cm diameter) and line each with 4 strips of corn husk so that husks extend above the rim of the cups.
❋ In a medium bowl, mix together the eggs, buttermilk, corn oil and brown sugar using an electric mixer. Sift the cornmeal, flour, baking powder, soda and salt into a large bowl. Fold the two mixtures together just until flour mixture is moist; stir in the blueberries. Divide mixture among the 12 muffin cups.
❋ Bake for 25–30 minutes, or until a toothpick inserted into the center of a muffin comes out clean. Using the corn husks as handles, transfer to a rack to cool.

MAKES 12

PIÑON PANCAKES

Native Americans made bread from ground piñons, along with corn, nuts and seeds before wheat flour was introduced by Europeans. This updated version combines ground pine nuts and flour, and if pine nuts are not readily available, pecans may be substituted. Serve these pancakes with maple syrup for a delicious breakfast or brunch, or make quarter-sized pancakes, top with sour cream and caviar and serve as an elegant hors d'oeuvre.

¾ cup (4 oz/125 g) unbleached all-purpose (plain) flour
½ cup (2½ oz/75 g) piñon (pine) nuts, toasted and finely ground (see glossary)
½ teaspoon salt
2 eggs
1 cup (8 fl oz/250 ml) milk
2 tablespoons melted butter
2 tablespoons vegetable oil

❋ In a food processor or blender, process the flour, nuts and salt until the mixture resembles coarse meal. Add the eggs, milk and butter and mix until just combined. Refrigerate for 30 minutes.
❋ Heat the oil in a heavy skillet over medium heat. Drop about 2 tablespoons of batter per pancake into the hot pan. When bubbles form on the surface, turn each pancake over and cook until lightly browned on both sides. Repeat with the remaining batter.

MAKES ABOUT 16

Top to bottom: Jalapeño Scones, Piñon Pancakes

JALAPEÑO SCONES

Jalapeño chilies and dried red pepper add zip to these delicate scones. They may be served with butter (try Avocado Butter on page 196) or Jalapeño Jelly (recipe on page 192), or sliced in half and filled, but in any event, they're best served on the day they are made. For a cocktail party, cut them in half horizontally and fill with chicken salad or thinly sliced smoked turkey breast. Split in half, these scones are a good base for poached eggs; for a Southwestern version of eggs Benedict, serve them with Orange-Cilantro Hollandaise (recipe on page 197).

1½ cups (6 oz/185 g) cake (soft-wheat) flour
½ cup (2½ oz/75 g) cornmeal
1½ cups (12 oz/375 g) grated Cheddar cheese
1½ teaspoons baking powder
½ teaspoon baking soda (bicarbonate of soda)
½ teaspoon salt
2 jalapeño chilies, seeded and minced
¼ teaspoon dried red pepper flakes
¼ cup (2 oz/60 g) chilled unsalted butter, cut into ½-in (12-mm) pieces
½ cup (4 fl oz/125 ml) heavy (double) cream (or more as needed)

❋ Preheat an oven to 350°F (180°C). Butter a baking sheet.
❋ In a large bowl, combine the flour, cornmeal, 1 cup (4 oz/125 g) of the cheese, baking powder, baking soda, salt, chilies and red pepper. Mix thoroughly. With a fork or pastry blender, cut in the butter until it is well combined and the mixture resembles coarse meal. Sprinkle the cream over the surface and stir into the flour mixture until a soft dough is formed, adding more cream if necessary.
❋ On a lightly floured surface, pat the dough into a circle and then roll it out to a ½-in (12-mm) thickness. Cut rounds using a 2-in (5-cm) cutter and transfer them to prepared baking sheet. Sprinkle the remaining ½ cup (2 oz/60 g) cheese on top of the scones. Bake for 20–25 minutes, or until firm and golden brown. Let cool on a rack.

MAKES ABOUT 24

RED ENCHILADAS

Throughout the Southwest there are numerous versions of red enchiladas: stacked or rolled, with red chili sauce or chili gravy, with or without meat, baked or served hot from the skillet. This Arizona recipe calls for filling the tortillas with red chili sauce, cheese, and onions, then rolling them into cylinders and baking them until the cheese melts.

vegetable oil for frying
12 corn tortillas (6 in/15 cm in diameter)
2 cups (16 fl oz/500 ml) Red Chili Sauce (recipe on page 195)
2 cups (8 oz/250 g) grated Cheddar cheese
1 cup (5 oz/155 g) finely chopped onions

❁ Preheat an oven to 350°F (180°C). Oil a 9-by-12-in (23-by-30-cm) casserole dish.
❁ Pour oil into a skillet to a depth of ½ in (12 mm). Heat over medium-high heat to 375°F (190°C), or until a bread cube browns in 60 seconds. Dip the tortillas one at a time, in the hot oil, about 5 seconds per side; drain on paper towels.
❁ Place about 1 cup (8 fl oz/250 ml) of red chili sauce in a shallow dish. Dip each tortilla into the sauce. Sprinkle 2 tablespoons Cheddar cheese, 1 tablespoon chopped onion and 1 tablespoon of the remaining sauce on each coated tortilla. Roll up and place seam-side down in the prepared dish. Repeat with the remaining tortillas. Cover with the remaining sauce, onions and cheese and bake for 30 minutes, or until hot and bubbly.

MAKES 12

VEGETABLE TAMALES

A perfect appetizer or a lovely side dish, these tamales are the inspiration of John Sedlar, author of Modern Southwest Cuisine *and chef-owner of Bikini in Santa Monica.*

MASA

2 cups (10 oz/315 g) masa harina (see glossary)
1¼ teaspoons baking powder
½ teaspoon salt
⅓ cup (3 oz/90 g) lard, vegetable shortening (vegetable lard) or softened butter
1 cup (8 fl oz/250 ml) lukewarm water

FILLING

2 cups (10 oz/315 g) mixed diced zucchini (courgette), potato and yellow squash (vegetable marrow)
1 tablespoon vegetable oil
¼ cup (2 oz/60 g) jalapeño chilies, diced and roasted (see glossary)
1 teaspoon chili powder
salt and freshly ground pepper to taste
2 tablespoons minced fresh epazote
1 package dried corn husks (20 corn husks), soaked in warm water for 30 minutes

SAUCE

juice of 10 carrots (about 2½ cups/20 fl oz/625 ml)
½ cup (4 fl oz/125 ml) olive oil
salt and freshly ground pepper to taste

corn husks, cooked baby vegetables and fresh cilantro (coriander) sprigs for garnish

❁ To make the masa, in the bowl of an electric mixer, beat together the masa harina, baking powder and salt. Gradually add approximately one fourth of the masa mixture into the lard, shortening or butter, then add 2 tablespoon of the water. Continue adding the masa mixture alternately with the water until they are fully blended and the mixture is smooth and light. Cover and chill until ready to use.
❁ To make the filling, blanch the vegetables in boiling water for 3–5 minutes; drain. In a large skillet, heat the oil over medium heat and add the vegetables

Left to right: Vegetable Tamales, Red Enchiladas

and chilies. Add the chili powder, salt, pepper and epazote and cook, stirring, for about 5 minutes, or until vegetables are tender.

❁ Drain the soaked corn husks. Spread ¼ cup (3 oz/90 g) masa over half the surface of each husk, beginning at the large end. Put 2 tablespoons vegetable filling in the center of the husk and fold the sides of the husk toward the center, one side at a time. Fold the bottom of the husk up and the top down, tying with a strip of soaked corn husk. Cook the tamales in a steamer until firm and heated through, about 15–20 minutes.

❁ To make the sauce, in a large saucepan over high heat, cook the carrot juice to reduce it to approximately 2 cups (16 fl oz/500 ml). Remove from heat and transfer to a blender. Blend the reduced juice with the olive oil; add salt and pepper.

❁ Place 2 clean unsoaked corn husks in the center of each of 10 plates. Place an unwrapped tamale on top of the corn husks. Spoon 2 tablespoons sauce over each tamale and garnish with baby vegetables and cilantro.

SERVES 10

143

SAN ANTONIO, TEXAS

CHIPOTLE PASTA WITH MEXICAN CREAM

The heat of the chipotle, a dried jalapeño chili, is tempered by the lime-flavored cream, and the delicately balanced pasta that results is the perfect enhancement for a grilled entrée. To make this pasta a main dish, add bits of grilled chicken, seafood or vegetables.

MEXICAN CREAM

½ cup (4 fl oz/125 ml) heavy (double) cream
½ cup (4 oz/125 g) sour cream
1 teaspoon fresh lime juice
salt and freshly ground pepper to taste (optional)

PASTA

1 cup (4 oz/125 g) cake (soft-wheat) flour
1 cup (5 oz/155 g) unbleached all-purpose (plain) flour
2 eggs
½ teaspoon salt
2 chipotle chilies in adobo sauce, puréed
about 2 tablespoons heavy (double) cream

2 tablespoons unsalted butter
1 zucchini (courgette), shredded and well drained

2 red bell peppers (capsicums), roasted, peeled, cored, seeded and julienned (see glossary)
¼ cup (⅓ oz/10 g) minced fresh cilantro (coriander)
½ cup (2 oz/60 g) grated cotija, Asiago or Parmesan cheese

❋ To make the Mexican cream, combine the heavy cream, sour cream and lime juice in a nonaluminum bowl; cover with plastic wrap and refrigerate for at least 2 hours. Just before serving, taste for seasoning and add salt and pepper, if desired.

❋ To make the pasta, process the flours, eggs, salt and chilies in a food processor. Add as much cream as is needed to make a smooth dough. Turn the dough out onto a lightly floured board and knead slightly; divide into 4 pieces. Using a pasta machine, roll out each piece to the thinnest setting. Using the fettuccine cutter of the machine, cut into strips.

❋ To cook, bring a large pot of salted water to the boil. Add pasta and cook for 2–3 minutes, or until al dente. Drain.

❋ In a large skillet, heat the butter over medium heat and add the zucchini; cook until tender, about 3 minutes. Add the red pepper strips and cilantro. Stir in the Mexican cream and cooked pasta. Cook until the pasta is heated through and coated with the cream. Divide among 6 serving plates and sprinkle the grated cheese over the pasta.

SERVES 6

Chipotle Pasta with Mexican Cream

Avocado Pasta with Shiitake Mushrooms, Tomatoes, Goat Cheese and Piñons

AVOCADO PASTA WITH SHIITAKE MUSHROOMS, TOMATOES, GOAT CHEESE AND PIÑONS

If time doesn't allow for making the pasta, purchase a good-quality fresh variety (spinach fettuccine is a good substitute). A perfect main dish for a light meal, this is also a good side dish with grilled or broiled fish.

PASTA

1 ripe avocado
1 teaspoon fresh lemon juice
2 large eggs
3 cups (15 oz/470 g) unbleached all-purpose (plain) flour
½ teaspoon salt
1 tablespoon heavy (double) cream if needed

SAUCE

2 tablespoons olive oil
6 oz (185 g) fresh shiitake mushrooms, stemmed and diced
¾ cup (6 fl oz/180 ml) chicken stock (see glossary)
1 teaspoon minced fresh thyme leaves, or ½ teaspoon crumbled dried thyme
freshly ground black pepper to taste
2 plum (egg) tomatoes, diced
3 tablespoons unsalted butter
4 oz (125 g) mild fresh goat cheese, cut into pieces
¼ cup (1 oz/30 g) piñon (pine) nuts, toasted, for garnish (see glossary)

❁ To make the pasta, mash the avocado with the lemon juice; add the eggs and mix well. In a large bowl, stir together the flour and the salt; add the avocado mixture and mix until smooth. If the mixture seems dry, add the cream a little at a time. Knead for 5 minutes, or until smooth, soft and elastic. Put through a pasta machine, following the manufacturer's directions; cut into fettuccine noodles.

❁ To make the sauce, heat the olive oil in a heavy skillet and sauté the mushrooms for 1 minute over high heat. Add the stock and bring it to a boil. Add the thyme, pepper, tomatoes, butter and goat cheese. Stir the mixture until the cheese melts; remove from heat.

❁ To prepare, cook the pasta in a large amount of boiling salted water for 3–4 minutes, or until al dente. Toss the cooked pasta with the sauce and divide evenly among 6 plates. Garnish with pine nuts.

SERVES 6

BLUE CORN AND PEPPER BREAD

Used widely by the Zuni and other Pueblo people in New Mexico, blue corn has a more intense flavor than does yellow or white corn. Blue cornmeal acquires its distinctive lavender-blue color when the ground blue corn (which is actually a dark gray) is treated with an alkaline substance such as juniper ashes or calcium carbonate. Because cornmeal contains no gluten, it should be mixed with wheat flour to create a lighter bread. This is a good bread to use in Blue Corn Chorizo Stuffing (recipe on page 136).

3 tablespoons corn oil
3 tablespoons unsalted butter
1 red bell pepper (capsicum), cored, seeded and diced
1 jalapeño chili, cored, seeded and minced
2 garlic cloves, minced
¾ cup (3½ oz/105 g) unbleached all-purpose (plain) flour
1 cup (5 oz/155 g) blue cornmeal
4 teaspoons sugar
2 teaspoons baking powder
¼ teaspoon baking soda (bicarbonate of soda)
½ teaspoon salt
2 eggs
¾ cup (6 fl oz/180 ml) buttermilk

❋ Preheat an oven to 375°F (190°C). Lightly grease an 8-in (20-cm) square baking pan.
❋ In a small skillet over medium heat, heat the oil and butter; when the butter has melted, add the pepper, chili and garlic; sauté until just soft, about 3 minutes. Set aside and let cool.
❋ Sift together the flour, cornmeal, sugar, baking powder, baking soda and salt. Set aside.
❋ In a large bowl, beat together the eggs and buttermilk; whisk in the butter-pepper mixture. Fold in the dry ingredients until just moistened. Pour the batter into the prepared pan and bake until a wooden skewer inserted into the center comes out clean, about 45–50 minutes. Let cool, cut into squares and serve.

SERVES 8–10

PUMPKIN BREAD WITH PECANS AND SUNFLOWER SEEDS

Three New World contributions to cuisine—pumpkin, pecans, and sunflower seeds—come together in this sweet bread. Serve it with cream cheese at tea or with salads at lunch or supper. Unsalted sunflower seeds are best, but if they are unavailable, use the salted variety and omit the salt in the bread recipe.

2 eggs, lightly beaten
½ cup (4 fl oz/125 ml) vegetable oil
1 cup (12 oz/375 g) pumpkin purée
2 cups (10 oz/315 g) unbleached all-purpose (plain) flour
1 cup (8 oz/250 g) sugar
1 teaspoon baking soda (bicarbonate of soda)
½ teaspoon ground cinnamon
½ teaspoon ground nutmeg
½ teaspoon ground ginger
½ teaspoon ground allspice
¼ teaspoon salt
¼ cup (1 oz/30 g) unsalted shelled sunflower seeds
¾ cup (4 oz/125 g) pecans, toasted and finely chopped (see glossary)

❋ Preheat an oven to 350°F (180°C). Butter and flour an 8½-by-4½-in (21-by-11-cm) loaf pan.
❋ In a small bowl, whisk together the eggs, oil and pumpkin until smooth.
❋ In a large bowl, stir together the flour, sugar, baking soda and spices. Add the egg-pumpkin mixture, then the sunflower seeds and pecans; stir just until combined. Spoon into the prepared pan and bake for about 1 hour, until a wooden skewer inserted into the center comes out clean.
❋ Let the bread cool on a rack and cut into slices to serve.

MAKES 1 LOAF

Clockwise from top: Pumpkin Bread with Pecans and Sunflower Seeds, Onion Biscuits, Blue Corn and Pepper Bread

ONION BISCUITS

Images of cowboys on the trail may come to mind when these flavorful biscuits are baking. After a hard day—either on the range or in the office—enjoy them with soups, stews and chilies, or as a treat for breakfast. They are best served warm from the oven.

2 cups (10 oz/310 g) diced onions
2 tablespoons water
2½ cups (12½ oz/390 g) unbleached all-purpose (plain) flour
1 tablespoon baking powder
1 teaspoon salt
⅛ teaspoon freshly ground pepper
1 teaspoon minced fresh thyme, or ½ teaspoon crumbled dried thyme
½ cup (4 oz/125 g) unsalted butter
¾ cup (6 fl oz/180 ml) buttermilk

❀ Preheat an oven to 375°F (190°C). Put the onions and water in a heavy saucepan, cover and cook over medium heat for 5 minutes. Drain and let cool.

❀ Place the flour, baking powder, salt, pepper and thyme in a medium bowl or a food processor; blend. Cut in the butter with a pastry cutter, 2 knives or the processor. Mix until it resembles coarse meal. Add the onions; pulse or mix once or twice. Add the milk, mix until just moistened.

❀ Turn the dough out onto a lightly floured board. Roll to a ¾-in (2-cm) thickness and cut into rounds with a 2-in (5-cm) cutter. Place on a lightly greased baking sheet. Bake for 12–15 minutes, or until lightly browned.

MAKES 18

RIO GRANDE VALLEY

RIO GRANDE VALLEY

W ith its valley floor more than a mile above sea level, its towering snowcapped mountains and its quaint settlements filled with adobe dwellings, the high Rio Grande Valley of north-central New Mexico captures the very heart and soul of the Southwest.

"The world is very wide here, and it's very hard to feel that it's wide in the East," were the simple words used by twentieth-century painter Georgia O'Keeffe to explain the area's appeal. After her first visit to Santa Fe in 1917, she claimed that "I was always on my way back." She kept that promise, finally settling in the village of Abiquiu to paint her ravishing still-lifes of sun-bleached steer skulls and awe-inspiring scenes of towering mountains, erosion-scarred plateaus and rocky buttes. Not surprisingly, myriad other artists and writers have been drawn by this dramatic landscape to visit or make permanent homes here as nowhere else in the United States.

The earliest humans to live in the area were the Anasazi, whose descendants may be found in the many pueblos that line the valley: Tesuque, Nambe, Pojoaque, San Ildefonso, Santa Clara, San Juan, Picuris and Taos. Each pueblo sustained itself over the

Previous pages: Aspens' fall colors contrast strikingly with the evergreens that surround Sunshine Peak at Mount Wilson in southern Colorado.
Left: The Oldest House in Santa Fe is a superb example of ancient adobe construction; its foundation may have been built by Pueblo Indians as early as the thirteenth century.

151

Possibly the oldest church in America, Mission San Miguel dates from the founding of Santa Fe in 1610 and contains some of the finest examples of New Mexican religious art.

The high plateaus and mountains of the Sangre de Cristo (Blood of Christ) Range provided welcome relief to the early colonists who migrated north through a stretch of New Mexico they referred to as La Jornada del Muerto or Journey of Death.

centuries by cultivating corn, squashes and beans, supplemented with such hunted and gathered foods as fish, rabbits, deer, piñon nuts and wild greens.

The adobe edifice of Taos Pueblo impresses in particular. Built around A.D. 1450, its five stepped-back levels with their rounded corners and recessed painted wooden doorways form one of the greatest architectural monuments in the world. Occupied today, along with another smaller building, by about one thousand members of the tribe, the pueblo—backed by the Sangre de Cristo Mountains—forms a dramatic setting for annual ceremonial dances that members of the non-native public are welcome to view.

Many of these ceremonies revolve around corn, which the Taos have always imbued with weighty spiritual significance. In a legend echoed by other Southwestern peoples, they believe that the Creator gave their ancestors six different colors of corn to bring to Mother Earth, teaching them to plant and harvest the seeds and use each type in every aspect of their daily lives. For example, yellow corn, they were told, came from the south, and was associated with springtime and rebirth. Red came from the west and the setting sun, and held in it the promise of long life. The north brought white corn, which embodied the strength of the tribe's elders. Blue corn, from the east and the rising sun, was perhaps the most powerful of all, conveying knowledge and playing an important role in healing and prayer. Not surprisingly, blue corn—with

its discernibly richer and earthier flavor—is a favored variety in New Mexico, particularly in the high valley of the Rio Grande.

Under the Spaniards, Taos was an important pueblo, particularly as a gateway for trade with the Plains tribes to the north. But it was relegated to secondary status following the founding of Santa Fe by the Spanish in 1610. As the northernmost stop on the Camino Real, the "royal highway" from Mexico City, Santa Fe served as the region's major trading center. In that capacity, it naturally became a focal point for the mingling of cuisines. Hispanic settlers introduced the natives to domesticated livestock and many new fruits and vegetables—most notably the chili. Today, chilies thrive throughout the Rio Grande Valley, most notably in such villages as Chimayó and Española, whose names have become synonymous with the pungent pod.

The capital city grew more important with the forging of the Santa Fe Trail, which in 1821 provided the eastern United States with a link to the heart of the Southwest by way of Franklyn, Missouri, the great state of Kansas and Bent's Fort, Colorado. The trickle of Anglo visitors who first came along the trail turned to a flood when New Mexico passed into American hands in 1846. By that time, the chili was well established as a hallmark of the Southwestern kitchen, as noted two years earlier by trader Josiah Gregg, who wrote that the "extravagant use of red pepper . . . enters into nearly every dish at every meal, and often so predominates as entirely to conceal the character of the viands." Likewise, U.S. Army surveyor William Emory's first bite of a New Mexican meat-stuffed red chile relleno led to "tears trickling down my cheeks, very much to the amusement of the spectators with their leather-lined throats."

Though chili novices such as Gregg and Emory no doubt became aficionados in good time, Anglos had a revenge of sorts beginning in the late nineteenth century with the arrival of the Santa Fe Railroad. Always seen as a civilizing influence, the railroad in this case brought conventional Midwestern and East Coast fare to New Mexico in the form of the dining cars, hotels, station restaurants and cafes run by the Kansas-based Fred Harvey Company.

The English-born Harvey brought unequaled reliability, quality and good service to railroad meals that before his time could be counted on only for cold, unappetizing food that promised indigestion. But the Harvey Company menus for the most part ignored or slighted the specialties of the Southwest. Chugging northward toward the Rio Grande Valley, a passenger in a Santa Fe dining car might be offered such lunch choices as Chilled Tomato Juice, Filets of Sea Bass Sauté Anglaise, Melted Cheese Sandwich on Toast, Fresh Fruit Salad with Cottage Cheese, and Apple Pie à la Mode, all served on exquisite china decorated with prehistoric Mimbres pottery patterns. In the land of tortillas, there were no tortillas in sight.

Santa Fe's commerce relies heavily on tourism; here, native American arts and crafts vendors manage a lively summer sidewalk trade.

Taos Pueblo, one of the more traditional and picturesque of New Mexico's native American settlements, is still inhabited by the descendants of those who built it nearly 700 years ago.

Blankets of snow on the sculpted peaks of the San Juan Mountains of New Mexico create a surreal landscape.

*Contemporary pottery of Santa Fe is inspired by the
original patterns and designs of the old Southwest.*

Even the dinner menu at the Harvey Company's magnificent La Fonda, a pueblo-inspired hotel that opened in Santa Fe in 1926, included as recently as 1954 only two regionally inspired dishes among some four dozen selections: a Special Mexican Plate (Taco, Tamale, Enchilada, Salsa, and Fried Egg) and a Santa Fe Omelette (Green Chili, Hot Rarebit, French Fried Potatoes, Green Salad); a single capitalized line at the bottom of the menu discreetly informed guests of the availability of a MEXICAN FOOD MENU ON REQUEST. And here is how the company Anglicized that Southwestern standard, guacamole: At the Harvey-run El Tovar hotel on the Grand Canyon's South Rim, a popular recipe for Guacamole Monterey "(pronounced Gwah-ka-mo-leh)," called for mashing the avocado with cottage or cream cheese, green onions, chives and a dash of Worcestershire sauce. Not a trace of chili or drop of salsa to offend sensitive taste buds!

That sort of gastronomic bastardization may help explain a schizophrenia that seemed to have descended over dining in Santa Fe by the mid-twentieth century. Sure, small cafes and diners might offer red chili and green chili, bowls of the chili-laced hominy stew known as posole, blue corn enchiladas and any number of other traditional dishes. But such cuisine was generally thought of as poor people's fare. Southwestern food was just as likely to mean a hamburger topped with strips of roasted green chili, or that much-revered specialty of the Woolworth's store on the Plaza: Frito

pie, made by slitting open the side of an individual-serving bag of Fritos corn chips, spooning in hot canned chili con carne with beans, and topping to taste with chopped white onion and shredded sharp Cheddar cheese.

Frito pies and green chili burgers remain popular, and certainly have their own down-to-earth appeal. But the status of Southwestern cooking has shot skyward in recent decades with the growing popularity of Santa Fe and its outlying areas as an elite enclave of the artistically and spiritually inclined, coupled with a nationwide revolution in American cooking. Now, the hottest restaurants in Santa Fe serve innovative, contemporary and often pricey variations on traditional Southwestern food.

Chefs like Mark Miller, who came to Santa Fe by way of his native New England and the San Francisco Bay Area, have become passionate scholars and spokespersons for the intrinsic merits of regional ingredients and preparations, exciting people about Southwestern cuisine as never before. Those who come to eat at Miller's Coyote Cafe in Santa Fe might be inspired to visit the nearby Rancho de las Golondrinas, a living-history museum just outside of town, where crops are grown, corn and wheat are milled and bread is baked in beehive-shaped *hornos,* just as in ages past. By radically changing the future of Southwest cuisine, modern chefs of the region are honoring its past.

Once a rowdy cowboy town, Durango, Colorado, is now a popular destination for outdoor recreation; here, adventure seekers run the rapids of the Animus River.

VEGETABLES, RICE AND BEANS

Pinto beans have been a life-sustaining food in the Southwest for as long as 1500 years.

Vegetables, Rice and Beans

Those who regard the Southwest as an inhospitable desert region would do well to consider New Mexico's most traditional vegetable recipe: *calabacitas*. Though its name humbly translates as "little squashes," the dish is as rich, abundant, and varied as a French ratatouille, combining green or yellow squash, fresh sweet corn and green chilies—all bound together by a melting sauce of mild white cheese.

Though they sometimes have had to work hard to scratch a living from the earth, native and immigrant Southwesterners have produced a cornucopia of colorful, flavorful and filling vegetable dishes. For several millennia, the earth has provided the region's people with the squashes, corn and chilies that combine in *calabacitas*. These same vegetables also star on their own in other familiar dishes of the Southwest, from whole chilies stuffed and deep-fried to make chiles rellenos; to exquisitely simple grilled or boiled corn on the cob; to the delicate squash blossoms long beloved of the Zuni tribe and now the darlings of nouvelle-style cuisine.

First from Latin America and then from European shores, a wide variety of other vegetables were transported to the Southwest, to be warmly welcomed and readily assimilated into the culture and the cuisine. Potatoes were brought up from the Andes, sweet potatoes from the Caribbean. Carrots and onions were carried by European settlers. Broccoli was introduced to the Southwest, as it was to the rest of the United States, from Mediterranean climes.

Any of these vegetables, indigenous or immigrant, gains new zest from familiar Southwestern seasonings. Roasted green chilies, for example, transform an otherwise mild-mannered New England corn pudding into a seductive creation that would give a Puritan pause. Sharp-tasting fresh cilantro throws the natural sweetness of carrots into sharp relief. Red chili powder adds punch to all-American beer-battered onion rings. And chilies, once again, when whipped into unsalted butter, provide a simple embellishment that might make even an adopted Texan and former United States president beg for broccoli.

Rice was another transatlantic transplant to the Southwest, carried here by the Spaniards. Their way of cooking the grain owed much to the influence of the Moors on their own native land, the rice being gently simmered with tomato, chilies and other seasonings to make a moist and fragrant dish resembling a pilaf. So-called "Spanish rice" became such a classic Mexican recipe that it long ago gained the alternative name of "Mexican rice." Yet Southwest cooks do their best to put that culinary cliché to rest by cooking the grain with onions and garlic alone; or by adding breathtakingly hot habanero chilies; or by using milder green chilies and

Previous pages, clockwise from left: Creamy Sauté of Chayote Squash (recipe page 176), Steamed Broccoli with Green Chili Butter (recipe page 172), Cherry Tomatoes Sautéed with Tequila (recipe page 168)

160

a handful of finely chopped, fresh-picked *yerba buena*—a "good herb" belonging to the mint family.

Rice thus cooked shares many Southwestern plates with another definitive element of the regional kitchen: beans. In New Mexico, they may be boiled pintos, so named for their mottled brown-and-tan surfaces before cooking, or black beans in a rich inky gravy of their own making. Or they may be the familiar Mexican-style *frijoles refritos,* "refried beans," cooked and mashed in fat after first being boiled to absolute tenderness. Texas cooks may elaborate dried pinto or kidney beans with a liberal dose of powdered red chilies to make a dish known as "chili beans."

Though commonly relegated to the role of side dish today, beans provided primary sustenance for Southwestern peoples as many as fifteen hundred years ago. Indeed, they may have had a civilizing influence on the region. As New Mexican writer John Crenshaw points out in his "Paean to the Pinto Bean," reprinted in *New Mexico Magazine's More of the Best from New Mexico Kitchens*, corn, that other Southwestern staple, didn't require much in the way of agricultural attention, whereas beans "took more tending, indicating the beginnings of a more settled life—perhaps even requiring it."

Meals in some Southwestern kitchens today still center on a generous pot of beans—enough for at least two days' meals—augmented with rice, tortillas and salsas to provide a well-rounded and healthy diet. To a palate used to a wide and varied menu,

Vegetables were grown in home gardens until the advent of irrigation encouraged commercial production. Here, cabbage is harvested along the Rio Grande in west Texas.

The Verde River brings Arizona's desert valley to life; farmers have taken advantage of the fertile land in this area for hundreds of years.

such a regimen might seem boring, but beans offer incredible variety to the daily table, particularly with the success of efforts to revive the cultivation of dozens of ancient bean species once considered extinct. Local home gardeners, small-scale farmers and such organizations as Native Seeds/SEARCH in Tucson are responsible for making available such bean varieties as Aztec, Bisbee red, black valentine, Hopi yellow, Mitla black, New Mexico bolita, Paiute white, Pima beige, Tohono O'odham, Yaqui string, wild cocolmeca and Zuni shalako—names that read like a mystic incantation, with a range of colors, shapes, sizes, textures and flavors that is nothing short of astonishing.

No discussion of beans would be complete without addressing the prevalent digestive problem that comes with eating them. Over the centuries, cooks have persistently addressed the challenge of de-gassing beans. Presoaking them overnight, with as many as three changes of water, is often prescribed as the best way to tame the hard-to-digest sugars that cause gastric distress; while other cooks are content merely to "fast-soak" the beans, bringing them to a rolling boil for a minute and then setting them aside to sit in the hot water for one hour. In Mexico and the borderlands, the herb *epazote* is added to the cooking water in the pot with the aim of further defusing the gaseous factor. Elsewhere, the cooking water is supplemented with baking soda or with ashes from a wood fire. Dallas restaurateur Stephan Pyles recalls his grandmother tossing in an aspirin while reassuring the incredulous young chef-to-be that the beans didn't have a headache.

As many lovers of Southwestern cuisine discover, none of these methods is guaranteed to produce entirely satisfactory results. The best way of dealing with the problem may well be the practical approach suggested by John Crenshaw in his aforementioned essay. When all attempts fail to subdue the bean's most volatile element, he says, you should simply "let its flaw pass."

161

BLACK BEANS

*These beans are delicious as a side dish either with or without a
cheese topping. The beans may also be used as the base for black
bean cakes (recipe follows) or served as an appetizer topped with
sour cream and salsa. Oaxaca (pronounced wa-ha-ka), is a good
melting cheese similar to mozzarella in texture and flavor.*

1 lb (500 g) dried black beans, about 2 cups (14 oz/440 g)
2 tablespoons olive oil
1 cup (4 oz/125 g) chopped red (Spanish) onion
4 garlic cloves, minced
1 red bell pepper (capsicum), cored, seeded and diced
1 yellow bell pepper (capsicum), cored, seeded and diced
2 teaspoons ground cumin
2 tomatoes, diced
2 Anaheim chilies, roasted, peeled, seeded and diced
  (see glossary)
salt to taste
½ cup (2 oz/60 g) grated Oaxaca, Monterey jack or
  mozzarella cheese (optional)

❀ Put the beans in a large pot and cover with cold water; let
sit for 1 hour. Drain the beans and put them back into the
pot; add water to cover by 1 in (2.5 cm). Bring to a boil and
cook, uncovered, over medium heat for 1–1½ hours, or until
tender, adding more water if necessary.
❀ In a medium, heavy skillet, heat the olive oil over
medium-high heat; add the onion and cook for 5 minutes.
Add the garlic and peppers and cook until all the peppers
are tender, about 5 more minutes. Set aside.
❀ When the beans are tender, add the onion-pepper
mixture, cumin, tomatoes, chilies and salt. Cook an
additional 15–20 minutes, or until all the flavors are blended
and the mixture is slightly thickened. Sprinkle the cheese on
top of the beans if you like and serve immediately.

SERVES 8; MAKES 4 CUPS (32 FL OZ/1 L)   *Photograph pages 8–9*

BLACK BEAN CAKES

❀ Drain any excess liquid from the cooked black beans, let
the beans cool and purée in a food processor or blender until
smooth. Spoon 2 tablespoons purée onto a nonstick grill or a
large nonstick skillet and flatten to form each cake; cook
over medium heat for 1 minute per side, or until lightly
browned. Serve 2 cakes per serving and garnish with a
dollop of sour cream and salsa.

MAKES 32 CAKES   *Photograph pages 8–9*

SANTA FE HOMINY

*Hominy is dried corn that has been treated with slaked lime to
dissolve and remove the hulls, then slightly cooked. Canned yellow
or white hominy is available in grocery stores. The "heat" of this
dish may be altered by using various types of chilies; use Anaheims
instead of poblanos and eliminate the jalapeño to make it milder.
To make this a main dish, add 8 oz (250 g) of crumbled, cooked
and drained chorizo.*

2 tablespoons corn oil
2 garlic cloves, minced
1½ cups (6 oz/185 g) chopped red (Spanish) onions
two 15-oz (470-g) cans hominy, rinsed and drained
3 large ripe tomatoes, diced
2 poblano chilies, roasted, peeled, cored, seeded and diced
  (see glossary)
1 jalapeño chili, seeded and minced

1 cup (4 oz/125 g) grated asadero or Monterey jack cheese

❀ Heat the oil in a large, heavy skillet; when hot, add the
garlic and onions; cook, stirring, over medium heat until the
onions are translucent. Stir in the hominy, tomatoes and
chilies; cover and simmer over low heat for about 15 minutes, or until all the ingredients are well blended and the
vegetables are tender. Remove the cover and sprinkle the
cheese over the hominy. Stir just until the cheese is melted
and serve immediately.

SERVES 6

Left to right: Refried Beans, Santa Fe Hominy

Refried Beans

Refried beans (frijoles refritos) are beans that have been cooked, then fried with melted lard. Although higher in calories and cholesterol than most bean dishes, they are sinfully good, especially as an accompaniment to chili dishes. You may also use them in layered dips or as a topping for tostadas or Indian Fry Bread (recipe on page 132).

2 tablespoons bacon drippings or lard
4 cups (32 fl oz/1 l) Frijoles (recipe on page 171)

2 cups (8 oz/250 g) grated ranchero, shredded longhorn or
   Monterey jack cheese
½ cup (1½ oz/45 g) finely chopped green (spring) onions

✿ Melt the bacon drippings or lard in a large, heavy skillet. Add the beans, a few at a time, mashing them with a potato masher or a fork. Cook over low heat until they are thick, about 1 hour, stirring occasionally and adding water if needed. Top each serving with ¼ cup (1 oz/30 g) cheese and 1 tablespoon green onion.

SERVES 8

Left to right: Zucchini Pancakes, Black Bean Torta

ZUCCHINI PANCAKES

These colorful morsels are good on their own or with salsa as a vegetable side dish. Be sure to drain the shredded zucchini well to remove excess moisture.

2 eggs, separated
½ cup (5 oz/155 g) unbleached all-purpose (plain) flour
½ teaspoon salt
½ teaspoon freshly ground pepper
1 Anaheim chili, roasted, peeled, cored, seeded and diced (see glossary)
2 cups (8 oz/250 g) shredded zucchini (courgettes), well drained
1 tablespoon corn oil

❀ Beat the egg yolks and stir in the flour, salt and pepper; add the chili, then the zucchini. Beat the egg whites until stiff but not dry; gently fold into the zucchini mixture. Heat the oil in a nonstick skillet over medium-high heat. When hot, drop the zucchini mixture by tablespoonfuls into the hot oil. Cook, turning once, until lightly brown on both sides and cooked through.

SERVES 6

BLACK BEAN TORTA

A hearty vegetable side dish or meatless main course, this torta can be made with pinto beans rather than black beans. Asadero cheese, available in specialty or Latino markets, has the flavor of provolone and the texture of mozzarella.

3 cups (24 fl oz/750 ml) cooked black beans
¼ cup (2 fl oz/60 ml) chicken stock (see glossary)
1 tablespoon corn oil
2 cups (10 oz/315 g) finely chopped red (Spanish) onion
2 red bell peppers (capsicums), cored, seeded and julienned
2 zucchini (courgettes), halved and thinly sliced
2 garlic cloves, minced
1 cup (6 oz/185 g) corn kernels
1 teaspoon cumin seed, ground to a powder, or ¾ teaspoon ground cumin
¼ teaspoon cayenne pepper
salt to taste
6 flour tortillas (8 in/20 cm in diameter)
2 cups (16 fl oz/500 ml) Salsa Fresca (recipe on page 201)
2 cups (8 oz/250 g) grated asadero or Monterey jack cheese

❀ Preheat an oven to 375°F (190°C).
❀ Purée the beans and chicken stock in a food processor or blender. Set aside. In a large skillet, heat the corn oil over medium heat and add the red onions, bell pepper, zucchini and garlic. Sauté the vegetables, stirring, until they are tender, about 10 minutes. Add the corn, cumin, cayenne and salt; cook another 2–3 minutes.
❀ Lightly oil an 8-in (20-cm) springform pan with 3-in (7.5-cm) sides. Place 1 flour tortilla in the bottom of the springform pan. Spread ½ cup (4 fl oz/125 ml) of the bean purée over the tortilla and top with 1 cup (6–8 oz/185–250 g) of the sautéed vegetable mixture, then spoon ⅓ cup (3 fl oz/80 ml) salsa over vegetables and sprinkle ⅓ cup (1 oz/30 g) cheese over the salsa. Repeat with the remaining ingredients, ending with cheese.
❀ Bake for 45 minutes, or until the torta is warmed through; let stand for 5 minutes before cutting into wedges.

SERVES 10–12

SPICY SWEET POTATO FRIES

On his first voyage to the West Indies, Columbus discovered the sweet potato and brought it back to Europe. Sweet potatoes are similar to yams in taste and appearance, and yams also may be used in this Southwest version of french fries. Double frying is the classic method for making french fries; fries are crisper on the outside and lighter on the inside when cooked using this method.

2 lb (1 kg) sweet potatoes
8 cups (64 fl oz/2 l) corn oil
1 tablespoon Southwest Seasoning Mix (recipe on page 196)

❀ Peel the sweet potatoes and cut them into julienned strips. Put the sweet potatoes in a large bowl of cold water; rinse, drain and dry well on paper towels. The sweet potatoes should be as dry as possible so that the hot oil won't spatter when they are added.
❀ In a large, deep pot, heat the oil over high heat to 325°F (170°C), or until a cube of bread takes 90 seconds to brown. Add the fries in batches and cook until almost brown, about

Left to right: Chili Onion Rings, Spicy Sweet Potato Fries,
Chili-Corn Fritters

CHILI-CORN FRITTERS

Served with Pineapple Salsa, or any other salsa of your choice,
these light, tasty fritters are a perfect side dish for a sauceless
main course. The creation of Eddie Matney, chef-owner of Eddie's
Grill in Phoenix, they are also delicious as an appetizer.

2 cups (12 oz/375 g) corn kernels, about 5 ears (cobs) of corn
2 eggs
2 green (spring) onions, chopped
2 tablespoons Anaheim chilies roasted, peeled, cored,
   seeded and diced (see glossary)
1 garlic clove, minced
2 tablespoons chopped fresh cilantro (coriander)
2 teaspoons ground coriander
2 teaspoons freshly ground pepper
2 teaspoons sugar
2 teaspoons salt
½ cup (2½ oz/75 g) unbleached all-purpose (plain) flour
½ cup (2½ oz/75 g) cornmeal
½ teaspoon baking powder
vegetable oil for frying
Pineapple Salsa (recipe on page 201) or other salsa

❉ Place all the ingredients except the salsa and oil in the
bowl of a food processor and process until blended but still
slightly lumpy; don't over-process. Or, to make in a blender,
combine all ingredients except the salsa and oil in a medium
bowl and blend in batches. Let stand for 1 hour at room
temperature.
❉ In a heavy skillet, pour oil to a depth of ½ in (12 mm) and
heat over medium-high heat to 375°F (190°C), or until a
cube of bread browns in 60 seconds. Drop batter by
teaspoonfuls into the hot oil and cook until golden brown
and cooked through. Drain on paper towels and keep warm
in a low oven. Repeat until all the batter is used.

MAKES 48

CHILI ONION RINGS

Chili powder and cayenne add extra zest to these crunchy onion
rings. They are terrific on their own, dipped in Chile Catsup
(recipe on page 189), or as an accompaniment to steaks and
hamburgers.

2 large onions, separated into rings
2 cups (16 fl oz/500 ml) cold milk
1 cup (8 fl oz/250 ml) beer
1 cup (5 oz/155 g) unbleached all-purpose (plain) flour
½ teaspoon cayenne pepper
½ teaspoon chili powder
½ teaspoon salt
vegetable oil for frying

❉ Soak the onion rings in milk in a large bowl and set aside.
❉ In a medium bowl, make the batter: Whisk together the
beer, flour, cayenne pepper, chili powder and salt. Fill a
medium, heavy pot or deep-fryer with enough oil for deep-
frying (about 3 in/7.5 cm) and heat over medium-high heat
until the oil is almost smoking. Remove the onion rings one
at a time from the milk, coat with the batter and fry in small
batches until golden brown. Drain on paper towels and keep
hot in a low oven while preparing the remainder of the
onion rings.

SERVES 6

5 minutes. Remove from the oil and drain on paper towels.
Repeat until all the potatoes have been cooked. Set aside,
reserving the oil.
❉ Just before serving, reheat the oil to 360°F (185°C),
or or until a cube of bread takes 75 seconds to brown.
Add the partially cooked potatoes in batches and cook
until golden brown, about 1 minute. Drain on paper
towels and sprinkle to taste with Southwest seasoning
mix. Repeat until all the fries have been cooked.
Serve immediately.

SERVES 6

NEW MEXICO

CORN PUDDING

This creamy casserole goes well with grilled chicken or meat and would be a welcome addition to a brunch buffet. If desired, add a serrano or jalapeño chili to make it slightly more spicy. Ranchero, a fresh milk cheese, has a crumbly texture and adds a unique flavor to the pudding.

2 cups (12 oz/375 g) creamed corn
1 cup (5 oz/155 g) yellow cornmeal
½ cup (4 oz/125 g) unsalted butter, melted
1 cup (8 fl oz/250 ml) buttermilk
2 cups (10 oz/315 g) finely chopped onions
2 eggs, slightly beaten
½ teaspoon baking soda (bicarbonate of soda)
2 cups (8 oz/250 g) grated ranchero or sharp Cheddar cheese
3 New Mexico chilies, roasted, peeled, cored, seeded and diced (see glossary)

❊ Lightly butter an 8-cup (64–fl oz/2-l) casserole. Preheat an oven to 350°F (180°C).
❊ Purée the corn in a processor or blender until creamy.
❊ In a large bowl, stir together the cornmeal, butter, buttermilk, onions, puréed corn, eggs and baking soda. Pour half of the batter into the prepared casserole dish. Spread the cheese and chilies over the batter; pour the remaining batter over the top. Bake for 1 hour, or until set and slightly browned; let sit 10 minutes before serving.

SERVES 6–8

SOUTHWEST

EGGPLANT-TOMATO CASSEROLE

This casserole of vegetables of the vine may be varied by using zucchini (courgettes) or cucumber instead of yellow squash and yellow or red bell peppers in place of the green.

5 tablespoons (3 fl oz/80 ml) olive oil
2 cups (10 oz/315 g) finely chopped onions
2 garlic cloves, minced

Top to bottom: Squash, Corn and Peppers Medley; Corn Pudding

2 cups (8 oz/250 g) sliced yellow squash (vegetable marrow)
2 teaspoons salt
1 teaspoon dried oregano, or 2 teaspoons fresh oregano
½ teaspoon ground cumin
freshly ground pepper to taste
4 Japanese (long narrow) or 1 large (globe) eggplant (aubergine), sliced
2 green bell peppers (capsicums), cored, seeded and cut into ½-in (12-mm) wide slices
2 ripe tomatoes, cored and sliced

❊ Preheat oven to 350°F (180°C). In a medium skillet, heat 2 tablespoons of the olive oil over medium heat; when hot, add the onions and garlic and sauté until the onions are translucent, about 5 minutes. Spoon half of the onions over the bottom of an 8-cup (64-fl oz/2-l) casserole. Layer the yellow squash slices over the onions. In a small bowl, combine the salt, oregano, cumin and pepper. Sprinkle about 1 teaspoon of the spice mixture over the squash. Drizzle 1 tablespoon of the olive oil over all. Add a layer of sliced eggplant, 1 teaspoon of spices and 1 tablespoon of oil. Top the casserole with a layer of the green peppers and the remaining spices and 2 tablespoons oil.
❊ Cover the casserole and cook for 1 hour. Remove the cover, add a layer of sliced tomatoes and the remaining onions; bake, uncovered, for 15 more minutes. Serve immediately.

SERVES 6–8

SOUTHERN ARIZONA

CHERRY TOMATOES SAUTÉED WITH TEQUILA

This simple vegetable dish is a perfect last-minute addition to almost any main course and goes well with egg dishes. For additional color, use a mixture of red and yellow cherry tomatoes.

2 tablespoons olive oil
1 garlic clove, minced
2 cups (12 oz/375 g) cherry tomatoes, stemmed
2 tablespoons tequila
2 tablespoons minced fresh cilantro (coriander)
¼ cup (1½ oz/45 g) piñon (pine) nuts, toasted (see glossary)
salt and freshly ground pepper to taste

❊ In a heavy skillet, heat the oil over medium heat. Add the minced garlic and cherry tomatoes; sauté until the garlic is soft but not brown, about 5 minutes. Add the tequila, mix well, and sauté for 1 minute. Add the cilantro and pine nuts; cook, stirring, for 1 minute. Add salt and pepper and serve immediately.

SERVES 6   *Photograph pages 158–159*

NEW MEXICO

SQUASH, CORN AND PEPPERS MEDLEY

Native Americans have traditionally gathered wild sunflower seeds, using them whole and ground for meal. This New Mexican dish is a good example of the marriage of the indigenous cuisine with that of Mexico and Europe. To make it less rich, eliminate the cream and cream cheese and substitute safflower oil for the butter.

Eggplant-Tomato Casserole

2 tablespoons unsalted butter
1 cup (5 oz/155 g) finely chopped onions
2 garlic cloves, minced
3 yellow squash (vegetable marrows), cut into ¼-in (6-mm) rounds
2 ripe tomatoes, diced
1 cup (5 oz/155 g) corn kernels
1 poblano chili, roasted, peeled, cored, seeded and diced (see glossary)
¼ teaspoon dried oregano
1 teaspoon cumin seed, ground to a powder, or 1 teaspoon ground cumin
salt and freshly ground pepper to taste
1 cup (8 fl oz/250 ml) light (single) cream or half & half (half cream and half milk)
¼ teaspoon red hot pepper sauce
3 oz (90 g) cream cheese, cut into cubes
¼ cup (1½ oz/45 g) sunflower seeds

❁ Melt the butter in a heavy skillet over medium-high heat; sauté the onions and garlic over medium heat for 5 minutes, or until tender. Add the squash and cook another 5 minutes. Add the tomatoes, corn, chili, oregano, cumin and salt and pepper; lower heat and simmer for 15–20 minutes, or until the squash is tender, stirring occasionally. Stir in the cream, hot pepper sauce and cream cheese. Cook until heated through and the cheese is melted; add the sunflower seeds and stir until mixed in.

SERVES 6

HABANERO PILAF

The small lantern-shaped habanero is considered the hottest chili in the world (30 to 50 times hotter than the jalapeño) and is closely related to the Scotch bonnet, or bonnie, chili. Wear rubber gloves when working with this spicy devil. Make this picante side dish into a main dish by adding diced cooked chicken, pork or beef.

2 tablespoons unsalted butter
½ cup (2 oz/125 g) chopped red (Spanish) onion
2 habanero chilies, seeded and minced
½ teaspoon cumin seed, crushed, or ¼ teaspoon ground cumin
1 cup (7 oz/220 g) basmati rice
2 cups (16 fl oz/500 ml) chicken stock (see glossary)
2 cups (12 oz/375 g) chopped seeded tomatoes
1 teaspoon chopped fresh cilantro (coriander)
salt to taste

❁ In a large, heavy saucepan over medium heat, melt the butter and add the onion, chilies, cumin seed and rice. Cook, stirring, until the onions are soft and the rice is lightly browned, about 8 minutes. Add the chicken stock and bring to a boil; add the tomatoes, cilantro and salt and stir together once. Cover, reduce heat and simmer for 20–25 minutes, or until all the liquid has been absorbed and the rice is tender.

SERVES 6   *Photograph pages 8–9*

CHILES RELLENOS

The components of chiles rellenos, or "stuffed chilies," vary from region to region. In Mexico, poblano chilies are most common, while in the Southwest the chili of choice is the green New Mexican. A classic relleno is stuffed with cheese before being dipped in batter and fried, but this version includes corn to add flavor and texture. Shredded chicken may be added to the filling for an even heartier dish. Serve these plain or with Green Chili Sauce (recipe on page 195) or Ranchero Sauce (recipe on page 190).

2 tablespoons vegetable oil
1 cup (5 oz/155 g) finely chopped onions
2 garlic cloves, minced
2 cups (12 oz/375 g) corn kernels, cooked
½ teaspoon dried oregano, or 1 teaspoon fresh oregano
salt and freshly ground pepper to taste
¼ cup (2 oz/60 g) sour cream
2 cups (8 oz/250 g) grated Monterey jack cheese
6 New Mexico green or Anaheim chilies, roasted, peeled and seeded with stems left intact (see glossary)
3 eggs, separated
2 tablespoons unbleached all-purpose (plain) flour
¼ teaspoon salt
¼ teaspoon baking powder
vegetable oil for frying

170

batter and fry in the hot oil until golden on one side; turn over and fry until golden on the other side. Drain on paper towels and keep warm while frying the remaining rellenos. Serve on warmed plates with green chili or ranchero sauce.

MAKES 6

FRIJOLES

Frijoles, the Mexican word for beans, usually refers to boiled and simmered pinto beans, so named because of their spotted appearance. They should be cooked slowly in unsalted water, because salt toughens the skins. Served as a side dish, cooked into refried beans or used as the topping for tostadas, frijoles are an essential part of any Southwestern cook's repertoire.

2 cups (14 oz/440 g) dried pinto beans
1 onion, halved and sliced
1 garlic clove, minced
8 oz (250 g) bacon, diced
1 guajillo chili, toasted, stemmed and seeded (see glossary)
1 *chile de árbol*, toasted, stemmed and seeded (see glossary)
salt to taste
grated cotija, Cheddar or Monterey jack cheese for garnish
  (optional)

❀ Pick over the beans to remove any stones. Place the beans in a large pot, add water to cover by 2 in (5 cm) and soak overnight.
❀ Rinse and drain the beans; put back in the pot with the onion, garlic, bacon and chilies. Add water to cover by 1 in (2.5 cm). Bring to a boil; lower heat and simmer for 2–3 hours, or until the beans are tender and most of the liquid is evaporated. Add salt. If using as a side dish, sprinkle each portion with grated cheese. Serve immediately.

SERVES 6–8; MAKES 4 CUPS (32 FL OZ/1 L)

MEXICAN RICE

Rice and beans are standard components in almost every combination plate in Mexican restaurants. The beans are usually refried pinto beans; this is the typical rice dish.

¼ cups (2 fl oz/60 ml) vegetable oil
1 cup (7 oz/220 g) long-grain white rice
2 tablespoons diced red bell pepper (capsicum)
¼ cup (1 oz/30 g) finely chopped onion
1 tablespoon minced fresh parsley
⅓ cup (2½ oz/75 g) tomato paste (purée)
2 garlic cloves, minced
2½ cups (20 fl oz/625 ml) cold water
¾ teaspoon salt

❀ Heat the oil in a large, heavy saucepan over medium heat. Add the rice and cook, stirring constantly, until the rice is golden, about 5 minutes. Add the red pepper and onion and cook another 5 minutes, stirring. Reduce heat; add the parsley, tomato paste and garlic; stir well. Add the water and salt, raise heat and bring to a boil. Cover tightly and reduce heat to low; simmer for 20–30 minutes, or until the water is absorbed. Remove from heat and let sit for 10 minutes before serving.

SERVES 6

Clockwise from left: Chiles Rellenos, Frijoles, Mexican Rice

❀ Heat the oil in a medium skillet over medium heat. Add the onions and garlic and sauté until the onions are soft, about 5 minutes. Add the corn, oregano, salt and pepper and heat, stirring, until well blended, about 2 minutes. Remove from heat, let cool slightly and add the sour cream and cheese. Stuff the chilies with the cheese mixture and refrigerate for 1 hour.
❀ In a small bowl, beat the egg yolks with the flour, salt and baking powder. In a large bowl, whip the whites until soft peaks form. Fold the whites into the yolks.
❀ Fill a heavy skillet with oil to a depth of 1 in (2.5 cm). Heat the oil to 375°F (190°C), or until a cube of bread browns in 60 seconds. Dip a few chilled rellenos in egg

STEAMED BROCCOLI WITH GREEN CHILI BUTTER

Chili butter is delicious on almost any fresh vegetable. New Mexico green chilies are rather mild; to make the butter hotter, use poblano chilies.

BUTTER

6 tablespoons (3 oz/90 g) unsalted butter
¼ teaspoon ground cumin
2 ripe tomatoes, seeded and finely chopped
3 New Mexico green chilies, roasted, peeled, seeded and finely chopped (see glossary)

4½–5 lb (2.25–2.5 kg) broccoli, trimmed, cut into flowerets, steamed and kept warm
salt and freshly ground pepper to taste

❈ Melt the butter over medium heat in a large, heavy saucepan. When it bubbles, add the cumin, stir and add the tomatoes and chilies. Lower heat and cook until the mixture is hot. Add the steamed broccoli, toss quickly and add salt and pepper. Serve immediately.

SERVES 6   *Photograph pages 158–159*

CALABACITAS

Calabacitas means "little squash" and usually includes three native American crops: corn, squash and chilies. Queso fresco is a mild white cheese available in Latino markets. This colorful and flavorful side dish goes well with almost any main course.

¼ cup (2 oz/60 g) butter
½ cup (2 oz/60 g) chopped onion
1 garlic clove, minced
6 cups (30 oz/950 g) cubed zucchini (courgettes) or yellow squash (vegetable marrow)
1 red bell pepper (capsicum), cored, seeded and diced
½ cup Anaheim chilies, roasted, cored, seeded, peeled and diced (see glossary)
1 cup (6 oz/185 g) corn kernels
1 teaspoon Southwest Seasoning Mix (recipe on page 196)
freshly ground pepper to taste
1 cup (4 oz/125 g) crumbled queso fresco or shredded Monterey jack cheese

❈ In a large skillet, melt the butter over medium heat; add the onion and garlic and sauté for 2 minutes. Add the zucchini or squash and bell pepper and cook another 2 minutes. Stir in the chilies, corn and seasonings; cover, lower heat and simmer until the squash is tender, about 5 minutes. Uncover, sprinkle with the cheese and cook, stirring, until cheese is melted. Serve immediately.

SERVES 6

SAUTÉED POTATOES WITH GREEN CHILIES

Good either at home or on a camping trip, these potatoes are a great accompaniment to barbecue, steak or ribs. If red bell peppers are unavailable, use green ones.

¼ cup (2 fl oz/60 ml) vegetable oil
4 unpeeled russet potatoes, thinly sliced
2 cups (8 oz/250 g) diced red (Spanish) onion
1 red bell pepper (capsicum), cored, seeded and diced
1 Anaheim chili, cored, seeded and diced
salt and freshly ground pepper to taste

❈ In a large, heavy skillet, heat the oil over medium-high heat until hot. Add the potatoes and sauté, stirring constantly, until tender, about 10 minutes. Add the onion and red bell pepper; cook another 3 minutes, stirring occasionally. Stir in the Anaheim chili, salt and pepper and cook 5 minutes more.

SERVES 6

Clockwise from bottom left: Green Beans with Piñons, Calabacitas,
Sautéed Potatoes with Green Chilies

GREEN BEANS WITH PIÑONS

Good hot or cold, these beans are a nice accompaniment to roasts
or grilled meats. The piñon nuts add a crunchy texture, and the
Manchego, a mellow cheese found in Latino markets, adds a
creamy contrast.

1 lb (500 g) green beans
⅓ cup (1½ oz/45 g) piñon (pine) nuts, toasted (see glossary)
¼ cup (2 fl oz/60 ml) olive oil
¼ cup (2 fl oz/60 ml) red wine vinegar
1 teaspoon fresh oregano, or ½ teaspoon dried oregano

1 teaspoon chopped fresh cilantro (coriander)
1 garlic clove, minced
salt and freshly ground pepper to taste
¼ cup (1 oz/30 g) grated Manchego or Parmesan cheese

❂ Cook the beans in boiling water until just tender; drain
and rinse with cold water.
❂ In a large skillet, stir together the nuts, olive oil, vinegar,
oregano, cilantro and garlic. Add the beans and cook,
stirring, over medium low heat until all the ingredients are
heated through. Add salt and pepper and sprinkle the cheese
over all.

SERVES 6

173

ZUCCHINI TARTA

A rich, creamy side dish or part of a brunch, this savory pie freezes well. It is also good at room temperature and a perfect addition to any picnic.

PASTRY

1⅓ cups (6½ oz/190 g) unbleached all-purpose (plain) flour
½ cup (4 oz/125 g) chilled unsalted butter, cut into 8 pieces
1 teaspoon salt
1 tablespoon sugar
¼ cup (2 fl oz/60 ml) ice water

FILLING

2 tablespoons Dijon mustard
3 cups (12 oz/375 g) grated zucchini (courgettes)
salt
2 tablespoons unsalted butter
8 large mushrooms, sliced
2 cups (8 oz/250 g) grated Monterey jack cheese
1 package (8 oz/250 g) cream cheese at room temperature
1 cup (8 fl oz/250 ml) heavy (double) cream
2 egg yolks
1 egg
salt and freshly ground pepper to taste

❀ To make the pastry, place the flour, butter, salt and sugar in a food processor and pulse until the mixture resembles coarse meal. With the machine running, pour the water through the feed tube; stop the machine as soon as the dough forms a ball. Or, to make by hand, combine flour, sugar and salt in a large bowl. With a fork or pastry blender, cut in butter until mixture resembles course meal. Add water gradually until a smooth dough is formed. Chill the dough if not using immediately, or roll out on a lightly floured board into a circle 14 in (35 cm) in diameter. Line a 10-in (25-cm) quiche pan with the dough.
❀ Preheat an oven to 450°F (230°C). Spread the mustard on the bottom of the pastry shell and bake for 10 minutes. Remove the pastry shell from the oven and reduce oven temperature to 350°F (180°C).
❀ Place the zucchini in a colander, sprinkle with salt and allow to drain. In a medium skillet, heat the butter over medium heat; add the mushrooms and sauté until soft; set aside. Sprinkle one half of the cheese over the bottom of the pastry shell; top with the sautéed mushrooms. Squeeze the zucchini to remove all the moisture; spread evenly over the mushrooms.
❀ In a medium bowl with an electric mixer, beat together the cream cheese, cream, egg yolks and egg until smooth. Add salt and pepper. Slowly pour the mixture over the zucchini. Sprinkle the remaining cheese over all and bake until the top is golden and a knife inserted in the center comes out clean, about 45 minutes. Let sit 5 minutes before serving.

SERVES 8–10

BATTER-FRIED SQUASH BLOSSOMS

Considered a special delicacy by the Zuni tribe, squash blossoms have been revered by native Americans for centuries. Golden yellow and extremely fragile, the blossoms are picked early in the morning before they open and should be used the same day. Although any squash produces a blossom, the most beautiful are those from zucchini, and male blossoms are preferred because they are larger and will not bear fruit. To make an even simpler, delicious vegetable side dish, batter fry the blossoms without stuffing them.

18 squash blossoms

CHEESE FILLING

3 oz (90 g) goat cheese
3 oz (90 g) cream cheese
½ teaspoon red pepper flakes
1 clove garlic, minced
salt and freshly ground pepper to taste

BATTER

½ cup (2½ oz/75 g) unbleached all-purpose (plain) flour
¼ cup (2 fl oz/60 ml) water
¼ cup (2 fl oz/60 ml) milk
1 egg
⅛ teaspoon salt

vegetable oil for frying
salt and freshly ground pepper to taste
salsa for garnish

❀ Dip the squash blossoms in cold water and drain them thoroughly on paper towels. If stuffing them, remove the stamens from the male blossoms.
❀ In a small bowl, mix all filling ingredients with a whisk or an electric mixer until smooth. Fill each squash blossom with 2 teaspoons of filling.
❀ To make the batter, in a medium bowl, stir together the flour, water, milk, egg and salt. Let sit for 1 hour.
❀ Fill a large, heavy saucepan or skillet with oil to a depth of 2 in (5 cm). Heat over medium heat to 375°F (190°C). Dip a few squash blossoms into the batter, covering each entire blossom, and drop into the hot oil. Fry until golden brown, about 1 minute, turn over and fry on the other side. Remove with a slotted spoon and drain on paper towels. Repeat with the remaining blossoms, being careful not to overcrowd the pan. Add salt and pepper and serve immediately.

SERVES 6

SOUTH-OF-THE-BORDER ZUCCHINI

Adjust the "heat" of this savory side dish by using mild to hot salsa. If time doesn't allow for making Salsa Fresca, use a good commercial salsa.

2 tablespoons olive oil
4 cups (16 oz/500 g) thinly sliced zucchini (courgettes)
½ cup (2½ oz/75 g) finely chopped celery
1 cup (5 oz/155 g) finely chopped red (Spanish) onion
1 red bell pepper (capsicum), cored, seeded and diced
2 tablespoons minced fresh basil
½ cup (4 oz/125 g) Salsa Fresca (recipe on page 201)
salt and freshly ground pepper to taste
1 cup (4 oz/125 g) grated asadero or Monterey jack cheese

❀ Heat the olive oil in a large, heavy skillet over medium-high heat. Add the zucchini, celery, onion and bell pepper; sauté, stirring constantly, until the vegetables begin to soften, about 5 minutes. Add the basil, salsa, salt and pepper. Cover and lower heat; simmer for another 5 minutes. Uncover, add the cheese and stir until the cheese is melted and the vegetables are tender. Serve immediately.

SERVES 6

*Clockwise from top left: Zucchini Tarta, Batter-fried Squash
Blossoms, South-of-the-Border Zucchini*

CARROTS WITH SOUR CREAM AND CILANTRO

Cilantro's distinctively pungent taste blossoms when heated, enhancing the carrots and sour cream to create a distinctive side dish. Because the perfume of cilantro is very volatile, do not wash it until ready to use; discard any thick stems.

3 tablespoons unsalted butter
2 lb (1 kg) carrots, peeled and cut into 2-by-¼-in (5-cm-by-6-mm) julienne
1 tablespoon minced fresh cilantro (coriander)
½ cup (4 fl oz/125 ml) chicken stock (see glossary)
2 teaspoons honey
3 tablespoons sour cream

❋ In a large skillet, melt the butter; add the carrots and sauté, stirring, for 5 minutes. Add the cilantro, stock and honey. Cover, lower heat, and simmer until the carrots are tender, about 5 minutes. With a slotted spoon, transfer the carrots to a bowl. Increase the heat to high and cook the liquid in the pan, uncovered, until only 1 tablespoon of liquid remains. Whisk in the sour cream; pour this sauce over the carrots and serve immediately.

SERVES 6–8

HERBED ZUCCHINI FANS

Use baby zucchini for an elegant dinner party: the delicious little fans will add color and interest to the plates.

2 tablespoons fine fresh bread crumbs
3 tablespoons grated ranchero or Parmesan cheese
¼ cup (2 oz/60 g) unsalted butter, at room temperature
¾ teaspoon crumbled dried tarragon
3 tablespoons minced fresh parsley
⅛ teaspoon cayenne pepper
salt and freshly ground pepper to taste
6 zucchini (courgettes) (each about 6 in/15 cm long), stems intact, steamed

❋ In a small bowl, toss the bread crumbs with the cheese. In another small bowl, cream together the butter, tarragon, parsley, cayenne, salt and pepper. Keeping the stem attached, cut each zucchini lengthwise into four ¼-in (6-mm) thick slices. Spread some of the herb butter carefully between the layers and separate the slices slightly to form a fan. Place the fans on buttered baking sheets.
❋ Sprinkle the fans with the bread crumb mixture and broil them under a preheated broiler about 4 in (10 cm) from the heat for 1–2 minutes, or until they are golden.

SERVES 6

CREAMY SAUTÉ OF CHAYOTE SQUASH

Chayote is a tropical summer squash. It is available in many grocery stores, but yellow squash or zucchini (vegetable marrows or courgettes) may easily be substituted. Serve this with grilled fish, poultry or meat.

3 tablespoons unsalted butter
1 jalapeño chili, seeded and minced
2 chayote squash (vegetable pears), peeled and thinly sliced
salt and freshly ground pepper to taste
½ cup (4 fl oz/125 ml) heavy (double) cream
1 tablespoon minced fresh chives
1 tablespoon minced fresh cilantro (coriander)

❋ Heat the butter in a large, heavy skillet over medium heat. Add the jalapeño and cook, stirring, for 1 minute. Add the squash, salt and pepper and reduce heat. Cover the pan, reduce heat and cook until the squash is just tender, about 5 minutes. Remove the cover and add the cream to the squash; toss gently. Raise heat and simmer the mixture, uncovered, until the cream is almost evaporated and has coated the squash. Add the chives and cilantro. Correct the seasoning.

SERVES 6   *Photograph pages 158–159*

Left to right: Carrots with Sour Cream and Cilantro,
Herbed Zucchini Fans

CORN ON THE COB

Native Americans showed the Europeans how to eat corn on the cob, but it was the Old World that, by introducing dairy products to the New World, contributed the custom of slathering the corn with butter. Here are two versions of corn on the cob that don't use butter, but if butter is a must, try boiled or grilled corn with Avocado Butter (recipe on page 196).

VERSION NO. 1

12 ears (cobs) corn, husks intact
salt, chili powder and lime juice to taste

❁ Light a fire in charcoal grill. Pull back the husks from the corn and remove the silk; pull the husks back into place around the corn. Soak the corn in warm water for 30 minutes. When the coals are hot, drain and roast the corn with its husks until the sugar in the corn has caramelized and the kernels are lightly browned, about 15–20 minutes, turning occasionally. Remove the husks, sprinkle each ear with salt and chili powder and sprinkle with a little lime juice. Or, pass salt, chili powder and wedges of lime so that guests can season their own.

VERSION NO. 2

6 cups (48 fl oz/1.5 l) water
1 cup (8 oz/250 g) sugar
1 jar (16 oz/500 g) pickled jalapeños, sliced, plus liquid from jar
12 ears (cobs) corn, husked
salt to taste (optional)

❁ Bring a large pot of water to a boil over high heat. Add the sugar, jalapeño slices and their juice to the boiling water. Add the corn and cook for 5–7 minutes, or until tender. Serve immediately, passing the salt, if desired.

MAKES 12   *Photograph pages 8–9*

Llano Estacado

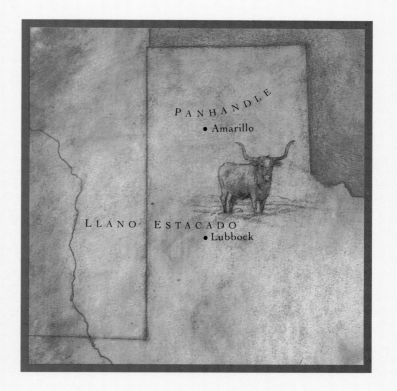

LLANO ESTACADO

S traddling the New Mexico–Texas border stretches
the southern extension of the Great Plains which
form the heart of the North American continent. At
the northeastern corner of the Southwest, where New
Mexico meets the Texas Panhandle, these gently slop-
ing, virtually featureless plains are broken only by the
remnants of hundreds of small volcanoes once active in
this region. Farther south, the plains break up into the
flatlands and eroded bluffs of the vast Llano Estacado.

Translated from the Spanish, Llano Estacado means
"Staked Plain." Several explanations exist for this name.
Some believe that pioneers marked the presence of
water on the plain by driving stakes into the mostly
arid earth. Others think that the name came from the
region's many yucca plants, whose stalks rise from the
plain like—yes—stakes.

(Some present-day pundits might note that the
stakes marking the plain today are the towers and
rocking horses of oil and gas wells that dot the region.)
Geologically minded sorts hold that the rugged wall-
like cliffs of the region bring to mind a stockade—in
Spanish, *estacada*. Some historians of native American
culture claim that the name derives from the stakes the

*Previous pages: Delicate cornflowers thrive during the wet season in the
open plains of the Texas Panhandle, a region that receives only 16–20
inches of rain annually. Left: The otherworldly beauty of Carlsbad
Caverns was created by groundwater eating through a limestone reef
formed 250 million years ago when southeastern New Mexico was
submerged beneath the sea.*

Comanches placed as trail markers for the Great Chief who, legend had it, would come out of the East to save them from oppression.

As many as eleven thousand years ago, as the Ice Age drew to a close, great herds of Pleistocene bisons and wooly mammoths roamed these plains, and nomadic tribes hunted them for food. The descendants of those early hunters, the Comanches, Apaches and Kiowas, hunted the American bison—more commonly known as the buffalo—into the nineteenth century A.D., and in their use of these animals practiced an economy perfected over the centuries. Before Spaniards introduced the horse to the New World, the natives probably donned animal-hide disguises to approach the more-than-one-ton beasts. They killed them with arrows shot from bows strung with buffalo hide. The women of the tribe butchered the animals with buffalo-bone tools, then scraped and tanned the hides. And they sun-dried thin strips of the meat as jerky or cooked it over buffalo chips: dried dung sometimes referred to as "prairie coal." They added extra nutrition to their buffalo stews by adding such organ meats as liver, heart, brains and testicles, creating a precursor of the Southwest cowboy's colorfully named son-of-a-gun or son-of-a-bitch stew.

By the late nineteenth century, the buffalos had been hunted to virtual extinction by the Anglos. But they were replaced on the Llano Estacado and in the Panhandle by ranches of sheep and cattle, animals well suited to grazing on the endless stretches of prairie grass. Some farmers also managed to make a living here, irrigating their crops—as the ranchers do to water their herds—by tapping a deep underground aquifer that stretches more than 250 miles north into Kansas. Farther west, toward the foothills of the Sacramento Mountains, artesian wells and the waters of the Pecos River and its tributaries, Salt Creek and the Rios Hondo and Penasco, provide water for farms of corn and beans, as well as for fruit orchards.

The cooking style that evolved in this region and still brings it distinction today is the honest sort of grub dished up by the cowboy chuck wagon: Eye-opening coffee strong enough to bend a spoon, brewed over the campfire in a pot and poured into mugs after the grounds have had a chance to settle. Masses of pinto beans simmered in an iron kettle with a hunk of bacon or a ham hock and maybe a sprinkling of crushed chilies. Steaming biscuits leavened with a much-cherished sourdough starter and baked in a Dutch oven. Great roasts of beef, or beef stews—sometimes supplemented with organ meats to turn it into son-of-a-gun stew. Fragrant casseroles of potatoes and onions. Tart-sweet preserves and dried fruit compotes. And on special occasions, pies filled crust to crust with spiced pumpkin purée or wild plums.

Though the horse-drawn chuck wagon is pretty much a thing of the past, replaced by sturdy trucks, that tradition of no-nonsense, pile-the-plate-high cooking continues to this day. And it carries over into the region's cafes and restaurants as well. In Amarillo, home of the Western Stockyards, where over 600,000 cattle are sold each year in the state's largest livestock

Green clusters of salt cedar trees herald intermittent springs in the vast, dry expanse of the Llano Estacado.

The vibrant blossoms of the spring star cactus look better suited to the tropics than the dry grass plains of northern Texas.

auction, there's a place known as the Big Texan Steak Ranch & Emporium. Its specialty: a complete dinner featuring a seventy-two-ounce steak, offered free of charge to any guest who can finish off the entire 4½ pounds of meat plus all the trimmings in under an hour.

Gastronomical accomplishments of a more refined sensibility also may be found today in the Llano Estacado. The unbroken horizons of Lubbock are beginning to yield wines worthy of Texan pride.

At Pheasant Ridge Winery, for example, they're growing and producing excellent Chardonnay, Chenin Blanc, Sauvignon Blanc, Barbera and Cabernet Sauvignon. And the Llano Estacado Winery, with its fine Chardonnay, Riesling, Chenin Blanc and both red and rosé versions of Cabernet, enjoys an ever-growing reputation.

To which the only appropriate response must be, "Cheers, y'all!"

Salsas, Sauces and Condiments

Inhabitants of the desert have long known the benefits of the prickly pear; cooks utilize both the fruit (tunas) and the pads (nopales) of the cactus.

SALSAS, SAUCES AND CONDIMENTS

Southwestern cuisine celebrated a milestone of sorts in the early 1990s, as nationwide sales of bottled salsas finally surpassed those of all-American tomato ketchup. But, truth be told, the competition wasn't fair.

Most ketchup, after all, is bought under the Heinz label, with few folks straying from that beloved standard-bearer. But consider the hundreds of different nationally advertised and regional brands of salsa consumers can choose from, each in its own way different from its shelf mates. All those ever-proliferating salsas just ganged up on poor old ketchup.

Ketchup's defeat may be news to some denizens of Des Moines, Portland or Ft. Lauderdale. But in the Southwest, salsa has always been the condiment of choice. That statement immediately demands a clarification of terms. *Salsa,* after all, is Spanish for "sauce." Yet not all Southwestern sauces are called salsas.

Sauces for the most part, are cooked mixtures that are served as an integral part of a savory dish. A prime example is the traditional Mexican mole of stock, tomatoes, onions, bitter chocolate, chilies, other seasonings and such thickeners as tortillas, sesame seeds, peanuts or pumpkin seeds. Whether used as the cooking liquid for meat or poultry, or served as it often is today as an accompaniment to grilled entrées, mole nevertheless remains the end product of extensive simmering.

Southwestern salsas, on the other hand, are usually—but not always—made fresh from raw ingredients. And they are most often—but again, not always—served condiment-style, as a tabletop seasoning for each person to add to taste.

Almost any number of fresh ingredients today can be combined to make a salsa. The most common are made of tomatoes or tomatillos, red or yellow onions and fresh cilantro. But salsas are also made from such contemporary-seeming ingredients as mangoes, black

Salsa, an essential element of most Southwestern meals, can be as diverse as the cook's imagination.

Previous pages, clockwise from top left: Guacamole (recipe page 191), Southwest Seasoning Mix (recipe page 196), Taco Sauce (recipe page 197), Salsa Fresca (recipe page 201)

186

Cascading chili garlands called ristras *are strung together by hand and are at once both ornamental and functional; the dried chilies can be picked off the wreath to be used in cooking.*

beans, papayas, sweet corn, peaches, pineapples, pumpkin seeds, zucchini, avocados, melons, cranberries and cactus pads.

Whatever goes into the mixing bowl, one common element gives the resulting concoction the right to bear the name of salsa: the chili. Even here, however, the opportunity for elaboration presents itself in vast profusion: dried red chilies. Mild New Mexican green chilies. Fiery jalapeños or serranos or pequíns. The absolutely incendiary habanero chili and other mind-blowing kin, whose presence justifies such popular salsa names as Maddog, Hellfire and Damnation, Dog's Breath, Across the Border Tangy Backfire, Prairie Fire, Snakebite and Pistol Packin' Picante.

With such variety and such intimations of danger, it's easy to understand why many Southwesterners regard salsa as the ideal opportunity for gustatory derring-do. "Even though I'm a gringo," admits Tucson writer Tom Danehy, "I was fortunate enough to grow up in an ethnic area of L.A., so I knew about salsa from the jump. I put it on my Malt-o-Meal, mixed it into my Ovaltine, and rubbed it on my chest when we ran out of Vicks Vap-o-Rub. but mostly I dipped chips in it. For days at a time, that's all I would eat." With such aficionados, ketchup never stood a chance.

The presence of chilies also welcomes into the salsa fold one of the Southwest's best-known specialties: guacamole. An almost-alchemical event occurs when a little chopped jalapeño is combined with avocado, the suave vegetable-fruit once commonly referred to as "Indian butter." Simultaneously, the chili is tamed and

refined, even as it adds boldness to the otherwise tame main ingredient.

The chili-laced salsa sensibility has infused itself into Southwestern sauces and condiments originally carried to the region by pioneers and settlers from the East Coast. What, after all, are jalapeño-spiced chutneys or jellies but sweet and spicy salsas made in quantity and preserved for storage? Oil-and-vinegar dressing becomes, in effect, a salsa for salad when chili, onion and cilantro are introduced and a blend of citrus juices replaces the traditional vinegar. And is it any surprise that chilies have infiltrated the ketchup bottle itself, to set the tongue afire with the first bite of a burger or french fries?

Other familiar elements of salsa have worked their way into the classic sauces of French cuisine. That luscious emulsion of egg yolks and butter known as hollandaise, for example, turns emphatically Southwestern with the addition of fresh cilantro and the juice of oranges grown in Arizona's Valley of the Sun.

Even when making dessert sauces, Southwestern cooks show their love for the flavors of the region, perhaps by throwing a handful of toasted piñon nuts into a rich caramel sauce, by enlivening a warm chocolate sauce with a Mexican-style sprinkling of ground cinnamon or by simmering prickly pears with wine to make a ruby-red topping for ice cream or baked goods.

You can count on Southwestern salsas and sauces, whether sweet or savory, to be—in the words of renowned Santa Fe–based chef Mark Miller—"a mini-fiesta for the tastebuds."

Left to right: Caramel Sauce with Piñons, Mexican Chocolate Sauce

MEXICAN CHOCOLATE SAUCE

In Mexico, chocolate has been associated with cinnamon since Spanish colonial times, and the hint of cinnamon in this rich sauce gives it a wonderful complexity. Melting chocolate with coffee brings out more of the chocolate flavor and, of course, the finer the chocolate used, the better the result. Serve over ice cream or Cookie Tacos (recipe on page 216).

8 oz (250 g) bittersweet or semisweet chocolate,
  coarsely chopped
¼ cup (2 fl oz/60 ml) strong coffee
½ cup (4 fl oz/125 ml) heavy (double) cream
¼ teaspoon ground cinnamon

❁ In a heavy saucepan, melt the chocolate and coffee over low heat; add the cream and cinnamon and whisk until blended and smooth. Serve warm. Keep refrigerated for up to 1 week.

MAKES ABOUT 1½ CUPS (12 FL OZ/375 ML)

CARAMEL SAUCE WITH PIÑONS

The toasted nuts and caramelized sugar enhance each other in this rich sauce, making it a perfect topping for ice cream or Mexican Chocolate Tart (recipe on page 217), Chilled Lemon Soufflé (recipe on page 214), or Apple Tart with Jalapeño (recipe on page 215). Serve it at room temperature or slightly warm.

1 cup (8 oz/250 g) sugar
¼ cup (2 fl oz/60 ml) water
1 cup (8 fl oz/250 ml) heavy (double) cream
½ cup (2½ oz/75 g) piñon (pine) nuts, toasted (see glossary)

❁ In a heavy saucepan, bring the sugar and water to a boil over high heat, stirring occasionally. Continue to boil until the sugar melts and begins to turn brown, about 10–15 minutes. Remove the pan from heat and immediately add the cream, stirring until completely blended. Stir in the toasted nuts and let cool to room temperature. Keep refrigerated for up to 1 week.

MAKES 1½ CUPS (12 FL OZ/375 ML)

CHILE CATSUP

Use vine-ripened tomatoes to make this healthful catsup with just a hint of heat. It is a perfect condiment for hamburgers and french fries.

2 lb (1 kg) ripe tomatoes
1 cup (5 oz/155 g) finely chopped onions
½ cup (2½ oz/75 g) chopped red bell pepper (capsicum)
1 habanero chili, seeded and minced
1 teaspoon celery seed
1 teaspoon mustard seed
1 teaspoon cumin seed
1 cinnamon stick
3 tablespoons sugar
¼ cup (2 fl oz/60 ml) distilled white vinegar
½ teaspoon paprika
¼ teaspoon ground allspice
½ teaspoon chili powder
salt and freshly ground pepper to taste

Chile Catsup

❁ Core and quarter the tomatoes and place them in a large, heavy saucepan. Add the onion, bell pepper and minced chili and bring to a boil, stirring occasionally, over medium-high heat. Lower heat and simmer, uncovered, until the tomatoes are soft, about 20 minutes. Transfer the mixture to a food processor or blender and purée. Strain the purée back into the saucepan and bring to a boil over medium-high heat. Lower heat and simmer, uncovered, until reduced by half, about 1 hour.
❁ Place the seeds and cinnamon stick in a double layer of cheesecloth and tie securely with cotton string. Add the packet to the simmering tomato mixture and continue to cook for 20 minutes. Remove the spice packet and discard.
❁ Stir the sugar, vinegar, paprika, allspice and chili powder into the tomato mixture and continue to simmer, stirring occasionally, until the mixture is reduced to about 2 cups (16 fl oz/500 ml), 30–45 minutes. Add salt and pepper. Let cool, place in storage containers and refrigerate for up to 2 weeks.

MAKES 2 CUPS (16 FL OZ/500 ML)

JALAPEÑO CHUTNEY

Louise DeWald, Scottsdale author of several Arizona Highways cookbooks, shares one of her favorite recipes from Tucson's famed Canyon Ranch Spa. To meet Canyon Ranch's dietary requirements, fructose (available at natural foods stores) is used, but sugar may be substituted. Jalapeño chutney is delicious on grilled chicken or meats, with crackers or tortilla chips as an appetizer, and combined with rice for a zesty side dish.

1¼ cups (10 fl oz/315 ml) cider vinegar
2 cups (12 oz/375 g) diced seeded tomatoes
¾ cup (5 oz/155 g) diced husked tomatillos
½ cup (4 oz/125 g) fructose or sugar
½ cup (2 oz/60 g) diced onion
¼ cup (2 oz/60 g) diced Anaheim or New Mexico
    green chilies
¼ cup (1½ oz/45 g) raisins
2 tablespoons chopped fresh cilantro (coriander)
½ tablespoon minced jalapeño chili
½ teaspoon ground cumin

❁ Combine all the ingredients in a heavy saucepan and, over medium heat, bring to a boil. Lower heat and simmer, uncovered, for 1½–2 hours, or until most of the liquid has evaporated. Let cool to room temperature and store covered in the refrigerator for up to 1 week.

MAKES 2 CUPS (16 FL OZ/500 ML)

RED PEPPER SAUCE

Red jalapeños and serrano chilies are green chilies that have been allowed to ripen. This beautifully colored and flavored sauce, which uses fresh red bell peppers and chili, is a festive addition to almost any entrée, but it is particularly good served warm with Baked Southwest Chicken (recipe on page 106) or grilled chicken or meats.

1 garlic clove, minced
2 shallots, chopped
1 red jalapeño or serrano chili, diced
1 cup (8 fl oz/250 ml) chicken stock (see glossary)
2 red bell peppers (capsicums), roasted, peeled, cored, seeded and diced (see glossary)
salt and freshly ground pepper to taste

❁ In a small saucepan over medium-high heat, bring the garlic, shallots, chili and chicken stock to a boil; reduce heat and simmer for 15 minutes. Transfer the mixture to a blender, add the diced bell peppers and purée until smooth. Add salt and pepper. This recipe can be made 2–3 days ahead and refrigerated, then reheated.

MAKES ABOUT 1½ CUPS (12 FL OZ/375 ML)

RANCHERO SAUCE

The same ingredients used in many raw salsas are transformed through cooking into a mild, smooth sauce. Serve on Huevos Rancheros (recipe on page 115) or Breakfast Burritos (recipe on page 102), or use as a substitute for any fresh tomato sauce—on pizzas or spaghetti, for instance.

2 tablespoons vegetable oil
1 cup (5 oz/155 g) finely chopped onion
1 garlic clove, minced

4 cups (1½ lb/750 g) finely chopped fresh or canned tomatoes
2 Anaheim or other mild chilies, cored, seeded and chopped
1 teaspoon sugar
salt and freshly ground pepper to taste
2 tablespoons minced fresh cilantro (coriander)

❁ In a large skillet, heat the oil over medium heat; add the onion and cook for 2 minutes, stirring. Add the garlic and cook for 2 minutes more, or until the onion is translucent. Add the tomatoes, chilies, sugar, salt and pepper. Simmer until slightly thickened, about 15 minutes, stirring occasionally. Stir in the chopped cilantro. Keep refrigerated for up to 1 week.

MAKES ABOUT 4 CUPS (32 FL OZ/1 L)

Clockwise from top left: Ranchero Sauce, Jalapeño Chutney, Red Pepper Sauce

GUACAMOLE

This versatile salsa, a combination of chilies, onion and avocado, is prevalent throughout the Southwest and California. Although it is possible to make guacamole in a food processor or blender, it is best when it is slightly chunky, so mashing the avocados with a fork or in a mortar is preferable. Guacamole is delicious served as a dip with tortilla chips and raw vegetables, as part of a layered appetizer, as a salad dressing or as a topping for chimichangas, tacos, enchiladas or tostadas.

3 large ripe avocados
2 tablespoons fresh lime juice
1 ripe tomato, diced
2 green (spring) onions, finely chopped
2 Anaheim chilies, roasted, peeled, seeded and diced
   (see glossary)
1 jalapeño chili, seeded and minced
¼ cup (2 oz/60 g) sour cream
salt to taste

❁ Peel the avocados and remove the pits. In a medium bowl, mash the avocados with the lime juice. Stir in the tomatoes, green onions, chilies and sour cream. Taste for seasoning and add salt. If not using immediately, cover and store in the refrigerator with an avocado pit pressed into the mixture (this helps to prevent discoloration).

MAKES ABOUT 1½ CUPS (12 OZ/375 G) *Photograph pages 184–185*

Top left: Jalapeño Jelly; top right: Prickly Pear Jelly;
bottom left: Margarita Jam

ARIZONA

PRICKLY PEAR JELLY

The beautiful color of this jelly is due to the deep, rich shade of the fruit, traditionally used by native Americans as a dye for yarn or thread. Prickly pears have a lovely mild flavor that makes a delicate-tasting jelly. Besides being delicious on breads, it may be thinned down with red wine to make a sauce for meats, or with sweet white wine for a dessert sauce.

3 cups (1½ lb/750 g) chopped, peeled prickly pear fruit
  (about 6 large pears)
2 cups (16 fl oz/500 ml) water
2 cups (16 oz/500 g) sugar
¼ cup (2 fl oz/60 ml) fresh lemon juice (optional)
⅓ cup (3 fl oz/90 ml) liquid pectin

✿ Place the chopped prickly pears and water in a heavy saucepan and bring to a boil over medium-high heat. Reduce heat and simmer for 15 minutes. Transfer the mixture to a food processor or blender and purée. Strain the mixture back into the saucepan; add the sugar and bring to a boil. Taste and, if desired, add the fresh lemon juice for a tarter flavor. Add the liquid pectin and bring to a boil; cook, stirring, for 1 minute. Pour into hot sterilized jars (see glossary); let cool and refrigerate up to 1 month.

MAKES 4 CUPS (32 FL OZ/1 L)

SOUTHWEST

JALAPEÑO JELLY

Lovely to look at, this unusual jelly makes a special holiday gift. For a quick, simple hors d'oeuvre, spread jalapeño jelly over a block of cream cheese and surround with crackers. It can also be served as a condiment for lamb.

1 cup (5 oz/155 g) finely chopped red bell
  pepper (capsicum)
1 cup (5 oz/155 g) finely chopped green bell
  pepper (capsicum)
½ cup (3 oz/90 g) seeded and minced jalapeño chili
6 cups (3 lb/1.5 kg) sugar
1½ cups (12 fl oz/375 ml) cider vinegar
¾ cup (6 fl oz/180 ml) liquid pectin

✿ In a heavy saucepan, stir together the peppers, chili, sugar and vinegar. Bring to a boil, stirring, until the sugar is dissolved. Stir in the pectin and cook for 1 or 2 minutes. Remove from heat, let cool until slightly thickened, then stir and ladle into hot sterilized jars (see glossary). If sealed with paraffin, the jelly will keep for 2 months unrefrigerated. If kept covered in the refrigerator, the jelly will keep up to 2–3 months.

MAKES 6 CUPS (48 FL OZ/1.5 L)

MARGARITA JAM

Like the popular Mexican cocktail, this jam blends the flavors of lime, tequila and Triple Sec, an orange-flavored liqueur. It is delicious over cream cheese on crackers, on corn muffins or as the base for a dessert sauce.

⅔ cup (5 fl oz/160 ml) tequila
⅓ cup (3 fl oz/80 ml) Triple Sec
⅔ cup (5 fl oz/160 ml) fresh lime juice
2 tablespoons grated lime zest
3 cups (1½ lb/750 g) sugar
⅓ cup (3 fl oz/80 ml) liquid pectin

✹ In a heavy saucepan, stir together the tequila, Triple Sec, lime juice, the zest and sugar. Bring to a boil over medium heat, stirring, until the sugar is dissolved. Add the pectin and stir for 1 minute. Ladle into hot, sterilized jars and seal (see glossary). If sealed with paraffin, the jam will keep for 2 months unrefrigerated. If kept covered in the refrigerator, the jam will keep up to 2–3 months.

MAKES 4 CUPS (32 FL OZ/1 L)

PRICKLY PEAR WINE SAUCE

Rich in color and flavor, this delicious sauce is good on both desserts and grilled meats. Prickly pears are available almost year round in specialty food stores or the produce section of Latino grocery stores.

2 cups (16 fl oz/500 ml) red wine, preferably Cabernet
    Sauvignon, Zinfandel, or Pinot Noir
8 oz (250 g) prickly pears (about 4), peeled and diced
½ cup (4 oz/125 g) sugar
¼ teaspoon freshly ground black pepper

✹ Combine all the ingredients in a heavy, nonaluminum saucepan and bring to a boil, stirring occasionally. Reduce by half, about 10–15 minutes, watching it carefully toward the end so that it doesn't burn. Remove from heat, strain into a clean bowl and let cool. This sauce will keep refrigerated for as long as a month. Serve it cold on ice cream or with cakes and tarts or serve warm with grilled chicken.

MAKES ABOUT 1⅓ CUPS (10½ FL OZ/325 ML)

Prickly Pear Wine Sauce

MOLE

Mole, an Aztec word meaning "mixture," usually refers to a complex sauce containing chilies. There are numerous kinds of moles, but most are rather elaborate and time-consuming. Turkey, chicken or meat may be cooked slowly in mole for special celebrations, but the sauce may also be used to top grilled poultry or meat. Roxsand Scoccos, chef-owner of RoxSand Restaurant in Phoenix, Arizona, shares her version of mole, which she uses with grilled pork tenderloin, although it also would be a wonderful sauce for duck, chicken or turkey.

6 ancho chilies
4 tablespoons lard
¼ cup (1½ oz/45 g) raw sesame seeds
4 corn tortillas (6 in/15 cm in diameter), cut into ½-in (12-mm) strips
1 cup (5 oz/155 g) finely chopped onions
1 cup (6 oz/185 g) chopped seeded tomatoes

½ cup (¾ oz/20 g) chopped fresh cilantro (coriander)
1 bay leaf, crushed
½ teaspoon ground cinnamon
½ teaspoon freshly ground black pepper
½ teaspoon salt
¼ teaspoon ground cloves
½ teaspoon ground cumin
½ teaspoon cayenne pepper
½ teaspoon oregano
4 oz (125 g) bittersweet chocolate, chopped
3½ cups (28 fl oz/875 ml) chicken stock (see glossary)
½ cup (2½ oz/75 g) cashews, toasted and chopped (see glossary)

❀ Cover the ancho chilies with hot water and soak for 30 minutes. Reserve ⅓ cup (3 fl oz/80 ml) of the soaking water. Stem and seed the chilies.
❀ In a medium skillet, heat 1 tablespoon of the lard over medium heat. Fry the chilies for 30 seconds on each side. Remove the chilies from the skillet and add the sesame seeds; stir until toasted lightly, about 1 minute. Remove the

Left to right: Mole, Green Chili Sauce, Red Chili Sauce

N E W   M E X I C O

GREEN CHILI SAUCE

One chili that has adapted extremely well to New Mexico is a mild, long green variety that turns red in the fall. Cultivated in Anaheim, California, since the early 1900s, the New Mexico variety is slightly hotter than the Anaheim. This versatile sauce is good over enchiladas or as an accompaniment to shrimp, grilled poultry, fish or meat. For a delicious sauce with lamb, substitute fresh mint for the cilantro.

1 jalapeño chili, seeded and diced
1 garlic clove, crushed
¼ cup (¾ oz/20 g) chopped green (spring) onions
4 tomatillos, husked and diced
1½ cups (12 fl oz/375 ml) chicken stock (see glossary)
2 New Mexico green or Anaheim chilies, roasted, peeled, cored, seeded and diced (see glossary)
¼ cup (⅓ oz/10 g) chopped fresh cilantro (coriander)
1 tablespoon fresh lime juice
1 tablespoon heavy (double) cream
salt and freshly ground pepper to taste

❀ In a medium saucepan, place the jalapeño, garlic, green onions, tomatillos and chicken stock. Bring to a boil over medium-high heat; reduce heat and simmer until the liquid is reduced to about 1 cup (8 fl oz/250 ml), about 15–20 minutes.
❀ Pour the chicken stock mixture into a blender or food processor. Add the Anaheim chilies, cilantro and lime juice; purée until smooth. Add salt and pepper. Add the cream and mix again. Serve warm. Keep 1–2 days, refrigerated.

MAKES 1½ CUPS (12 FL OZ/375 ML)

N E W   M E X I C O

RED CHILI SAUCE

This classic sauce is used in enchiladas, huevos rancheros, tamales, soups, beans and so on; it is also an excellent marinade for steak or chicken. New Mexico green chilies turn red when they dry and are strung together decoratively in cascades called ristras.

10 whole dried New Mexico chilies
1 tablespoon olive oil
1 cup (5 oz/155 g) finely chopped onions
2 garlic cloves, minced
about 2 cups (16 fl oz/500 ml) chicken stock (see glossary)
2 tablespoons lard or vegetable oil
salt to taste

❀ Preheat an oven to 250°F (120°C). Place the chilies in a heavy skillet and roast them dry in the hot oven for 3–4 minutes, being careful not to let them burn. Fill a pot just large enough to hold the chilies with water; bring the water to a boil and remove the pot from heat. Add the roasted chilies to the hot water and, using a weight such as a pot lid, keep them submerged until they are soft, about 20 or 30 minutes. Remove the chilies from the water, stem, seed and tear them into strips.
❀ Heat the olive oil in a medium skillet over low heat; add the onion and sauté until browned, about 5 minutes.
❀ Put the chili strips, sautéed onion, garlic and 1 cup (8 fl oz/250 ml) of the chicken stock into a food processor or a blender and purée until smooth; strain.
❀ Heat the lard or vegetable oil in a heavy skillet over medium heat. Add the chili mixture to the hot oil and cook, stirring, for about 5 minutes. Add chicken stock until the sauce is the desired consistency. Add salt to taste. Cover and refrigerate until ready to use. Keep 2–3 days, refrigerated.

MAKES ABOUT 2 CUPS (16 FL OZ/500 ML)

sesame seeds from the skillet and set aside. Add 1 tablespoon of lard to the skillet and, when hot, add the tortilla strips; fry until soft, about 2 minutes.
❀ Place the chilies, sesame seeds, tortilla strips and reserved soaking water in a blender and purée to a paste; set aside.
❀ In a large skillet, heat the remaining 2 tablespoons lard over medium-high heat; sauté the onions until translucent, about 3 minutes. Add the tomatoes and cilantro and cook for 2 minutes. Add the bay leaf, cinnamon, pepper, salt, cloves, cumin, cayenne and oregano and cook, stirring, for 2 minutes, or until well blended. Add the chopped chocolate and continue cooking and stirring until the chocolate is melted, about 2 minutes. Add the chicken stock and cashews and bring to a boil. Add the puréed chili mixture and stir well. Lower the heat and simmer, uncovered, stirring occasionally, for 15–20 minutes, or until the mixture thickens and the flavors have blended. Serve with grilled pork tenderloin, duck breasts, chicken or turkey.

MAKES ABOUT 3 CUPS (24 FL OZ/750 ML)

Avocado Butter served with corn bread sticks

SOUTHWEST SEASONING MIX

By combining the spices of the region in one mix, the earthy, pungent flavors of the Southwest are obtained as easily as reaching into the cupboard. Like all spices, however, this mix will lose its potency with age, so make it in small batches. Rub it on meats or poultry before grilling, add it to bread crumbs for a coating mixture or stir a spoonful into simmering vegetables.

1 tablespoon chili powder
1 tablespoon paprika
1 teaspoon cumin seed
1 teaspoon ground coriander
1 teaspoon sugar
1 teaspoon salt
½ teaspoon freshly ground pepper
½ teaspoon cayenne pepper

❉ Place all the ingredients in a blender or spice grinder and blend. Transfer to a glass jar and store for up to one month in a cool, dry place.

MAKES ABOUT ¼ CUP (2 OZ/60 G)   *Photograph pages 184–185*

AVOCADO BUTTER

Delicious on bread, grilled fish or chicken, or corn on the cob, this butter will keep its delicate color for several days if tightly covered with plastic wrap and refrigerated. For a special occasion, place the softened butter in a butter mold before refrigerating; unmold when firm.

½ cup (4 oz/125 g) unsalted butter at room temperature
½ cup (3 oz/ 90 g) mashed ripe avocado
¼ cup (2 fl oz/60 ml) fresh lemon juice
2 tablespoons minced fresh Italian (flat-leaf) parsley
2 garlic cloves, minced
⅛ teaspoon red hot pepper sauce
salt to taste

❉ Place all the ingredients in a food processor or blender and process until blended. Taste and correct the seasoning. Place in a decorative bowl or butter molds; cover and refrigerate up to 1 week.

MAKES 1 CUP (8 OZ/250 G)

196

TACO SAUCE

This mild yet zesty sauce is good with either shredded chicken or beef in tacos, and is also a good accompaniment to grilled meats, poultry and hamburgers.

4 cups (1½ lb/750 g) quartered ripe tomatoes
1 tablespoon vegetable oil
1 cup (5 oz/155 g) finely chopped onions
2 large garlic cloves, minced
1 teaspoon dried oregano
1 teaspoon ground cumin
1 teaspoon ground coriander
1 tablespoon tomato paste
1 jalapeño chili, seeded and minced
2 teaspoons sugar
1 tablespoon minced cilantro (coriander)
2 teaspoons red wine vinegar
salt and freshly ground pepper to taste

❀ Place the tomatoes in a food processor or blender and purée. In a large skillet, heat the oil over medium heat. Add the onions and garlic and sauté until the onion is translucent, about 3 minutes. Add the oregano, cumin and coriander and continue to cook, stirring, for 2 minutes. Stir in all the remaining ingredients. Reduce heat and simmer, stirring frequently, until mixture is thickened, about 15–20 minutes. Let cool to room temperature, cover and store in the refrigerator for up to 1 week.

MAKES 2 CUPS (16 FL OZ/500 ML)   *Photograph pages 184–185*

ORANGE-CILANTRO HOLLANDAISE

This flavorful variation on the classic recipe is delicious over split Jalapeño Scones (recipe on page 141) topped with smoked ham or salmon and poached eggs: a Southwest eggs Benedict. Try it over cooked fresh asparagus for an elegant first course.

1 cup (8 fl oz/250 ml) fresh orange juice
4 shallots, minced
2 egg yolks
¾ cup (6 oz/180 g) unsalted butter, melted and warm
2 teaspoons grated orange zest
¼ cup (⅓ oz/10 g) minced fresh cilantro (coriander)
salt and freshly ground pepper to taste

❀ Place the orange juice and shallots in a small saucepan and, over medium heat, cook until almost no liquid is left in the pan. In a nonaluminum bowl, whisk the egg yolks; add the shallot mixture. Place the bowl in a pan of simmering water over medium heat and whisk constantly until thick, about 3–5 minutes. Remove from heat and, in a slow stream, add the butter to the yolk mixture, whisking constantly. If the sauce is too thick, add a little hot water. Add the orange zest, cilantro, salt and pepper, and serve immediately. To hold the sauce for 1–2 hours, put it in a Thermos that has been rinsed with boiling water and dried.

MAKES ABOUT 1 CUP (8 FL OZ/250 ML)

Orange-Cilantro Hollandaise

SONORAN DESERT, ARIZONA

CILANTRO-CITRUS VINAIGRETTE

Because of its tangy combination of citrus juices, this versatile vinaigrette can be used in a number of ways: drizzled over lightly steamed vegetables, tossed with greens, used as a marinade for vegetables or poultry, and served as a lovely complement to avocados, tomatoes, and citrus. If achiote seeds are not available, you may make the vinaigrette without them, although it will not have the same deep orange color.

⅓ cup (3 fl oz/80 ml) vegetable oil
1 tablespoon achiote (annatto) seeds
1 red serrano chili, seeded and minced
1 garlic clove, minced
2 green (spring) onions, finely chopped
1 tablespoon minced fresh cilantro (coriander)
1 tablespoon fresh lemon juice
1 tablespoon fresh lime juice
1 tablespoon orange juice
salt and freshly ground pepper to taste

❀ Combine the vegetable oil and achiote seeds in a small saucepan and cook over medium heat, stirring, until the oil is a deep orange color, about 5 minutes. Remove from heat; strain the oil into a clean bowl and let cool.

❀ In a small bowl, whisk together the serrano chili, garlic, green onions, cilantro and citrus juices. Slowly whisk in the cooled oil. Add salt and pepper. Keep refrigerated up to 2 weeks if not using immediately.

MAKES ¾ CUP (6 FL OZ/180 ML)

SEDONA, ARIZONA

SPICY CUCUMBER DRESSING

This healthy, low-fat dressing is delicious on poached or grilled fish, tossed with lettuces or served as a dip with raw vegetables. For best results, use an English cucumber (unwaxed and usually wrapped in plastic).

¾ cup (3½ oz/105 g) peeled, seeded and finely chopped
  cucumber
2 tablespoons minced fresh dill
1 teaspoon minced jalapeño chili
3 garlic cloves
2 tablespoons fresh lemon juice
1½ cups (12 oz/375 g) non-fat plain yogurt
2 tablespoons olive oil
salt and freshly ground pepper to taste

Left to right: Cilantro-Citrus Vinaigrette, Spicy Cucumber Dressing

Green Chili Salsa

❀ Place the cucumber, dill, jalapeño and garlic in a blender and process until smooth and creamy. Pour into a bowl and fold in the remaining ingredients. Keep refrigerated up to 2–3 days.

MAKES ABOUT 2¼ CUPS (18 FL OZ/560 ML)

New Mexico

GREEN CHILI SALSA

A combination of chilies, tomatillos and nopalitos, this slightly tart salsa is good with grilled fish or poultry, on quesadillas or on tortilla chips. Nopalitos are julienned prickly pear cactus pads, available pickled in cans or jars at specialty foods markets and Latino grocery stores. If you are able to buy fresh cactus pads (nopales), clean off the little barbs and boil or steam the pads for about 15 minutes. When tender, scrape off the stickers with a sharp knife and cut the pads into julienne.

¼ cup (1½ oz/45 g) chopped nopalitos
4 New Mexico green or Anaheim chilies, roasted, peeled, seeded and diced (see glossary)
1 poblano chili, roasted, peeled, seeded and diced (see glossary)
1 green bell pepper (capsicum), cored, seeded and diced
1 red or yellow bell pepper (capsicum), cored, seeded and diced
1 serrano chili, seeded and diced
¼ cup (1 oz/30 g) chopped red (Spanish) onion
½ cup (3 oz/90 g) chopped husked tomatillos
½ cup (3 oz/90 g) chopped tomato
2 tablespoons fresh lime juice
1 tablespoon chopped fresh cilantro (coriander)
salt to taste

❀ Combine all the ingredients in a nonaluminum bowl and allow the flavors to blend at room temperature for at least 30 minutes. Salsa can be kept, covered in the refrigerator up to 1 week.

MAKES ABOUT 2 CUPS (16 FL OZ/500 ML)

TOMATILLO SALSA

Tomatillos look like small green tomatoes, except they have a papery husk. Now available in most grocery stores, they make a slightly more acidic salsa than tomatoes, which makes them a good foil for rich, buttery dishes. The apple juice in the recipe brings out the natural, slightly apple flavor of the tomatillos. This lovely green and red salsa enhances cheese quesadillas, tortilla chips and grilled fish, poultry or meat.

8 oz (250 g) tomatillos (about 5), husked
  and diced
2 Anaheim chilies, roasted, peeled, cored, seeded and
  diced (see glossary)

1 red bell pepper (capsicum), roasted, peeled, cored, seeded
  and diced (see glossary)
2 plum (egg) tomatoes, diced
1 jalapeño chili, seeded and diced
½ cup (1½ oz/45 g) finely chopped green (spring) onions
2 garlic cloves, minced
1 teaspoon cumin seed, crushed to a coarse powder
2 tablespoons cider vinegar
1 tablespoon apple juice
salt and freshly ground pepper to taste

❀ Combine all the ingredients in a nonaluminum bowl; let stand for 1 hour before serving to allow the flavors to mellow. Keep 1 week, refrigerated.

MAKES ABOUT 2½ CUPS (20 FL OZ/625 ML)

3 tablespoons minced fresh cilantro (coriander)
1 papaya, peeled, seeded and diced
2 tablespoons fresh lime juice
1½ teaspoons seasoned rice vinegar
3 green (spring) onions, finely chopped
1 habanero chili, finely chopped
⅛ teaspoon cayenne pepper
salt and freshly ground pepper to taste

❋ In a large, nonaluminum bowl, combine all the ingredients and adjust seasoning. Refrigerate until ready to serve. This is best the day it is made, but will keep for up to 1 week in the refrigerator.

MAKES ABOUT 4 CUPS (32 FL OZ/1 L)

S A N T A   F E ,   N E W   M E X I C O

PUMPKIN SEED SALSA

Green pumpkin seeds add a delightful crunch to this red, yellow and green salsa. Serve with poultry or fish for an intriguing combination of tastes and textures.

1 cup (6 oz/185 g) cooked corn kernels
1½ cups (9 oz/280 g) chopped tomatoes
1 New Mexico green or Anaheim chili, roasted, peeled, seeded and chopped (see glossary)
1 red serrano chili, seeded and diced
2 tablespoons fresh lime juice
¼ teaspoon ground cumin
1 cup (5 oz/155 g) unsalted green pumpkin seeds (pepitas), toasted (see glossary)
salt and freshly ground pepper to taste

❋ In a nonaluminum bowl, mix together the corn, tomatoes, chilies, lime juice and cumin. Stir in the toasted pumpkin seeds. Taste and adjust the seasoning with salt and pepper.

MAKES ABOUT 3½ CUPS (28 FL OZ/875 ML)

Clockwise from left: Pumpkin Seed Salsa, Tomatillo Salsa, Pineapple Salsa

P H O E N I X ,   A R I Z O N A

PINEAPPLE SALSA

Susan Fillhouer Begin, a caterer and an assistant at Les Gourmettes Cooking School in Phoenix, developed this sweet-spicy salsa. It is delicious on grilled fresh tuna, with chicken quesadillas or on blue corn chips. The habanero is one of the hottest chilies in the world, thirty to fifty times as spicy as a jalapeño, so be careful when handling it and use sparingly.

1 large pineapple, peeled, cored and diced
1 red bell pepper (capsicum), cored, seeded and diced
½ green bell pepper (capsicum), cored, seeded and diced
1 cup (5 oz/155 g) finely chopped red (Spanish) onion

S O U T H W E S T

SALSA FRESCA

Salsa is the new favorite condiment of American cooking. Also known as salsa fría, pico de gallo, salsa cruda, salsa picante and salsa Mexicana, this fresh relish may be made mild, medium or hot by adjusting the number of serrano chilies added. Serve with chips, quesadillas, burritos, eggs or meat.

3 ripe tomatoes, finely chopped
½ cup (2½ oz/75 g) finely chopped onion
1 to 3 serrano chilies, cored, seeded and minced
1 Anaheim chili, cored, seeded and finely chopped
2 tablespoons minced fresh cilantro (coriander)
1 teaspoon sugar
1 tablespoon fresh lime juice
salt and freshly ground pepper to taste

❋ Mix all the ingredients together in a nonaluminum bowl and allow the flavors to blend at room temperature for at least 1 hour. The salsa will keep in the refrigerator for up to 2 weeks.

MAKES ABOUT 1½ CUPS (12 FL OZ/375 ML) *Photograph pages 184–185*

BORDERLANDS

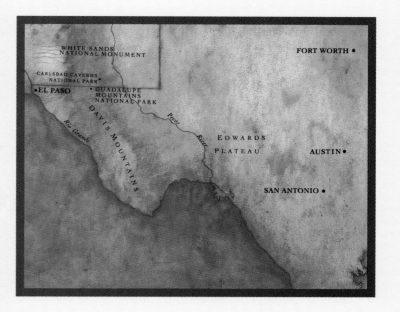

BORDERLANDS

F or more than eight hundred miles as the eagle flies, the Rio Grande winds its way along the border between Texas and Mexico. Starting at El Paso, it flows past the Davis Mountains and the Sierra Madre Oriental, through the canyons of Big Bend National Park and the vast reservoirs of Val Verde and Zapata counties, finally descending through the alluvial plain of the Lower Rio Grande Valley to enter the Gulf of Mexico at the city of Brownsville.

The Borderlands has long been an area of intense interaction between the Latino and Anglo worlds. Several major Texan cities enjoy sister status with Mexican cities across the narrow stretch of water: El Paso and Juarez, Laredo and Nuevo Laredo, Brownsville and Matamoros. That interaction infuses this easternmost region of the Southwest with a culture uniquely its own, reaching more than two hundred miles inland to central Texas to embrace historic San Antonio, the state capital of Austin and the Texas Hill Country to the west of those cities.

A unique version of Southwestern cooking has evolved here as well. The term "Tex-Mex" is used with pride inside Texas; but outside the state, and particularly in Mexico, folks sometimes use it with derision to

Previous pages: Mission Concepcion in San Antonio is the eighteenth-century legacy of the Spanish who first colonized Texas. Left: Originally built as a church in 1722, the Alamo became a fortress when a handful of Texas rebels defended themselves against overwhelming forces as they attempted to secede from Mexico in 1836.

*While in bloom, century plants attract such desert creatures as
hummingbirds, bats, butterflies and various insects.*

describe what they consider a sort of culinary bastard. *Hybrid* would be a better term for a cuisine that combines the best of northern Mexican cooking and the hearty fare of the cowboy chuck wagon with the foods of the American South and of the German and Czech immigrants who flocked to the Hill Country during the mid-nineteenth century.

Southerners lay claim to the barbecued and fire-grilled meats that are so much a part of Borderlands cuisine, and you can see their influence in the bastes and sauces that harken back to good old Dixie-style "mops" daubed onto beef or pork while it slowly cooked. But Texas cowboys and their south-of-the-border counterparts, the *caballeros,* deserve some of the credit as well: what simpler way could there be, after all, to cook your meat out on the range than over an open campfire? Middle and Eastern Europeans played their part, too, by bringing a tradition of smoked meats with them to the Hill Country.

But, truth be told, barbecuing predates all these Johnny-come-latelies. Before the arrival of Europeans, a hodgepodge of migrating tribes such as the Conchos and Chisos, the Sumas and Jumanos, the Tobosos and Mansos lived in what is now the Borderlands, hunting animals ranging in size from rabbits to buffalo. Archaeological evidence shows that they cooked these meats in fire pits or impaled on sticks over the flames. Of course, many others had their hands in the evolu-

tion of the carefully tended, smokey, barbecue served in Texas today; but, in the strictest sense, they were only contributors to a tradition that came long before.

The same mixed heritage produced what is possibly the best-known Tex-Mex dish: chili con carne. You'll find any number of authoritative, scholarly explanations for that definitive stew of meat, chilies and other ingredients—either mixed with or accompanied with the ubiquitous boiled pinto beans of the region. To his eternal credit, Dallas journalist and high chili priest Frank X. Tolbert covers them all in his definitive, richly anecdotal history, *A Bowl of Red.* Tolbert himself supports the theory that chili originated among the poorer citizens of San Antonio sometime around the third decade of the nineteenth century. He cites an 1828 account of a visit to that city by one J.C. Clopper, who observed that when a family there could only afford a small amount of meat, "it is generally cut into a kind of hash with nearly as many peppers as there are pieces of meat—this is all stewed together."

But Tolbert also cites the story of Sister Mary of Agreda, as told in George Leonard Herter's book *Bull Cook and Authentic Historical Recipes and Practices.* Legend has it, according to Herter, that in the early seventeenth century a young Spanish nun slipped into trances in her convent in Castile and appeared as a miraculous vision preaching Christianity to the Jumano tribe some six thousand miles away near the

Still an active parish, Mission San Juan, built in the eighteenth century in San Antonio, evokes the architecture of the Mediterranean.

Rio Grande. She supposedly recorded their recipe for venison or antelope cooked with musk hog, onions, tomatoes and the fiery little chiltepín chilies that grow wild in the region. Even if you don't buy the Mary of Agreda tale, a grain of plausible truth remains: The basic ingredients for chili were available in the Borderlands for many years before the earliest verifiable accounts of the dish.

Whatever the actual origin of chili con carne, San Antonio has made it its own. By 1880, the city was noteworthy for its "chili queens." Come nightfall, these Mexican-American women would roll rustic carts into the plazas of the downtown area and set up tiny open-air cafes—each with a table covered with a checkered oilcloth, some stools, a brightly colored lamp and a charcoal or mesquite fire over which an iron cauldron of chili bubbled. Bedecked in colorful Mexican dresses with bunches of flowers pinned to their bosoms, these women were as enticing as the spicy aromas their food sent wafting into the air.

The chili queens were a fixture of the city until 1943, when they were forced to conform to strict health ordinances that quickly closed them down; today, they are remembered in a Return of the Chili Queens festival on Memorial Day weekend each year. Yet, by the time of the queens' passing, San Antonio was winning millions of chili converts across the nation, thanks largely to the efforts of William Gebhardt. Starting in 1896 at his first factory in the Hill Country town of New Braunfels, he began manufacturing and selling what may well have been the first commercial chili powder: a finely ground blend of dried chilies, oregano, cumin and garlic. Twelve years later, at larger quarters in San Antonio, he began to package chili con carne in a can: the well-known Gebhardt's Chili that for decades was most Americans' first taste of anything remotely resembling Southwestern food.

A similar tale of individual enterprise leading to nationwide fame is recounted by food historian Betty Fussell in her marvelous and exhaustive *The Story of Corn:*

> In San Antonio in 1932, a man named Elmer Doolin bought a five-cent package of corn chips at a small cafe, liked what he ate and tracked down the Mexican who made them. For $100, Doolin bought the Mexican's 'recipe' for *tortillas fritos* and his manufacturing equipment, an old potato ricer. Doolin handed over both to his mother, whereupon Mrs. Daisy Dean Doolin and son began to turn out ten pounds of fritos a day until they could afford to move to Dallas and expand. Expand they did through World War II, when they joined with H.W. Lay potato chips to fill America's eternal hunger for the salty, the crisp and the portable.

Most of us who grew up munching Fritos corn chips never knew they were born in San Antonio from a Mexican's recipe for fried corn tortillas. In their own humble way, over the years these chips have been subtly priming American taste buds for the present-day popularity of Southwestern food.

Farmlands follow the course of the Rio Grande in southwestern Texas; here, a hand attends to his windmill.

*El Paso has long served as a major link
between Old and New Mexico.*

DESSERTS AND BEVERAGES

Early European settlers brought a new dimension to the ancient cuisine of the Southwest when they introduced fruits such as apples; here, orchards thrive in southeastern Utah.

DESSERTS AND BEVERAGES

Nature has offered many sweet gifts to the native peoples of the Southwest. Throughout the sometimes desolate desert region, as summer mellows into autumn, the prickly pear cactus yields its plump fruit. Called *tunas* by Hispanic settlers, this spine-covered fruit conceals a rich, sugary, ruby-colored pulp ready to be eaten fresh, or to be juiced and boiled down for a range of syrups, sorbets, preserves and confections. Wild berries, such as elderberries and manzanita berries, have long been treasured by desert inhabitants.

Various species of succulents and cacti, including the agave and the saguaro, yielded up their sugary pulps to be eaten as a sweet by native peoples. Fresh corn kernels, naturally rich and creamy, could be blended with honey and water and then left outside on subfreezing winter nights to make a sort of ice cream.

Nuts, too, have long provided Southwesterners with a generous measure of sweet savor, along with rich sources of fat and protein. Black walnuts thrive along foothill and mountain streams and canyons. In fact, the town of Nogales, Arizona, takes its name from the Spanish word for *walnut*.

The Southwest's signature nut, without doubt, is the seed of the piñon pine, or pine nut, in these parts more properly called the *piñon*. Consisting of some 60 percent fat, 17 percent carbohydrates and 15 percent protein, the sweet, slightly resinous-tasting nuts were a staple of Hopis, Navajos and other tribes, who ground the nuts

and their shells into a nutritious flour, and even boiled them in water to make a nutritious soup that was given to motherless infants.

Native Americans still derive income from pine nuts, gathering the nuts in the autumn and selling them for use in a myriad of baked goods, candies and other specialties. Piñon brittle, piñon fudge, piñon cookies, piñon pancakes: wherever tourists throng, there will be piñon treats to entice them.

Other fruits, though not indigenous, have found welcome homes both in the parched valleys and high, cool mountains of the Southwest. Early European settlers carried with them the seeds, pits and seedlings for the various types of peaches, apricots and apples that now thrive in Cochise County, Arizona; Lincoln County, New Mexico; Gillespie County, Texas; and high-altitude points all over the area. As a result, cobblers and fruit pies are now part of the Southwestern table.

During the eighteenth century, citrus trees made their way northward into Arizona's Sonora Desert along with the Spanish missionaries. These trees were the progenitors of now-thriving orchards of grapefruit and lemons, juice oranges and tangerines, which add their gemlike color and bracing tartness to pastries and ices, fruit salads and soufflés.

Dates arrived more recently in 1917, when the Department of Agriculture acquired some palms from

Ice cream is the perfect dessert for a hot summer afternoon in the Southwest.

Arabia and planted them in the Phoenix area. Soon acres of date palms surrounded the city's environs. Today most of these have been replaced by houses and businesses, but a few date "ranches," as they are called, survive—along with the local taste for sticky-sweet date-based desserts.

A strong Hispanic influence may also be seen in the region's desserts. Natillas, Mexico's version of French *oeufs à la neige* or *îles flotantes,* poise ethereal egg-white meringues atop custard sauce. The Mexican-style anise-flavored sugar cookies known as biscochitos, also spelled *bizcochitos* in some places, remain *the* definitive Christmas treat among Hispanic families, and cooks take immense pride in their own little twists on the recipe and their skill at shaping the biscuits.

Traditional recipes or native or locally grown ingredients aren't the only factors that make a dessert typically Southwestern. As leading chefs of Arizona, New Mexico and Texas would have it, just the form and vernacular of local cooking alone can bestow regional status on desserts of farther-flung origins. Artfully fold or wrap French-inspired cookies or crêpes around any sweet filling of your choice and you can, without too great a stretch of the imagination, call them tacos, enchiladas or burritos. Add the merest hint of chili—which, after all, is botanically a fruit—to an apple tart or a chocolate dessert and you've infused it with the region's subtle fire. Mold imported French or Belgian chocolate in the form of a chili or an arrowhead and—presto!—it becomes an astonishing Southwestern confection.

Like the desserts of the Southwest, the region's most famous beverages combine New and Old World offerings—some of them to mind-bending effect. The popular cocktail known as the Margarita begins with tequila, a Mexican spirit distilled from the juice of the agave plant, or *mescal.* Add to that the juice of the lime, introduced by Spanish missionaries, and a splash of orange-flavored Triple Sec or Cointreau liqueur, and the liquor takes on a companionable demeanor that almost completely masks its potency.

Many have taken credit for originating the Margarita. But the most convincing claim seems to have come from one Francisco "Pancho" Morales, who came up with the now-classic formula in 1942 while tending bar at Tommy's Place in Juarez, just across the border from El Paso. From there the drink spread throughout the Southwest and across the United States, largely accounting for the fact that tequila remains one of the best-selling spirits in North America.

While a Margarita may be just the thing to wash down a pile of nachos or some guacamole and chips, beer is an equally refreshing and moderately less intoxicating bet to accompany a Southwestern meal. The many beers of Mexico admirably partner hearty, spicy food and are popular north of the border. Regional beers of the Southwest also enjoy a well-deserved following, from the German-style brews of the Texas Hill Country to the award-winning ales and porters of boutique breweries in the Santa Fe area.

The elegance of contemporary Southwestern cooking, with its subtle flavors and fine sauces, understandably calls for wine. And regional wine makers have responded admirably, following a tradition first established by Spanish missionaries. Early wines probably lacked distinction and were best enjoyed combined with fruit juices and ice in the refreshing Spanish punch known as sangría. But, just as in California's Napa Valley, the latest techniques of modern wine science and the dedication of ambitious, visionary vintners have brought distinction to wines from central Texas to Lubbock County; from Las Cruces, New Mexico to Tucson, Arizona; and from the Espanola Valley north of Santa Fe to Colorado Springs, Colorado. Such locally grown and produced varietal wines as Chenin Blancs and Rieslings, Cabernets and Muscat Canellis can complement every course of a fine Southwestern meal.

Indigenous to the desert, piñons have long been an important uncultivated crop to native Americans and are the signature nut of the Southwest.

MARGARITA ROULADE

Vary the taste and presentation of this refreshing, light dessert by serving it with different sauces: Prickly Pear Wine Sauce (recipe on page 193), Caramel Sauce with Piñons (recipe on page 189), or raspberry sauce.

CAKE

4 eggs, separated
¼ cup (2 oz/60 g) granulated sugar
1 tablespoon fresh lime juice
2 teaspoons grated lime zest
¼ teaspoon salt
½ cup (2½ oz/75 g) sifted unbleached all-purpose (plain) flour

SOAKING SYRUP

1 tablespoon fresh lime juice
2 tablespoons Triple Sec
1 tablespoon tequila

LIME CREAM

3 egg yolks
¼ cup (2 fl oz/60 ml) Triple Sec
2 teaspoons grated lime zest
2 tablespoons fresh lime juice
2 tablespoons tequila
1 teaspoon unflavored gelatin, dissolved in 2 tablespoons of cold water
½ cup (4 fl oz/125 ml) heavy (double) cream, whipped until stiff

FILLING AND TOPPING

½ cup (5 fl oz/160 ml) Margarita Jam (recipe on page 193) or lime marmalade
sifted confectioners' (icing) sugar for dusting

❀ To make the cake, preheat an oven to 375°F (190°C). Butter a 10-by-15-in (25-by-38-cm) jellyroll pan. Line the bottom with a sheet of waxed paper and butter the paper. Dust the pan with flour and tap out any excess.

❀ Beat the egg yolks in a medium bowl with an electric mixer. Gradually add the sugar, then the lime juice, lime zest and salt. Beat until the mixture is thick and pale, about 5 minutes. In a large bowl, beat the egg whites until stiff but not dry. Fold one third of the beaten egg whites into the egg yolk mixture. Sift one third of the flour over the batter and gently fold in until blended. Repeat with another one third of whites, then flour. Finish folding in the whites and flour and fill the prepared pan with the batter, spreading it evenly. Bake for 15 minutes, or until the cake is lightly browned and the edges have started to pull away from the sides of the pan. Let cool for 5 minutes.

❀ Place a damp towel on 2 wire racks placed side by side and turn the cake out onto the towel. Remove the waxed paper. Stir together all the soaking syrup ingredients and sprinkle it evenly over the cake. Starting with a long side, fold one edge up about 2 in (5 cm). Continue to roll up the cake in the towel, with the towel between the layers. Let sit until cool, at least 15 minutes but not longer than 1 hour.

❀ To make the lime cream, in a heavy nonaluminum saucepan, combine the egg yolks, Triple Sec, lime zest, lime juice and tequila. Whisk over medium heat until the mixture is thick enough to leave a trace as the whisk is pulled through it, about 10 minutes. Beat in the dissolved gelatin and whisk over heat just until well blended. Strain into a bowl and cool over a bowl of ice water, stirring occasionally, for about 10 minutes, or until cold. Fold the cooled mixture into the whipped cream. Cover and refrigerate until almost set, about 30 minutes.

❀ To serve, unroll the cake. Spread a thin layer of the jam evenly over the cake. Spread the lime cream over the jam. Roll the cake up again without the towel, allowing 2–3 in (5–7.5 cm) for the first fold. Wrap in plastic wrap and refrigerate for at least 3 hours or up to 2 days before serving. Just before serving, sprinkle with confectioners' sugar and cut into slices. If desired, serve with a fruit or caramel sauce.

SERVES 12

Top to bottom: Chilled Lemon Soufflé, Margarita Roulade

CHILLED LEMON SOUFFLÉ

After a spicy meal, a cold citrus soufflé hits the spot. Serve with Caramel Sauce with Piñons (recipe on page 189), if desired.

1 envelope unflavored gelatin
¼ cup (2 fl oz/60 ml) cold water
4 eggs, separated
1 cup (8 oz/250 g) sugar
½ cup (4 fl oz/125 ml) fresh lemon juice
1½ tablespoons grated lemon zest
1½ cups (12 fl oz/375 ml) heavy (double) cream
candied violets or candied lemon peel for garnish

❀ Place the gelatin in the cold water and set aside to soften. Prepare a 4-cup (32-fl oz/1-l) soufflé dish by tying a collar of waxed paper around the dish, extending 2 in (5 cm) above the rim. Lightly oil the inside of the dish and the paper collar.

❀ In a heavy saucepan over low heat, whisk the egg yolks until smooth. Whisk in the sugar, lemon juice and zest. Cook, stirring, until slightly thickened, about 10 minutes. Stir in the softened gelatin and cook until dissolved, 1–2 minutes. Remove from heat and pour into a bowl set over ice water; whisk until cool but not set.

❀ In a deep bowl, beat 1 cup (8 fl oz/250 ml) of the cream until soft peaks form; do not overbeat or it will not fold well into the egg mixture. Fold into the chilled lemon mixture until blended.

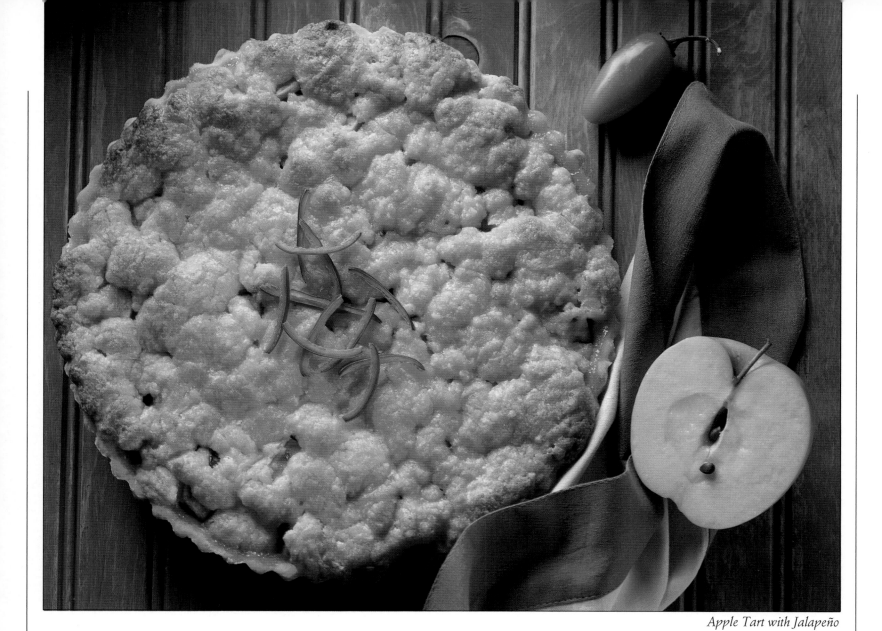

Apple Tart with Jalapeño

In a large bowl, beat the egg whites until stiff but not dry. Fold into the chilled lemon-cream mixture until blended. Scrape the mixture into the prepared dish and refrigerate until set, about 2 hours.

Remove the paper collar. In a deep bowl, beat the remaining heavy cream until stiff and place it in a pastry bag fitted with a star tip. Pipe rosettes around the top of the soufflé and top each rosette with a candied violet or a piece of candied lemon peel.

SERVES 6

APPLE TART WITH JALAPEÑO

The jalapeño in this tart does not overpower; it simply brings out the flavor of the apples and leaves a hint of spiciness on the tongue. The tart may be made without the Jalapeño Jelly and jalapeño chili but it will not have the same pizzazz.

PASTRY

½ cup (4 oz/125 g) chilled unsalted butter, cut into 8 pieces
1½ cups (7½ oz/235 g) unbleached all-purpose (plain) flour
3 tablespoons granulated sugar
¼ teaspoon salt
1 egg
3–4 tablespoons cold water

FILLING

2 tablespoons Jalapeño Jelly (recipe on page 192)
4 cups (16 oz/500 g) Granny Smith apples (about 3), peeled, cored and sliced
1 tablespoon fresh lemon juice
1 tablespoon granulated sugar
1 tablespoon unbleached all-purpose (plain) flour

½ teaspoon ground cinnamon
¼ teaspoon freshly grated nutmeg
2 tablespoons packed brown sugar
2 teaspoons minced jalapeño chili

TOPPING

½ cup (4 oz/125 g) granulated sugar
½ cup (2½ oz/75 g) unbleached all-purpose (plain) flour
¼ cup (2 oz/60 g) cold unsalted butter, cut into 8 pieces
¾ cup (3 oz/90 g) grated Monterey jack cheese

To make the crust, place butter, flour, sugar and salt in a food processor or a medium bowl and process or cut with a 2 knives or a pastry cutter until the mixture resembles a coarse meal. Add the egg and enough water to form a stiff dough. Shape the dough into a ball, cover with plastic wrap and refrigerate for 2 hours or overnight. With a rolling pin, roll the dough onto a lightly floured board to a thickness of ⅛ in (3 mm) and fit the dough in a 10-in (25-cm) springform tart pan. Prick the bottom of the shell with a fork and refrigerate until ready to use.

Preheat an oven to 350°F (180°C). To make the filling, spread the jalapeño jelly evenly over the bottom of the tart shell. Toss the apples and lemon juice together in a large bowl. In another bowl, stir together the granulated sugar, flour, cinnamon, nutmeg and brown sugar. Sprinkle the dry mixture over the apples; toss well and turn into the prepared tart shell. Sprinkle the minced jalapeño over the apples.

To make the topping, in a medium bowl, mix together the sugar and flour; cut in the butter with a fork or pastry blender. Add the cheese and mix well.

Spoon the topping evenly over the apple filling. Bake the tart until the topping and crust are golden brown, about 45 minutes. Serve warm or at room temperature.

SERVES 8–10

COOKIE TACOS

Flavorful brandy snaps are molded into a taco shape while still warm, filled with ice cream or fruit and served with a chocolate or fruit sauce. These versatile "tacos" are as good as they look!

¼ cup (2 oz/60 g) unsalted butter
¼ cup (2 fl oz/60 ml) dark corn syrup
¼ cup (2 oz/60 g) light brown sugar
¼ teaspoon ground ginger
¼ teaspoon ground cinnamon
6 tablespoons (3 oz/90 g) unbleached all-purpose
  (plain) flour
Espresso-Cinnamon Ice Cream (recipe on page 226), and
  Mexican Chocolate Sauce (recipe on page 189), or fresh
  fruit and Prickly Pear Wine Sauce (recipe on page 193)

❁ Preheat an oven to 375°F (190°C). Butter well a rolling pin. In a heavy saucepan over medium heat, melt the butter with the corn syrup, sugar and spices, stirring. Remove from heat and whisk in the flour until the mixture is smooth. Return to heat and whisk constantly for another 2 minutes.

❁ Spoon 1 tablespoon of batter per cookie onto ungreased cookie sheets, leaving at least 3 in (7.5 cm) between the cookies. Bake 1 cookie sheet at a time until the cookies are golden brown, about 6–8 minutes. Remove from the oven and let cool for 30 seconds to 1 minute. Remove a cookie from the baking sheet and mold it around the buttered rolling pin to form a U-shaped "taco." If they are too crisp to mold, return them to the hot oven for 1–2 minutes. Repeat with the remaining cookies. Let the cookies cool and harden for 2–3 minutes, then remove them from the rolling pin.

❁ Fill each cookie taco shell with espresso-cinnamon ice cream and drizzle Mexican chocolate sauce over the ice cream, or fill the shell with fresh fruit and sauce the plate with prickly pear wine sauce.

SERVES 12–16   *Photograph pages 210–211*

Left to right: Mexican Chocolate Tart, Chocolate Chimichangas

1¼ cups (10 fl oz/315 ml) heavy (double) cream
sifted cocoa or powdered sugar for garnish (optional)

❁ To make the pastry, in the bowl of an electric mixer, beat together the butter and sugar until light and fluffy; add the cinnamon and vanilla. Sift the cocoa and flour together; add to the butter-sugar mixture and mix just until combined. Shape the dough into a circle and, if the dough is very soft, refrigerate it for 30 minutes.

❁ Lay a sheet of plastic wrap on the counter, place the circle of dough on top of the plastic and cover with a second sheet of plastic. With a rolling pin, roll the dough out to a circle about 12 in (30 cm) in diameter and ⅛ in (3 mm) thick. Remove the top sheet of plastic wrap and invert the pastry circle into the bottom of a 10-in (25-cm) tart pan with a removable bottom. Pat the dough against the bottom and sides of the pan and refrigerate for 30 minutes, or until firm.

❁ Preheat an oven to 375°F (190°C). Prick the bottom of the tart shell with a fork. Bake until the tart shell is dry, about 15 minutes. Let cool.

❁ To make the filling, place the chopped chocolate in a large heatproof bowl. Heat the cream to just boiling and pour it over the chocolate. Let sit for 3 minutes, then stir until the chocolate is melted and the mixture is smooth. Pour into a cooled tart shell and refrigerate until the filling has hardened, about 3 hours. Decorate with sifted cocoa or powdered sugar, if desired.

SERVES 16

PHOENIX, ARIZONA

CHOCOLATE CHIMICHANGAS

The creation of Norman Fierros, a Phoenix chef, these bite-sized morsels will literally melt in your mouth. The hot oil barely melts the chocolate wrapped inside the crisp tortilla, and the combination is sensational.

1 bar (1 lb/500 g) milk chocolate with almonds
16 flour tortillas (6 in/15 cm in diameter)
vegetable oil for deep frying
sifted powdered sugar for sprinkling

❁ Cut the chocolate into sixteen 1-oz (30-g) bars along the lines in the bar. Using a ruler and a sharp knife, cut 1 in (2.5 cm) off the sides and bottom of the tortillas to make straight edges, then cut the top half in the shape of a wide upside-down V. The final shape will be like that of an envelope with its flap open. Heat the tortillas over the direct heat of a stove burner to soften, about 30 seconds on each side. As the tortillas are warmed, place them in a plastic bag to keep them soft.

❁ Place a piece of chocolate 1 in (2.5 cm) from the bottom of each tortilla. Fold the bottom part of the tortilla over the chocolate. Holding the folded tortilla firmly in place, fold the right side of the tortilla over the chocolate and bottom fold. Holding the first 2 folds in place, fold the left side over, then roll the tortilla toward the top until you have a folded packet. Secure with a wooden skewer.

❁ Fill a large, heavy pan with oil to a depth of 1 in (2.5 cm). Heat to 375°F (190°C) over medium-high heat, or until a bread cube dropped in the oil browns in 45 seconds. Fry the chimichangas in batches in the hot oil until golden, about 3–5 minutes. Drain on paper towels and remove the wooden skewer. Sprinkle with powdered sugar and serve warm.

MAKES 16

SAN ANTONIO, TEXAS

MEXICAN CHOCOLATE TART

Like the delicious drink chocolate con leche, this rich tart combines cocoa, cinnamon and cream. Although it's elegant without any adornment, it can be decorated easily by sifting cocoa or powdered sugar over a stencil (such as a petroglyph, a cactus or a free-form design) on top of the finished tart.

PASTRY

½ cup (4 oz/125 g) unsalted butter at room temperature
½ cup (4 oz/125 g) sugar
½ teaspoon ground cinnamon
1 teaspoon vanilla extract (essence)
¼ cup (1 oz/30 g) unsweetened cocoa powder, preferably not Dutch cocoa
¾ cup (4 oz/125 g) unbleached all-purpose (plain) flour

FILLING

10 oz (315 g) bittersweet or semisweet chocolate, finely chopped

FUDGE PIE WITH ANCHO CHILI

The chili in this chocolate sensation is detectable only as an enhancement to the chocolate flavor and as a slight tingle in the mouth. Serve this pie with butter pecan ice cream for a winning combination.

PASTRY

1½ cups (7½ oz/235 g) unbleached all-purpose (plain) flour
½ cup (4 oz/125 g) chilled unsalted butter, cut up
1 tablespoon granulated sugar
⅛ teaspoon salt
about ¼ cup (2 fl oz/60 ml) cold water

FILLING

½ cup (2 oz/125 g) walnuts, coarsely chopped
1 ancho chili
¾ cup (6 oz/180 g) unsalted butter
8 oz (250 g) bittersweet or semisweet (plain) chocolate, chopped
2 eggs
½ cup (4 oz/125 g) granulated sugar
½ cup (3½ oz/105 g) packed brown sugar
1 tablespoon vanilla extract (essence)
½ cup (2½ oz/75 g) unbleached all-purpose (plain) flour

❀ Preheat an oven to 350°F (180°C).
❀ To make the pastry, in a medium bowl or food processor, combine all of the dry ingredients. Cut in the butter with a pastry cutter, 2 knives, or the processor until it resembles coarse meal. Gradually add the water until a ball of dough forms. Shape the dough into a ball, flatten, wrap in plastic and refrigerate for 1 hour. Roll out on a lightly floured board and fit into a 9-in (23-cm) springform pan. Refrigerate until the filling is made.
❀ To make the filling, place the walnuts in boiling water to cover in a small saucepan and cook for 2–3 minutes. Drain and place on a baking sheet. Toast in the oven for 10 minutes, or until browned and crisp. Turn the oven temperature down to 325°F (170°C). Place the ancho chili in a small bowl; cover with boiling water and let steep until soft, about 30 minutes. Remove from the water (reserve the water), discard the seeds and stem and place the chili in a blender with 1 tablespoon of the soaking water. Strain and set aside. Melt the butter and chocolate together in a double boiler over simmering water; set aside. In a large bowl, beat the eggs with an electric mixer until foamy; gradually add the sugars, then the vanilla, ancho purée and chocolate-butter mixture. Fold in the flour and toasted walnuts.
❀ Pour the filling into the pastry shell and bake for 1 hour, or until firm.

SERVES 8–10   *Photograph pages 210–211*

APRICOT-PECAN TARTLETS

These bite-sized morsels are easy to prepare, as the dough is pressed into muffin cups, so it need not be rolled or cut.

CRUST

½ cup (4 oz/125 g) unsalted butter at room temperature
3 oz (90 g) cream cheese at room temperature
1 cup (5 oz/155 g) unbleached all-purpose (plain) flour
1–2 tablespoons heavy (double) cream, if necessary

FILLING

1 cup (4 oz/120g) dried apricots, diced
¾ cup (6 fl oz/180 ml) water
¾ cup (3 oz/90 g) pecans, toasted and chopped (see glossary)
¼ cup (2 oz/60 g) sugar
2 tablespoons orange marmalade
½ teaspoon ground cinnamon
½ teaspoon ground cloves

❀ Preheat an oven to 325°F (170°C). To make the crust, with an electric mixer, mix together the butter and cream cheese in a small bowl. Stir in the flour. If the dough is dry, add the cream a little at a time until it is soft and pliable. Shape the dough into 1-in (2.5-cm) balls and place each ball in the center of a miniature muffin cup; press the dough evenly against the bottom and sides of the cups. Refrigerate the molds while making the filling.
❀ To make the filling, combine the apricots and water in a small saucepan and bring to a boil. Reduce heat, cover and simmer for 8–10 minutes, or until the fruit is tender. Drain the apricots and place back in the saucepan and add the pecans, sugar, marmalade, cinnamon and cloves; stir well.

Top to bottom: Natillas, Apricot-Pecan Tartlets

❀ Divide the filling among the muffin cups and bake for 25–30 minutes, or until the crust is lightly browned. Place the muffin tins on a cooling rack for 10 minutes; remove the tartlets from the tins and cool completely on wire racks.

MAKES 24

NATILLAS

Also known as Spanish cream, this mild custard is a traditional Mexican dessert. Modify it by adding a little brandy or liqueur to the custard before folding in the egg whites. Instead of topping with cinnamon and raisins, garnish with shaved chocolate or fresh fruit.

4 cups (32 fl oz/1 l) whole milk
4 eggs, separated
¼ cup (1½ oz/45 g) unbleached all-purpose (plain) flour
¾ cup (6 oz/185 g) sugar
¼ teaspoon freshly ground nutmeg
ground cinnamon and raisins for garnish

❀ Butter eight ½-cup (4-fl oz/125-ml) ramekins. In a medium bowl, mix together 1 cup (8 fl oz/250 ml) of the milk, the egg yolks, and flour; set aside.
❀ In a medium saucepan, bring the remaining 3 cups (24 fl oz/375 ml) milk and the sugar to a boil over medium-high heat. Whisk 1 cup (8 fl oz/250 ml) of the hot milk into the egg yolk mixture. Pour the egg yolk mixture back into the saucepan and continue to cook, stirring, over medium heat until thickened to the consistency of soft custard, about 8–10 minutes. Stir in the nutmeg, cover the surface with a piece of buttered waxed paper and let cool.
❀ Beat the egg whites in a large bowl until soft peaks form. Stir a small amount of the whites into the cooled custard to lighten it. Fold in the remaining whites just until blended. Divide the custard among the 8 ramekins and refrigerate until well chilled. Sprinkle with cinnamon and raisins just before serving.

SERVES 8

Top to bottom: Toffee Caramel Flan (recipe page 229), Fried Ice Cream

❀ Refrigerate 6 serving bowls. In a medium bowl, beat the cream with the sugar until whipped. Do not overbeat; set aside. Fill a medium, heavy saucepan with enough oil to cover an ice cream ball. Heat the oil over medium-high heat to 400°F (200°C), or until a bread cube dropped in the oil browns in 45 seconds. Drop the frozen balls 1 at a time in the hot oil and cook for about 5 seconds, or until the coating is crispy. Remove with a slotted spoon and drain very briefly on a paper towel. Immediately place the fried ball in a cold serving bowl. Repeat with the remaining balls.

❀ Drizzle the ice cream with a little honey and top with whipped cream. Sprinkle with additional cinnamon and garnish with strawberries if desired. Serve immediately.

SERVES 6

NORTHERN ARIZONA

CRANBERRY–PRICKLY PEAR TART

This brilliant, red tart would be a welcome addition to any holiday table. It is best made with fresh cranberries, but frozen ones may be substituted. Prickly pears are available almost year round in the produce departments of Southwestern and Latino grocery stores, but if they are not available, replace the prickly pears with 1 cup (4 oz/125 g) of raspberries. The pastry dough makes excellent cookies: Bake on a greased baking sheet in a preheated 350° F (180°C) oven for 7–9 minutes, or until lightly browned.

PASTRY

¾ cup (3 oz/90 g) slivered almonds
½ cup (2 oz/60 g) sifted confectioners' (icing) sugar
½ cup (4 oz/125 g) chilled unsalted butter, cut into pieces
½ teaspoon salt
1 teaspoon vanilla extract
1 egg
1 cup (5 oz/155 g) plus 2 tablespoons unbleached
  all-purpose (plain) flour

FILLING

4 prickly pears, peeled
2 cups (8 oz/250 g) cranberries
¼ cup (2 fl oz/60 ml) water
1 tablespoon Grand Marnier
¾ cup (6 oz/185 g) granulated sugar

❀ To make the pastry, place the almonds in a food processor and process until they resemble coarse meal; add the confectioners' sugar and mix again. Add the butter, salt, vanilla and egg; process until creamy. Add the flour and quickly mix it in by pulsing the machine. Or, to make by hand, finely chop the almonds. Add the confectioners' sugar. With a whisk, mix in the butter (which should be at room temperature), salt, vanilla and eggs. Add the flour and mix until just moistened. Turn the dough out onto plastic wrap, wrap and refrigerate overnight, or until firm enough to roll. Roll out to an ⅛-in (3-mm) thickness and turn into an 8-in (20-cm) round springform pan. Refrigerate until ready to use.

❀ To make the filling, place the prickly pears in a food processor or blender and purée until smooth; strain and set aside. Mix the cranberries, water, Grand Marnier and sugar together in a small saucepan. Cook over medium heat, stirring occasionally, until the cranberries begin to pop, about 5 minutes. Remove from heat and stir in the prickly pear purée; let cool.

❀ Preheat an oven to 400°F (200°C). Spoon the filling into the chilled tart shell and bake until the crust is brown and the cranberries are bubbly, about 20 minutes. Let cool on a rack and remove the tart from the pan.

SERVES 8

SCOTTSDALE, ARIZONA

FRIED ICE CREAM

An often-requested dessert in Mexican restaurants, fried ice cream is usually ordered the first time as a novelty. Once people have tasted ice cream with cinnamon-flavored, warm crunchy topping, however, they always come back for more.

1½ cups (12 fl oz/375 ml) good-quality vanilla ice cream
4 teaspoons ground cinnamon
4 cups (4 oz/125 g) corn flakes, crushed, or ground nuts
1½ cups (12 fl oz/375 ml) heavy (double) cream
2 tablespoons sugar
vegetable oil for frying
¼ cup (3 oz/90 g) honey
ground cinnamon and strawberries for garnish (optional)

❀ Using an ice cream scoop or 2 tablespoons, divide the ice cream into 6 balls about 2 in (5 cm) in diameter. Mix the cinnamon and 3 cups (3 oz/90 g) of the cornflakes or nuts and roll each ball in the mixture, making sure it is completely coated. Place on a freezer-proof plate or baking sheet sprinkled with the remaining crushed cornflakes or nuts and repeat with the remaining balls. Freeze until very hard, about 2–3 hours.

Cranberry–Prickly Pear Tart

DATE BARS

Dates are plentiful year-round in the desert and, puréed, they make a wonderful filling for these bar cookies. Substitute pecans for walnuts if desired.

¾ cup (2 oz/60 g) quick-cooking oats
½ cup (2½ oz/75 g) unbleached all-purpose (plain) flour
¼ cup (1 oz/30 g) walnuts, toasted and chopped (see glossary)
¼ teaspoon baking soda (bicarbonate of soda)

½ cup (4 oz/125 g) unsalted butter, cut into ½-in (12-cm) pieces and chilled

FILLING

8 oz (250 g) dates, pitted
½ cup (3½ oz/105 g) packed brown sugar
⅓ cup (3 fl oz/80 ml) water
1 teaspoon vanilla extract (essence)

❀ Preheat an oven to 350°F (180°C). Butter an 8-in (20-cm) square baking pan. In a medium bowl or a food processor, combine the oats, flour, nuts and baking soda. Cut in the butter with a pastry cutter, 2 knives or the processor until

222

Top to bottom: Mexican Hot Chocolate, Orange Bizcochitos, Date Bars

NEW MEXICO

ORANGE BIZCOCHITOS

Bizcochitos are New Mexican favorites at Christmastime served with hot chocolate. Traditionally, they are made with lard rather than butter and flavored with anise. This lighter, updated version is perfect with sorbet for a refreshing dessert.

2½ cups (12½ oz/375 g) unbleached all-purpose (plain) flour
1 teaspoon baking powder
1½ cups (12 oz/375 g) plus 1 tablespoon sugar
1 cup (8 oz/250 g) unsalted butter at room temperature
1½ teaspoons aniseed, crushed
2 eggs, lightly beaten
2 teaspoons Triple Sec or Grand Marnier
½ teaspoon finely grated orange zest
1 tablespoon ground cinnamon

❋ Sift together the flour and baking powder. Cream together 1½ cups (12 oz/375 g) sugar and the butter; add the aniseed, eggs, Triple Sec or Grand Marnier and orange zest. Stir in the flour mixture and mix to a soft dough. Shape the dough into a disk, wrap in plastic and refrigerate for at least 2 hours, or until firm enough to roll.
❋ Preheat an oven to 375°F (190°C). Lightly butter a baking sheet. On a floured board, roll the dough to ¼-in (6-mm) thickness and cut out with cookie cutters (try cactus or coyote cutters). Mix the cinnamon and the remaining 1 tablespoon sugar together and sprinkle liberally over the cookies. Transfer to the prepared baking sheet and bake for 10 minutes, or until lightly browned. Let cool on a rack.

MAKES ABOUT 24 BIZCOCHITOS

NEW MEXICO

MEXICAN HOT CHOCOLATE

Mexican chocolate is characterized by a hint of cinnamon, and this delicious drink is perfect after skiing, as a morning treat or to soothe the soul on a cold winter's night.

⅓ cup (1½ oz/45 g) unsweetened cocoa powder, preferably not Dutch cocoa
⅓ cup (3 oz/90 g) sugar
1 teaspoon ground cinnamon
5 cups (40 fl oz/1.25 l) whole milk
½ cup (4 fl oz/125 ml) half & half (half milk and half cream), optional
1 vanilla bean (pod), split in half lengthwise, or 1 teaspoon vanilla extract (essence)
½ cup (4 fl oz/125 ml) heavy (double) cream, whipped
1 oz (30 g) bittersweet chocolate, cut into shavings with a vegetable peeler

❋ Mix the cocoa, sugar and cinnamon together in a small bowl. In a medium saucepan, stir together the milk and the optional half & half. Add the vanilla bean, if using, and, over low heat, bring the mixture to a simmer. Whisk in the cocoa mixture and cook, whisking, until the mixture is blended. Remove the vanilla bean and save for another use or discard. Add the vanilla extract now, if using.
❋ Divide the hot chocolate among 6 mugs and top each one with 2 tablespoons whipped cream and about 2 teaspoons chocolate shavings.

SERVES 6

crumbly. Press half of the mixture evenly into the prepared pan and reserve the other half.
❋ To make the filling, put all the filling ingredients in a small saucepan and bring to a boil over medium-high heat, stirring occasionally. Lower heat and simmer for 3–5 minutes, or until the sugar is dissolved. Transfer the mixture to a food processor or blender and purée until smooth.
❋ Spread the filling evenly over the bottom crust. Pat the remaining crumb mixture over the filling and bake for 25–30 minutes, or until the top is browned. Let cool in the pan and cut into squares.

MAKES 16 BARS

BANANA TACOS WITH PAPAYA AND STRAWBERRY SALSAS

Dean Fearing, the innovative young chef at The Mansion on Turtle Creek in Dallas, composed this scrumptious dessert. The components may be used separately: the salsas are delicious on ice cream or with flan, the glazed bananas can be served by themselves, and the crêpes are a good base for any filling.

CRÊPE TACOS

1 cup (4 oz/125 g) cake (soft wheat) flour
1 cup (5 oz/155 g) bread flour
2 tablespoons granulated sugar
pinch of salt
2 cups (16 fl oz/500 ml) milk
4 large eggs, beaten
4 large egg yolks, beaten
½ cup (4 oz/125 g) unsalted butter, melted and hot
¼ cup (2 fl oz/60 ml) Cognac

GLAZED BANANAS

½ cup (4 oz/125 g) unsalted butter
1 cup (7 oz/220 g) packed light brown sugar
2 tablespoons fresh orange juice
2 tablespoons Grand Marnier
6 bananas, peeled and sliced

GRAND MARNIER SAUCE

5 large egg yolks
½ cup (4 oz/125 g) granulated sugar
3 tablespoons Grand Marnier

STRAWBERRY SALSA

1 pint (8 oz/250 g) strawberries, washed and hulled
3 tablespoons packed light brown sugar

PAPAYA SALSA

1 papaya, peeled, halved and seeded
3 tablespoons granulated sugar
1 teaspoon ground cinnamon

❀ To make the crêpe batter, in a large bowl, combine the flours, sugar and salt. Slowly beat in the milk, eggs and egg yolks. Whisk in the butter, then the Cognac; stir well to combine. Let sit for 15–20 minutes.

❀ To make the glazed bananas, combine the butter and brown sugar in a small saucepan over medium heat. Cook for 3 minutes, or until the sugar has dissolved. Stir in orange juice and Grand Marnier and cook for 5 minutes. Remove from heat and stir in sliced bananas.

❀ To make the Grand Marnier sauce, beat the egg yolks and sugar in the top half of a double boiler over simmering water for 10 minutes, or until very thick and pale and a small amount trailed from the whisk forms a 3-second ribbon on the surface of the mixture. Remove from heat and let cool slightly. Whisk in the Grand Marnier.

❀ To make the strawberry salsa, cut one half of the strawberries into ¼-in (6-mm) dice. In a blender, purée the remaining strawberries with the brown sugar. Pour the purée over the diced strawberries and stir to combine.

❀ To make the papaya salsa, cut 1 half of the papaya into ¼-in (6-mm) dice. In a blender, purée the remaining half with the sugar and cinnamon. Pour the purée over the diced papaya and stir to combine.

❀ To make the crêpes, lightly butter an 8-in (20-cm) sauté or crêpe pan and place over medium heat. Pour in approximately 1 tablespoon batter and swirl in a circular motion to cover the bottom of the pan. Cook for 2–3 minutes, or until lightly browned. Turn the crêpe over and cook for an additional 2–3 minutes, or until lightly browned. Continue until all the batter is used. Stack crêpes between sheets of waxed paper or they will stick together. Keep warm.

❀ To serve, preheat a broiler (griller). Spoon 6 or 8 slices of glazed bananas in the center of each crêpe and roll up like a soft taco. Place on ovenproof serving plates. Pour Grand

Banana Tacos with Papaya and Strawberry Salsas

Top to bottom: Piñon Cookies, Baked Grapefruit

Marnier sauce across the top of the tacos and place under the preheated broiler for 2 minutes, or until lightly browned. Spoon 4 or 5 more banana slices on top and serve the salsas on the side.

SERVES 8

PIÑON COOKIES

Piñons add a subtle, nutty flavor to these light, airy cookies. Their flavor is enhanced by toasting. Not very sweet, these simple cookies are perfect for an afternoon cup of tea or coffee.

2 eggs
⅔ cup (6 oz/185 g) sugar
1 cup (5 oz/155 g) unbleached all-purpose (plain) flour
¼ cup (1½ oz/45 g) piñon (pine) nuts, toasted
  (see glossary)

❀ Combine the eggs and sugar in a heavy saucepan and whisk constantly over low heat until the mixture is lukewarm and light in texture, about 3–5 minutes. Remove from heat and whisk until cool; gradually stir in the flour until the batter is smooth.

❀ Preheat an oven to 375°F (190°C). Butter 2 baking sheets and drop the batter by teaspoonfuls onto the pan, leaving about 1 in (2.5 cm) between cookies. Let sit 5 minutes. Place 4 or 5 pine nuts on top of each cookie and let them sit another 5 minutes.

❀ Bake for 12–15 minutes, or until golden brown. Remove from the baking sheets while still warm and let cool on racks.

MAKES 36 COOKIES

BAKED GRAPEFRUIT

Grapefruit has been cultivated in Phoenix since 1894, and, despite rapid commercial development, citrus groves are still abundant in the area. Serve this dish for brunch or as a refreshing finish to a heavy meal.

3 large grapefruits, halved
3 tablespoons sugar
2 teaspoons ground cinnamon
2 tablespoons unbleached all-purpose (plain) flour, sifted
2 tablespoons chilled unsalted butter, cut into pieces
6 fresh mint sprigs

❀ Preheat an oven to 450°F (230°C). Cut the sections of grapefruit away from the membrane with a grapefruit knife or small serrated knife.

❀ Combine the sugar, cinnamon and flour. Cut the butter into the dry mixture with a fork or pastry blender.

❀ Sprinkle equal amounts of the mixture over the grapefruit halves. Place the grapefruit on a baking sheet and bake until lightly browned, about 7 minutes. Place 1 grapefruit half on each plate and garnish with a sprig of mint.

SERVES 6

225

STRAWBERRY MARGARITA SORBET

Strawberry Margaritas are on the menus of restaurants throughout the Southwest. This sorbet, based on the cocktail, is a refreshing finish to any meal. Garnish with mint sprigs and serve with Orange Bizcochitos (recipe on page 223) or Mexican Shortbread (recipe follows). On a hot summer evening, this sorbet makes a delicious drink when partially frozen.

1 cup (8 oz/250 g) sugar
2 cups (16 fl oz/500 ml) water
4 cups (16 oz/500 g) fresh strawberries
⅓ cup (3 fl oz/80 ml) fresh lime juice
⅓ cup (3 fl oz/80 ml) tequila
¼ cup (2 fl oz/60 ml) Triple Sec or Grand Marnier
mint sprigs for garnish

❁ Place the sugar and the water in a medium, heavy saucepan; bring to a boil over high heat, stirring, until the sugar is completely dissolved; let cool. (This sugar syrup can be made in large quantities and refrigerated indefinitely.)
❁ In a food processor or blender, purée the strawberries. Stir in the lime juice, tequila, Triple Sec or Grand Marnier and sugar syrup. Taste and adjust the flavor, adding more lime juice if necessary. Chill completely.
❁ Place the strawberry mixture in an ice cream maker and freeze according to the manufacturer's instructions. Or, pour it into a shallow pan and freeze until almost solid. Remove from the freezer, stir with a fork or process in a food processor and refreeze. Repeat 2–3 more times, or until the mixture is smooth (the sorbet will be icier than if made in an ice cream maker). Scoop into glasses or bowls and garnish each serving with a sprig of mint.

SERVES 6–8

Espresso-Cinnamon Ice Cream

ESPRESSO-CINNAMON ICE CREAM

The aromatic flavors of coffee, cinnamon and vanilla are subtly infused into this rich ice cream, and toasted hazelnuts add the final touch. Delicious on its own, it is also terrific served in Cookie Tacos (recipe on page 216) with Mexican Chocolate Sauce (recipe on page 189).

2½ cups (20 fl oz/625 ml) milk
2 cups (16 fl oz/500 ml) heavy (double) cream
2 cinnamon sticks
1 vanilla bean (pod), halved lengthwise, or ½ teaspoon vanilla extract
¼ cup (2 oz/60 g) instant espresso powder
⅔ cup (5 oz/155 g) sugar
4 egg yolks
½ cup (2½ oz/75 g) hazelnuts, toasted and coarsely chopped (see glossary)

❁ Stir together the milk, cream, cinnamon sticks, vanilla bean and espresso powder in a heavy saucepan. Over medium heat, bring the mixture to a simmer. Remove from heat, cover and let steep for 45 minutes.
❁ Strain the milk mixture through a fine sieve and return it to the saucepan. Over medium heat, bring the mixture to a simmer. Whisk the sugar and egg yolks together in a medium bowl, then gradually whisk in 1 cup (8 fl oz/250 ml) of the hot milk. Return the egg-milk mixture to the milk mixture in the saucepan and stir over medium-low heat until the mixture thickens and coats the back of a spoon, about 8 minutes; do not boil. Strain into a clean bowl, let cool and refrigerate.
❁ Put the cooled mixture into an ice cream maker and freeze according to the manufacturer's instructions. When the mixture is almost frozen, add the chopped hazelnuts and finish freezing.

MAKES 6 CUPS (48 FL OZ/1.5 L)

MEXICAN SHORTBREAD

These melt-in-your-mouth cookies store well in an airtight container.

¾ cup (6 oz/180 g) unsalted butter at room temperature
¾ cup (6 oz/185 g) sugar
4 teaspoons ground cinnamon
2 egg yolks
1¾ cups (9 oz/280 g) unbleached all-purpose (plain) flour
¼ teaspoon salt

❁ In a medium bowl with an electric mixer, beat together the butter, ½ cup (4 oz/125 g) of the sugar and 2 teaspoons of the cinnamon until the mixture is light and fluffy. Add the yolks and mix well. Stir in the flour and salt and mix until the flour is incorporated. If the dough is too soft, add more flour a little at a time. Shape the dough into a log about 2 in (5 cm) in diameter and wrap tightly in plastic wrap. Refrigerate for at least 2 hours or overnight.
❁ Preheat an oven to 350°F (180°C) and lightly butter a baking sheet. Unwrap the refrigerated dough and cut it into ¼-in (6-mm) slices. Place the slices on the prepared baking sheet and bake for about 15 minutes, or until the cookies are light brown.
❁ Mix together ¼ cup (2 oz/60 g) of the sugar and the rest of the cinnamon on a shallow plate or bowl. While the cookies are still warm, roll them in the cinnamon-sugar mixture and transfer them to a cooling rack.

MAKES ABOUT 48 COOKIES

Clockwise from top left: Grapefruit and Champagne Sorbet, Strawberry Margarita Sorbet, Mexican Shortbread

GRAPEFRUIT AND CHAMPAGNE SORBET

A refreshing palate cleanser between courses or a delightfully refreshing finish to a meal, this tart sorbet can also be served as a terrific hot-weather drink when frozen just to the slushy stage. For a slightly sweeter, beautifully colored sorbet, use pink grapefruit. The alcohol in the champagne keeps the mixture from freezing too solidly.

4 cups (32 fl oz/1 l) fresh grapefruit juice
1 cup (8 oz/250 g) sugar
¼ cup (2 fl oz/60 ml) dry champagne, plus more for topping

❀ In a small saucepan over medium-high heat, dissolve the sugar in 1 cup (8 fl oz/250 ml) of the grapefruit juice. Add to the rest of the juice and refrigerate until well chilled.
❀ Stir the champagne into the grapefruit juice mixture and freeze in an ice cream maker according to the manufacturer's directions. If serving for dessert, pour additional champagne over scoops of sorbet, if desired.

MAKES 4 CUPS (32 FL OZ /1 L)

SOUTHERN ARIZONA

PRICKLY PEAR SORBET

The fruit of the prickly pear (called tunas*) are available almost year round in the Southwest. According to Navajo legend, the person picking the fruit must pluck a hair from his or her head so as not to offend the spirit of the plant. A dessert similar to this was made by native Americans in the winter months by leaving it outside overnight to freeze. Choose soft but not over-ripe pears*

to make this vibrant, unusual sorbet that can be served either as a dessert or as a palate cleanser.

2 cups (16 oz/500 g) prickly pears, peeled and
  coarsely chopped
1 cup (8 oz/250 g) sugar
1 cup (8 fl oz/250 ml) water
1 tablespoon Grand Marnier

❀ Place the prickly pears in a blender or food processor and purée. Strain into a bowl.

Left to right: Apple Cider Sorbet, Prickly Pear Sorbet

❀ Combine the sugar and water in a small saucepan and bring to a boil, stirring. Cook until the sugar is dissolved; let cool.

❀ Add the sugar syrup and Grand Marnier to the prickly pear purée and pour the mixture into an ice cream maker and freeze according to the manufacturer's directions. Or, pour the mixture into a shallow pan and freeze it. When almost frozen, remove from the freezer, break up with a fork and return to freezer until solid.

MAKES 2 CUPS (16 FL OZ/500 ML)

APPLE CIDER SORBET

Reminiscent of the fall when cider is pressed, this sorbet is a lovely palate cleanser or a refreshing dessert. It is also delicious scooped into a chilled bowl of Cold Apple Soup (recipe on page 77) on a hot summer's day.

1 cup (8 fl oz/250 ml) hard cider
1 cup (8 fl oz/250 ml) sweet cider
¾ cup (6 oz/185 g) sugar
1 tart apple, peeled, cored and thinly sliced
1 tablespoon Calvados

❀ Place the ciders and sugar in a heavy saucepan and cook over medium heat, stirring, until the sugar dissolves. Add the apple slices and cook until tender, about 3 minutes. Transfer the mixture to a food processor or blender and process until smooth. Stir in the Calvados. Freeze in an ice cream maker according to the manufacturer's instructions.

MAKES 2 CUPS (16 FL OZ/500 ML)

TOFFEE CARAMEL FLAN

Sarah Labensky, chef-instructor of Scottsdale Community College's Culinary Arts Program, developed this rich, creamy dessert while she was the pastry chef at Saguaro Restaurant, also in Scottsdale. It is delicious on its own or garnished with fresh fruit, caramelized almonds or whipped cream.

1¼ cups (10 oz/315 g) granulated sugar
½ cup (4 fl oz/125 ml) water
1½ cups (12 fl oz/375 ml) milk
1½ cups (12 fl oz/375 ml) heavy (double) cream
1 cinnamon stick
1 vanilla bean (pod), split
4 eggs
2 egg yolks
5 tablespoons (2½ oz/75 g) packed brown sugar
2 teaspoons molasses
1 tablespoon Amaretto liqueur

❀ Butter six ¾-cup (6–fl oz/180-ml) ramekins. Combine the granulated sugar with the water in a small, heavy saucepan and bring to a boil. Cook until the sugar reaches a dark golden brown. Immediately pour about 2 tablespoonfuls into each of the ramekins, tilting to spread the caramel evenly along the bottom. Arrange the ramekins in a baking dish 2-in (5-cm) deep and set aside.

❀ Combine the milk, cream, cinnamon stick and vanilla bean in a heavy saucepan. Bring just to a boil, cover and remove from the heat. Let steep for about 30 minutes.

❀ Preheat an oven to 325°F (165°C). Whisk the eggs, yolks, brown sugar, molasses and Amaretto together in a medium bowl. Uncover the milk mixture and return it to the stovetop. Bring just to the boil again. Whisk about one-third of the hot milk into the egg-sugar mixture to temper it. Whisk in the remaining hot milk. Strain the custard through a fine sieve. Pour into the caramel-lined ramekins, filling them to just below the rim. Pour enough warm water into the baking pan to reach halfway up the sides of the ramekins. Bake for 30–40 minutes, or until almost set but still somewhat liquid in the center.

❀ Chill completely before serving. To unmold, run a small knife around the edge of the custard, invert onto a serving plate and give the ramekin a firm, sideways shake.

MAKES 6–8   *Photograph page 220*

PEACH COBBLER

In 1864, Kit Carson destroyed the Navajo flocks and crops, including their prized peach orchards, and marched many of the people on "The Long Walk" to captivity. Today, Navajo people have flourished, and their peach trees have been replanted in Canyon de Chelly. Thus peaches have taken on both a symbolic and historical significance to the enduring Navajo. The desert peaches grown on the reservation are smaller but sweeter than commercially grown peaches, but any fresh, ripe peaches in season will work in this recipe.

5 peaches (2½ lb/1.25 kg), peeled and cut into ½-in
  (12-mm) slices (about 5 cups/2 lb/1 kg)
¼ cup (2 oz/60 g) sugar
1 tablespoon fresh lemon juice

TOPPING

⅓ cup (3 oz/90 g) unsalted butter at room temperature
¾ cup (6 oz/185 g) sugar
1 egg
¾ cup (4 oz/125 g) unbleached all-purpose (plain) flour
½ teaspoon baking powder

❀ Preheat an oven to 375°F (190°C). Butter an 8-in (20-cm) square baking dish. Layer the peach slices in the bottom of the prepared baking dish. Sprinkle with sugar and lemon juice and set aside while making the topping.

❀ In a medium bowl with an electric mixer, beat the butter and sugar until light and fluffy. Add the egg and beat another minute. Add the flour and baking powder and beat just until combined.

❀ Spoon the batter over the peaches. Do not try to cover the peaches completely with the topping; the fruit should bubble through it. Bake for 40 minutes, or until the top is lightly browned.

SERVES 6–8

Peach Cobbler

Left to right: White Sangría, Sangría

SANGRÍA

Sangría is the Spanish word for "bleeding," and this traditional drink is named for its blood-red color. A refreshing drink made with red wine and fruit, it's best served very cold, either over ice or well chilled and poured into stemmed glasses.

3½ cups (28 fl oz/875 ml) chilled dry red wine
½ cup (4 fl oz/125 ml) chilled fresh lemon juice
½ cup (4 fl oz/125 ml) chilled orange juice
½ cup (4 oz/125 g) sugar
¼ cup (2 fl oz/60 ml) brandy
1¼ cups (10 fl oz/310 ml) chilled sparkling water
1 lemon, thinly sliced
1 orange, thinly sliced
½ cup (3 oz/90 g) seedless red grapes (optional)

❀ In a large glass pitcher, stir together the wine, lemon juice, orange juice, sugar and brandy. Refrigerate until ready to serve. Just before serving, mix the sparkling water and fruit, if desired, into the wine mixture. Pour over tall glasses filled with ice.

SERVES 6

WHITE SANGRÍA

Like traditional sangría, this blend of fruit and wine is a refreshing drink on a warm evening, and it goes well with Southwestern foods. Serve it in a clear glass pitcher to highlight the fruit.

3½ cups (28 fl oz/875 ml) chilled dry white wine
½ cup (4 fl oz/125 ml) Cointreau, Triple Sec or
   Grand Marnier
¼ cup (2 fl oz/60 ml) brandy
¼ cup (2 oz/60 g) sugar
1¼ cups (10 fl oz/310 ml) chilled sparkling water
1 lemon, thinly sliced
2 limes, thinly sliced
½ cup (3 oz/90 g) seedless green grapes (optional)

❀ In a clear glass pitcher, stir together the wine, liqueur, brandy and sugar. Refrigerate until ready to serve. Just before serving, stir in the sparkling water and fruit, if desired. Fill tall glasses with ice and pour the sangría over the ice, or serve well chilled in cocktail glasses without ice.

SERVES 6

PEPPER VODKA

This spicy drink may be made with any chili, but with the chiltepín, available in specialty food markets or Latino markets, hot results are guaranteed. Chiltepíns are usually dried and crushed, then sprinkled into soups, stews and salsas—they are even used to cure acid indigestion. Here, a few of the fiery devils, which grow wild in southern Arizona, supply enough heat for an entire quart of vodka. The longer the chiltepín and vodka steep, the hotter the vodka will get, so check it regularly and remove the chili when the vodka is the right "temperature." Drink this spicy *vodka well chilled, over ice, mixed in Bloody Marys or in any vodka cocktail for an extra kick.*

4 chiltepín chilies
one 4-cup (32–fl oz/1-l) bottle of vodka

❀ Drop the whole chiltepíns into the vodka and reseal the bottle. Let steep for 7–10 days, testing occasionally for the desired level of heat. Strain the mixture through a fine sieve and return the strained vodka to the bottle.

MAKES 4 CUPS (32 FL OZ/1 L)

Pepper Vodka

Left to right: Margaritas, Southwestern Sunset, Tequila Sunrise

SOUTHWESTERN SUNSET

The orange and brilliant red colors of this cocktail resemble the spectacular sunsets that often paint the sky in Arizona and New Mexico. Not too sweet, it can be made easily without alcohol: Simply mix the prickly pear juice with sugar syrup or grenadine and pour over orange juice.

4½ cups (34 fl oz/1.1 l) orange juice
1 cup (8 fl oz/250 ml) tequila
6 prickly pears, peeled, puréed and strained to yield 1 cup
   (8 fl oz/250 ml)
½ cup (4 fl oz/125 ml) Triple Sec or Grand Marnier

❈ Mix together the orange juice and tequila; divide among 6 glasses filled with ice. Stir the prickly pear juice and Triple Sec or Grand Marnier together and gently pour 2 tablespoons over each orange juice- and tequila-filled glass. For the most dramatic effect, do not stir. Serve immediately.

MAKES 6

TEQUILA SUNRISE

Immortalized by the Eagles in their song of the same name, this popular drink contains the colors of sunrise in the Southwest. Tequila, which is made from the Mexican agave plant, is touted by some as containing vitamins. Serve this at your next brunch for an eye-opening morning.

1½ cups (12 fl oz/375 ml) tequila
1½ cups (12 fl oz/375 ml) orange juice
¾ cup (6 fl oz/180 ml) club soda
3 tablespoons grenadine
6 orange slices

❈ Put ¼ cup (2 fl oz/60 ml) tequila in each of 6 tall glasses. Fill the glasses three-fourths full with crushed ice. Pour ¼ cup (2 fl oz/60 ml) orange juice and 2 tablespoons club soda over the ice in each glass and stir. Spoon ½ tablespoon grenadine into each glass and do not stir again. Garnish each glass with an orange slice and serve immediately.

SERVES 6

MARGARITAS

Almost every Southwestern restaurant and host claims to make the perfect Margarita, and contests are often held for proof. There are almost as many recipes for Margaritas as there are bartenders: with or without salt on the rim; on the rocks; blended with crushed ice; shaken with ice and strained; with Triple Sec rather than Cointreau; or even puréed with fresh fruit such as strawberries. But the two most important ingredients remain fresh, not frozen, lime juice and a good-quality tequila. Here is a basic recipe; embellish and expand on it to suit your own taste.

½ cup (4 fl oz/125 ml) fresh lime juice (Mexican limes,
   if possible), lime shells reserved
coarse salt for dipping
½ cup (4 fl oz/125 ml) Cointreau or Triple Sec
1 cup (8 fl oz/250 ml) white tequila
1 cup (8 oz/250 g) crushed ice

❈ Rub the juiced lime shells around the rims of 6 cocktail or wineglasses; dip the rims into the coarse salt and set aside. Put the lime juice, Cointreau or Triple Sec, tequila and crushed ice into a blender. Mix well and pour into the prepared glasses.

MAKES 6

GLOSSARY

ACHIOTE
The Mexican name for the tiny, brick-red seeds of the tropical annatto tree, which are often used as a coloring agent, especially in Cheddar-like cheeses. Annatto seeds have an earthy, slightly musky taste. In the Yucatán Peninsula of Mexico, they are often ground up with garlic, chilies and spices for *adobos,* or seasoning pastes.

ANAHEIM CHILI see *Chilies, fresh.*

ANCHO CHILI see *Chilies, dried.*

ANISEED
Small, curved seeds of the anise plant, which add a sweet licorice flavor to baked goods and both sweet and savory dishes. Aniseed is widely available in grocery stores.

ASADERO CHEESE see *Cheeses, Mexican.*

CAYENNE CHILI see *Chilies, dried.*

CHAYOTE SQUASH
A pale green, pear-shaped member of the melon and gourd family, also called vegetable pear or choko. Chayote has a mild, white flesh that tastes similar to zucchini (courgette) and is a good carrier for other flavors. Use it raw in salads or as a substitute in any recipe calling for summer squash. Chayote squash are available in most grocery stores, especially during the winter months.

CHEESES, MEXICAN
The main producer of Mexican cheeses in North America is Cacique, and their products are found in Latino markets and specialty foods stores. Monterey jack, Cheddar and other more familiar cheeses may be substituted, as noted, but the dishes will taste slightly different.

ASADERO: A mild, soft cheese with the flavor of provolone and the texture of mozzarella. Asadero melts well, and therefore is a good cooking cheese, especially in quesadillas and enchiladas. Substitutes: mozzarella or provolone.

COTIJA: A hard, dry, aged full-flavored cheese similar to Parmesan, cotija is used either cubed or crumbled in enchiladas, salads and beans. Substitutes: feta, Parmesan or dry Monterey jack.

MANCHEGO: A rich, mellow-flavored table cheese that is delicious in casseroles, quesadillas and sandwiches. Substitutes: white Cheddar, Swiss or Gouda.

OAXACA: A versatile cheese similar to mozzarella in texture and flavor, and often found in long ropes rolled into a ball, which makes it appealing to children as a snack. Oaxaca (pronounced *wa-ha-ka*) melts easily, so it is delicious in quesadillas and enchiladas. Substitute: mozzarella.

QUESO FRESCO: A tangy cheese with the crumbly texture of farmer's cheese, good either crumbled in dishes or as a table cheese. Substitute: feta.

RANCHERO: A fresh cheese made with Grade A milk, good either as a table cheese or in cooking. Ranchero has the texture of farmer's cheese and the taste of jack, and it is best crumbled over huevos rancheros, beans or tacos or used in the fillings of chiles rellenos and enchiladas.

CHILE DE ÁRBOL see *Chilies, dried.*

CHILIES, DRIED
Fully ripened, or red, fresh chilies have an intense flavor when dried and may be stored indefinitely in airtight containers. When choosing dried chilies, select those that are slightly flexible and uniform in color with no white spots. To use dried chilies, toast them in a dry skillet for 3–4 minutes, or until flexible. Remove the ribs, stems and seeds and, depending on the recipe, tear the chilies into pieces and grind them in a blender or food processor, or soak them, weighted down, if necessary, in very hot (not boiling) water for 20–30 minutes, or until soft. To use soaked chilies in a sauce, purée them with a little of the soaking water in a blender or food processor, then add to the other sauce ingredients. Dried chilies vary considerably in their depth of flavor; to add even more interest to Southwest food, experiment with different combinations of them.

ANCHO: A dried poblano chili ranging in color from deep red to dark brown. Usually about 4 in (10 cm) long and 3 in (7.5 cm) wide, the ancho has a slightly fruity flavor and is sweeter than most dried chilies. It is often mislabeled as a pasilla, which is a long, thin and very dark brown dried chili.

CAYENNE: Usually dried and ground for use in powdered form, cayenne chilies are bright red, translucent and about 3 in (7.5 cm) long. They provide a pungent heat that is slightly acidic, tart and smoky-flavored.

CHILE DE ÁRBOL: A small, red chili about 2 in (5 cm) long and ½ in (12 mm) wide. Often used in powdered form, it adds a smoky heat to dishes.

CHILTEPÍN: Also called tepín. A medium red, round chili about ½ in (12 mm) in diameter, which grows wild in northern Mexico and southern Arizona. Chiltepíns are very hot and should be used sparingly; they are usually crushed before being sprinkled into soups, stews and salsas. Use the cultivated variety, pequín, as a substitute.

CHIPOTLE: The dried and smoked jalapeño. Tobacco colored and about 3 in (7.5 cm) long, chipotles are most often found canned in *adobo* sauce and are sweet and smoky in flavor.

DRIED RED PEPPER FLAKES: Crushed dried chilies, usually New Mexicos. Dried red pepper flakes are available in the spice department of any grocery store. Sprinkle them into salad dressings, salsas, sauces, soups or stews for a crisp, clear heat.

GUAJILLO: A shiny red chili about 5 in (13 cm) long and 1½ in (4 cm) across; grown in Mexico. The heat of the guajillo is somewhat sweet, and it is most often used in salsas, sauces and soups.

NEW MEXICO: A dried red New Mexico chili, about 6 in (15 cm) long and tapered. Sometimes called *chile colorado,* the scarlet-colored dried New Mexico provides a crisp heat. The chili most often used in traditional red sauces, it often hangs in strings called *ristras* on porches throughout the Southwest.

CHILIES, FRESH
The many varieties of fresh chilies differ in color, flavor and heat. While growing, chilies are green; as they ripen, they turn shades of yellow and red and become sweeter and more flavorful. Because their taste is affected by the soil in which they are grown, flavor and heat will vary even among chilies of the same variety. When purchasing fresh chilies, choose those that are shiny, unblemished, dry and heavy for their size. Store fresh chilies in the refrigerator, wrapped in paper towels rather than in plastic bags.
Most of the heat in a chili—60 percent—comes from the capsaicin contained in the ribs, while 30 percent of the heat is in the seeds and 10 percent in the flesh. Smaller chilies are hotter because the percentage of ribs and seeds is higher. It is important to handle chilies with care; wear rubber gloves, do not touch your eyes or face and wash your hands with soap and water when finished.
Many Southwestern and Mexican recipes call for roasted, peeled and seeded chilies, because roasting helps remove the sometimes bitter skin and also brings out the chili's earthy, smoky flavor. There are a number of ways to roast chilies: over an open flame, with a butane torch, under a broiler (griller) and on a grill. The object is to blister and blacken the skin without damaging

the flesh of the chili. When the skin is blackened all over, place the chili in a paper or plastic bag, close the bag and let the chili cool for 15–20 minutes. The steam created in the bag loosens the skin and allows its easy removal either with your hands or a knife. Do not remove the skin under running water, as the essential oils and smoky taste will be washed away. After skinning, cut the chili open and remove the ribs, seeds and core. Store peeled roasted chilies in the refrigerator for up to 2 days.

ANAHEIM: A bright green chili about 6 in (15 cm) long, often referred to as the long green or California chili. The Anaheim was originally grown in Southern California and is closely related to the New Mexico green chili. Green Anaheims are the most widely available chilies in produce markets; the ripe, red version is not as common. Mild in flavor, Anaheims are often roasted and stuffed.

HABANERO: Slightly spherical chilies about 1½ in (4 cm) in diameter and ranging in color from dark green to bright red. Habaneros are the hottest of all chilies, so it is important to use caution when handling them. They supply an intense heat and a slight fruitiness to salsas and marinades. Habaneros are also available in dried form.

JALAPEÑO: A bright green tapered chili about 2 in (5 cm) long and 1 in (2.5 cm) wide. Jalapeños are the most common hot chili in the United States. Because of their heat, caution should be used when working with them. Jalapeños may be added to almost anything, even desserts, to add extra spice. The ripe form is bright red and slightly sweeter than the green; both red and green jalapeños are good pickled.

NEW MEXICO GREEN, NEW MEXICO RED: The New Mexico green chili is medium green in color and about 7 in (18 cm) long and 1½ in (4 cm) wide. Often confused with the Anaheim, the New Mexico green is hotter, with a sweet, earthy flavor. It is usually roasted and used in green chili sauces, stews, rellenos and salsas. The fresh New Mexico red chili is the ripe form of the New Mexico green. Like the green, it is usually roasted and used in sauces, rellenos and salsas. The New Mexico red chili is dark red in color and is sweeter in flavor than the green. It is also available in dried form.

POBLANO: A dark green, triangular and thick-fleshed chili about 4 in (10 cm) long and 2½ in (6 cm) wide, the poblano is often mislabeled as a pasilla. Roasting brings out its smoky, earthy flavor, and it is usually stuffed or used in sauces.

SERRANO: A small, thick-fleshed, cylindrical chili with a tapered rounded end. Ranging in color from dark green to bright red, the serrano is 1–2 in (2.5–5 cm) and ½ in (12 mm) in diameter. Slightly hotter, smaller and a darker green than jalapeños, serranos are used raw in fresh salsas and roasted in cooked sauces.

CHILI POWDER AND POWDERED CHILI
A seasoning made of ground dried red chilies, garlic, oregano, cumin and other herbs, chili powder is used frequently in chilies, soups, stews, dressings and so on. Powdered chili is the ground form of one particular dried chili, without any other herbs or spices. Both substances have a short shelf life and should be kept in a dry, dark place so that they keep their pungency. Avoid buying chili powder or powdered chili in clear packages that may have been exposed to too much light, or they will be bitter and lack flavor.

CHILTEPÍN CHILI see Chilies, dried.

CHIPOTLE CHILI see Chilies, dried.

CHORIZO
A highly seasoned fresh sausage made with pork, garlic, chili powder and other spices and used in Mexican and Spanish cooking. Available in many markets, chorizo comes in bulk and link form. It should always be cooked before being eaten, and is usually removed from its casings and crumbled before cooking.

CILANTRO
A green herb, also known as Chinese parsley or fresh coriander. First introduced to Mexico by the Spanish, cilantro is one of the world's most widely used herbs, common in Mexican, Indian, Caribbean and Asian cuisines. Its dark green, lacy leaves have a pungent, sweet odor and add a distinctive flavor to salsas and other dishes. When buying cilantro, look for unwilted, evenly colored leaves. Store it in the refrigerator either washed, wrapped in paper towels and in a plastic bag, or standing with the stems in a glass of water and lightly covered with a plastic bag.

CORIANDER
The dried ripe fruits of the coriander plant are referred to as coriander seeds, which are slightly fragrant. Whole, they are used in pickling; ground, they are used in baked goods and as a seasoning.

CORN
A plant indigenous to North America, which produces grains that are the traditional food of most Pueblo people. Corn is considered sacred by many Native Americans. The six colors of the kernels (yellow, white, red, blue, black and speckled) each represent a different direction in some Pueblo cultures: north, south, east, west, up and down. Dried corn is used to make hominy, masa harina and cornmeal. Fresh sweet corn, harvested during the summer months, is best eaten as soon after picking as possible, because the natural sugar in the corn begins to turn to starch, lessening the sweetness of the corn. When choosing fresh corn, look for ears with tightly fitting husks, light brown silk and plump kernels in tightly spaced rows all the way to the tip of the ear (cob).

CORN HUSKS
The outer wrapping of ears (cobs) of corn, which are dried to use in making tamales and other Mexican specialties. Soak corn husks in hot water for about 30 minutes, or until soft and pliable, then use them as wrappings for dishes to be steamed. Dried corn husks are widely available in Southwestern grocery stores and Latino markets.

CORNMEAL
A meal ground from dried, processed corn kernels and used in baked goods. The color of cornmeal depends on the type of corn used; yellow and white are more common than blue. Blue cornmeal, which has a more intense flavor than yellow or white, acquires its distinctive lavender-blue color when ground blue corn (which is actually dark gray) is treated with alkaline substances such as juniper ashes or calcium carbonate.

COTIJA CHEESE see Cheeses, Mexican

CUMIN
The dried fruit of a parsleylike plant, cumin has a spicy, nutty flavor and is often mixed with chili powders and curries. It is widely available, either whole as seeds or ground into a powder. To get the maximum flavor from cumin, grind the seeds in a spice grinder rather than purchasing it already ground.

DRIED RED PEPPER FLAKES see Chilies, dried.

EPAZOTE
A Mexican herb often used in bean dishes to reduce gas and commonly known as wormseed or Mexican tea. Epazote grows wild throughout Mexico and the United States, and its flat, pointed leaves have a pungent taste similar to cilantro. If fresh epazote is not available, many Latino markets carry it dried.

FRIJOLES
The Mexican word for "beans," usually referring to boiled and simmered pinto beans, so named because of their spotted appearance. Dried pinto beans are widely available, either in bulk or packaged, in most grocery stores. Pick through the beans and discard any stones before soaking the beans in water overnight. They should be cooked slowly the next day in unsalted water, as salt toughens the skins.

GUAJILLO CHILI see *Chilies, dried.*

HABANERO CHILI see *Chilies, fresh.*

HOMINY
Whole, dried corn kernels that have been soaked in slaked lime or lye to remove their tough outer hulls. The alkaline processing of the corn improves its nutrient content, making it more valuable for consumption. Hominy is the basis for many native American dishes in almost every tribe and pueblo throughout the Southwest. It is also the main ingredient in a traditional New Mexican stew called posole (the Mexican version of this stew is called *pozole*). Yellow and white hominy are available canned in many supermarkets and dried in specialty or Latino markets (where it is called *maiz para pozole*). If using dried hominy, soak it in water before cooking. Coarsely ground dried hominy is called grits.

JALAPEÑO CHILI see *Chilies, fresh.*

JÍCAMA
A root vegetable, also known as the Mexican potato and the yam bean, with a fibrous, thick brown skin and crisp, white flesh. Slightly sweet, with a nutlike flavor, the crunchy flesh of the jícama is usually eaten raw, although it retains its water chestnut–like texture when cooked. Available almost year-round, jícama will keep a long time in the refrigerator if the skin is intact. It is delicious as a crudité or in salads.

JUNIPER BERRIES
The ripe blue fruit of an evergreen shrub, juniper berries are usually dried and used in robust meat dishes such as stews or in marinades, stuffings and sauces; they are also the flavoring used in gin. Juniper berries should be crushed to release their spicy, pine aroma and sweet, resinous flavor. They are sold in jars in the spice section of most grocery stores.

MANCHEGO CHEESE see *Cheeses, Mexican.*

MASA
The word masa means "dough," but refers specifically to dough made from dried corn kernels that have been cooked and soaked overnight in lime water, then ground. Masa may be purchased fresh or frozen from Latino markets or tortilla factories and used to make tortillas or tamales. It should be used within a few days, as it spoils easily.

MASA HARINA
A flour made from dried corn, which is combined with liquid and used to make corn tortillas and tamales. Masa harina is available in many grocery stores and may be stored indefinitely in an airtight container or in the freezer.

MESQUITE
A wild, tenacious hardwood tree that dots the landscape throughout the southwestern United States and northern Mexico. Mesquite is disliked by farmers and ranchers because it chokes out crops and grazing areas, but it also prevents erosion and provides a desert habitat for birds and animals. Its beans, which are rich in sugar, were a staple of the Native Americans of the Sonoran Desert, who dried them on rooftops and ground them into flour for making breads. Today, the variously shaded wood of the mesquite tree is prized not only by woodworkers but also by cooks, who use the wood and the charcoal made from it for grilling because their sweet smoke imparts a distinctive flavor to foods. Mesquite chips and charcoal are readily available in specialty cookware stores and many hardware stores.

NEW MEXICO GREEN CHILI, NEW MEXICO RED CHILI see *Chilies, fresh.*

NEW MEXICO CHILI, see *Chilies, dried.*

NOPALES
The fleshy, oval pads, or leaves, of the prickly pear cactus, ranging in color from light to dark green. The smaller, deep-green pads are the most tender, and their taste is similar to that of a green bean. Buy nopales fresh in specialty produce departments and keep them well wrapped in the refrigerator for up to a week. Before using, scrape the thorns away with a vegetable peeler and cut the pads into dice or slices to be used in salads, salsas, vegetable and egg dishes. Substitute: nopalitos (see below).

NOPALITOS
Diced or sliced nopales, available canned or pickled in the specialty section of many grocery stores.

OAXACA CHEESE see *Cheeses, Mexican.*

PEPITAS
Dark green, hulled pumpkin seeds, delicious toasted and salted as a snack. The delicate flavor and crunchy texture of pepitas enhance salads and main dishes; they are also ground and used in moles and sauces. They are available in Latino markets.

PIÑON NUTS (Spanish plural: *piñones*)
The seeds from the cones of a Southwestern pine tree called the piñon, the state tree of New Mexico. Skinned piñon nuts resemble small white corn kernels and are highly prized for their smooth texture and delicate flavor. They are often toasted and used in soups, sauces, salads, desserts, appetizers and main dishes. Native Americans grind the raw nuts into a meal used in breads. Substitute: Italian pine nuts, or pignolas.

POBLANO CHILI see *Chilies, fresh.*

PRESERVING, CANNING
Home preserves and canned goods must be put up in hot, sterilized jars. To sterilize canning jars, boil them gently in water to cover for 10 minutes; leave them in water until you are ready to fill them. In order to process any of the preserves in this book for shelf storage, further important steps must be followed for the safety of the product. Please contact your local County Cooperative Extension Office, found in the telephone book under your county listings. This office provides current information from the United States Department of Agriculture and the Land Grant University System for safe home-preserving procedures.

PRICKLY PEAR FRUIT
The purplish-red, pear-shaped fruit of the prickly pear cactus, called *tunas,* are available almost year-round in the Southwest. Always used peeled, the soft flesh of the prickly pear is filled with tough black seeds that should be removed before eating or cooking. The fruit can be sectioned and the seeds removed, or it can be puréed and strained, discarding the seeds. Prickly pear fruit smells similar to a melon and has a sweet, subtle flavor. Choose soft but not overripe fruit: look for those that are deep red, although green fruit may be stored at room temperature until it turns red, then refrigerated.

QUESO FRESCO see *Cheeses, Mexican.*

RANCHERO CHEESE see *Cheeses, Mexican.*

REFRIED BEANS (*FRIJOLES REFRITOS*)
Beans that have been cooked, then mashed and fried in lard. Almost always found on combination plates in Mexican restaurants, refried beans are also used in dips and as a topping for tostadas and Indian fry bread.

SERRANO CHILI see *Chilies, fresh.*

SQUASH BLOSSOMS
The flowers of various squash plants, revered by native Americans for centuries and ranging in color from golden yellow to orange. Although any squash produces a blossom, the most beautiful are those of the zucchini. Male blossoms are preferred because they are larger and will not bear fruit. Extremely fragile, squash blossoms should be picked early in the morning before they open and used the same day, if possible. They can be dipped in batter and sautéed or fried, either plain or stuffed with a soft cheese, or they can be used whole or cut into strips as a garnish for soups, salads or main dishes. Trim the stems to about

1 in (2.5 cm). Look for them in specialty foods markets from late spring to early fall and store them in a basket (not in plastic), for 1–2 days in the refrigerator.

STOCK, BEEF AND CHICKEN
Homemade stocks are easy to make and can be frozen for future use. Canned broth may be substituted for stock in most recipes, but it should be used with discretion because most of these products are very salty.

To make beef stock: Roast 4 lb (2 kg) beef bones (with some meat on them) in a 450°F (230°C) oven in a roasting pan for 30 minutes, turning once. Place the bones in a large pot and add 2 onions, peeled and halved, 3 whole carrots, 3 whole celery stocks, a bay leaf, a handful of parsley sprigs, 1 teaspoon salt and ½ teaspoon cracked peppercorns. Discard the fat from the roasting pan and deglaze the pan with two cups of water. Add to the pot with 3 additional quarts of water. Bring to a boil, then reduce the heat and simmer very gently, partially covered, for about 5 hours, skimming off any foam that rises to the surface for the first 30 minutes or so. Strain through several thicknesses of cheesecloth and let cool, uncovered. Makes about 3 quarts.

To make chicken stock: Place about 4 lb (2 kg) chicken pieces (backs, wings, necks and the remains of a roast chicken) in a large pot. Add 2 onions, peeled and halved, 2 whole carrots, 2 whole celery stocks, a handful of parsley sprigs, 1 bay leaf, 6 crushed peppercorns, 1 teaspoon dried thyme and 1 teaspoon salt. Pour in about 4 quarts of water, or enough to cover ingredients by 1 in (2.5 cm). Bring to a boil and reduce heat and simmer gently, partially covered for about 4 hours, skimming off any foam that rises to the surface for the first 30 minutes or so. Strain through several thicknesses of cheesecloth and let cool, uncovered. Makes 3 quarts.

SUNFLOWER SEEDS
The seeds of the sunflower, used for centuries by native Americans either whole or ground for meal. Sunflower seeds have a black-and-white-striped shell that must be removed. Often dried or roasted, the seeds add a delicious flavor and delicate crunch to salads, sandwiches, sauces, soups, vegetables, baked goods and main dishes.

TEQUILA
A colorless liquor that originated in Tequila, Mexico. Distilled from the sweet sap of a Central American century plant *(Agave tequilana)*, tequila is quite potent, usually 80–86 proof, and is used in many popular drinks in the Southwest, particularly the Margarita.

TOASTING NUTS
Toasting nuts brings out their rich flavor, deepens their color and increases their crunchiness. To toast nuts: Spread the nuts in a single layer on a shallow baking pan with edges and place under the broiler (griller) about 6 in (15 cm) from the heat for 3–5 minutes. Turn the nuts frequently until they are golden.

TOMATILLO
A ground cherry native to Mexico, with a slightly tart but mild flavor with hints of lemon and apple. Tomatillos look like small green tomatoes with thin, brown, paperlike husks, and are sometimes called husk tomatoes or Mexican green tomatoes *(tomates verdes)*. Tomatillos are available fresh sporadically and canned year round in many grocery stores. Use them raw in salads and fresh salsas and cooked in soups and cooked sauces.

TORTILLA
A thin round of dough either patted by hand, rolled out or pressed in a tortilla press, then quickly cooked on a hot skillet. The bread of Mexico, tortillas come in a variety of sizes, depending on their uses, and colors—white, yellow or blue (when made with different colors of corn). Red and green tortillas are popular at Christmas in the Southwest, but these are made by adding food coloring. Corn tortillas are made with fresh masa or with dough made from masa harina and water; flour tortillas are made with wheat flour and water. Flour tortillas are more common in northern Mexico and southern Arizona, where wheat is grown. Fresh tortillas are made daily and sold still warm in most of the Southwest and in areas of the United States with a large Latino population. Most are made by machine, but fresh hand-patted tortillas are available from some restaurants and markets. Packaged factory-made tortillas are available in the refrigerated section of most grocery stores.

To make your own tortillas, use a tortilla press (available in cookware stores), or roll dough between pieces of waxed paper or baking parchment with a rolling pin. Cook on both sides on a hot, ungreased skillet or griddle until speckled with brown spots but still pliable.

VANILLA BEAN
The cured and dried long, thin pod of a perennial orchid that grows in trees in tropical American forests. The vanilla bean was first cultivated by the Aztecs. Because the vanilla orchid has to be hand-pollinated and the pods must be hand-picked, then dried for months, vanilla beans and pure vanilla extract are costly. Whole beans may be added to hot liquid mixtures such as sauces, or mixtures such as ice cream bases that are then heated, and allowed to steep for 30 minutes or so. For maximum flavor, slit the bean open and scrape the tiny seeds into custards, ice cream, sauces and chocolate desserts (vanilla heightens the flavor of chocolate). If used whole and not split, the beans may be rinsed off and used again, but they should be tightly wrapped in plastic, then put into a glass jar and refrigerated. Vanilla beans are usually sold in glass jars or tubes in specialty foods markets or grocery stores.

To make vanilla sugar, take a used vanilla bean that has been rinsed off and dried and place it in a tightly covered jar with 1 cup (8 oz/250 g) of granulated sugar or 1 cup (4 oz/125 g) of powdered sugar. After a few days, the sugar will have a vanilla flavor. Vanilla sugar will keep indefinitely.

PHOTOGRAPHY CREDITS

ILLUSTRATION GUIDE

CONTENTS:
Although stylistically this horse motif resembles a prehistoric design, it was actually painted on a red clay canteen in 1938 by the Qahatika. The tribes of southern Arizona are distinguished by the polished red pottery which was developed within the last hundred years.

INTRODUCTION:
Pueblo communities attained one of the highest levels of prehistoric culture in ancient North America and pottery making evolved to an advanced art, far beyond the stage of simple utilitarian wares. Religious persecution in the Rio Grande Valley during the seventeenth century forced the pueblos to shield their rituals and related arts from outsiders. Thus, pottery painters began to fuse ritualistic symbols with the decorative art of their everyday wares. Simplicity and restraint characterize this bird motif from an Acomita polychrome jar of the Laguna Pueblo variety, circa 1770.

BASIN AND RANGE DESERTS:
The Pima, a river-dwelling people from the Sonoran Desert area of Arizona and Mexico, are renowned basket makers. Pima baskets are highly prized for the balance, symmetry and intricacy of their designs. This rare butterfly wing motif from a woven bowl-tray is an ancient design.

CENTRAL HIGHLANDS:
Apache women became adept basket makers; and the western Apache were thought to create the most ornate baskets of their people. Though their original designs were once austerely geometrical, the Apaches were encouraged by trading post operators to embrace more elaborate designs that would attract white collectors. The intricate design on this 1950 basketry plaque, with dominant male and female figures, reflects early commercial influence.

COLORADO PLATEAU:
The Anasazi (Navajo for "Ancient Ones") evolved from a tribe of pit dwellers and food gatherers into a culture of sophisticated farmers and architects. The Anasazi learned to make rudimentary pottery in A.D. 700, and by 1150 potters had advanced the art to include almost every type of bowl, mug, pitcher and ladle imaginable in daily use. Often elaborate, the imagery of Anasazi pottery is usually nonfigurative, consisting of stark geometric patterns executed with symmetrical regularity.

RIO GRANDE BASIN:
The people of the Mogollon cultures of New Mexico's Mimbres Valley created pottery that was unique to the prehistoric Southwest. The artists of the eleventh and twelfth centuries painted fanciful narratives on the interior surfaces of bowls, often incorporating nontraditional animal and human motifs. Many of the Mimbres bowls were found at burial sites and show evidence of having been pierced near the center, or ceremoniously "killed," to release the spirit of the painted figure.

RIO GRANDE VALLEY:
This motif was taken from a ceramic lampshade created between 1940 and 1960 and is representative of the Tewa Pueblo in New Mexico. The ancient Tewa tribe was one of the few Neolithic cultures to have created ceramic glazes. Although glazing died out around 1700, pueblo potters evolved a series of styles and designs that remained relatively independent from outside influences until the coming of the railroad in 1880.

LLANO ESTACADO:
Apache artifacts generally reflect the tribe's independence and nomadism: function is often stressed over form. While motifs recur, this symbol from a buckskin medicine shirt is unique and nontraditional. The shirts were considered sacred and sometimes supernatural.

BORDERLANDS:
This motif from pottery found at the pre-Columbian site of Casas Grandes in northern Chihuahua, Mexico, resembles the designs of both the Mogollon potters of the central highlands and the Anasazi from the Four Corners area. These similarities lead scholars to believe that the eleventh century communities of the Southwest and northern Mexico were closely linked.

ACKNOWLEDGMENTS

Barbara Pool Fenzl would like to thank her husband, Terry and their three children, Allison, Andrew and Ashley, for their patience, understanding and help with this book. Barbara's gratitude also goes to Linda Hopkins, Susan Begin and Patty Hart for their help in testing recipes and to Les Gourmettes Cooking School students for their encouragement and support. Norman Kolpas would like to thank John Sedlar.

The publishers and the photographers would like to thank the following people and organizations for their assistance in the preparation of this book: John Harrison, Sigrid Chase, Anne Greensall, Richard Van Oosterhout, Dawn Low, Janique Poncelet, Tori Ritchie, Fee-ling Tan, Jonette Banzon, Patty Hill, Angela Williams, Laurie Wertz, Wendely Harvey, Roger Smoothy, Jennifer Mullins, Jennifer Hauser, Bruce Bailey, Bob Firken. Derith Bogard who loaned props from her private collection; The Red Rooster, Whitney Arnold, Scottsdale, Arizona who loaned props for the jacket; Bill and Jan Frieder for the use of their beautiful hacienda as a backdrop for the jacket photograph; Barbara Pool Fenzl for her help with the on-location photography; Mike and Robin Showers of The Robin's Nest, Fred Cly, Duane Salisbury and David Salisbury.